Springer Series on LIFE STYLES AND ISSUES IN AGING

Series Editor: Bernard D. Starr, PhD
Marymount Manhattan College, New York, NY

Sheldon S. Tobin, Ph.D., has recently retired as a Professor Emeritus in the Schools of Social Welfare and Public Health and, from 1982–1990, was Director of the Ringel Institute of Gerontology at the University at Albany of the State University of New York. After receiving his doctorate in 1963 from the Committee on Human Development of the University of Chicago, he remained on the faculties of the Committee and the School of Social Service Administration until coming to Albany in 1982. Trained as a Clinical Psychologist, his geriatric experience includes two decades of consultation at Drexel Home for the Aged in Chicago and membership on the Geriatric Consultation team at Albany Medical Center. From 1985 through 1988, he served as Editor-in-Chief of *The Gerontologist*. He has authored eight books and has over 100 additional publications that are focused primarily on psychosocial aspects of aging and on services for the elderly. His most recent award was the University Award for Excellence in Research.

Preservation of the Self in the Oldest Years

With Implications for Practice

Sheldon S. Tobin, PhD

Springer Publishing Company

Springer Publishing Company, Inc.
536 Broadway
New York, NY 10012-3955

Cover design by Janet Joachim
Acquisitions Editor: Helvi Gold
Production Editor: Helen Song

99 00 01 02 03 / 5 4 3 2 1

Library of Congress Cataloging-in-Publication Data

Tobin, Sheldon S.
    Preservation of the self in the oldest years: with implications for practice / by Sheldon S. Tobin.
        p.   cm.
    Includes bibliographical references and index.
    ISBN 0-8261-7581-3
    1. Aged—Psychology.   2. Aging—Psychological aspects. 3. Aged—Counseling of.   I. Tobin, Sheldon S. Preservation of the self in the oldest years. II. Title.
BF724.8.T63   1999
155.67'182—dc21   98-31378
                                                                            CIP

Printed in the United States of America

Contents

Foreword

D*ementia is frightening,* both for those who experience it personally and those who see it in somebody they love. You see your mother sitting in the living room. She has the features of your mother and is wearing the clothes of your mother, but she isn't the mother you knew. Or there you are yourself, confused about who you are. Like what is your relation to the people around you, to the things around you, to your past life experiences? It is how this terrible loss of selfhood when very old is prevented that Sheldon Tobin's book is all about.

This comprehensive sequel to Tobin's 1991 volume on personhood expands both the empirical and clinical thrusts of the first book. By adding extensive reviews of his research and numerous illustrative vignettes, he builds a strong argument for his central thesis: The vital importance of feeling that one is still the same person one has always been. He convinces us that if that sense of continuity wavers in the process of aging, one of the most important services clinicians and other gerontologists can render is to help in its recovery. What is more, based essentially on normative processes that preserve selfhood, he proceeds to suggest many ways in which this can be done. Although he seems to have directed most of his discussion to clinical social workers, his primary targets, what he has to say is also valuable for anyone interested in the self, whether professionally or personally.

Maintaining a perception of the continuity of self is important at any time of life, not only in aging. Thirty years ago, in 1969, the psychologist Walter Mischel wrote that this sense of sameness acts "like an extraordinarily effective reducing value that creates and maintains the perception of continuity even in the face of perpetual observed changes in actual behavior." A year earlier, Erik Erikson had said, "No one who has worked with autistic children will ever forget the horror of observing how desperately they struggle to grasp the meaning of saying 'I' and 'you.'" Work with deeply disturbed young people confronts the therapist with the awful awareness of the patients' incapacity to feel the "I" and the "you." The primary developmental task of early life is the formation of a self. The primary developmental task of late life is the preservation of this self.

Perception of continuity of self is particularly relevant for those who are aging. Getting old makes one more vulnerable to discombobulating experiences like changes of habitat or losses of friends or family members, all of which serve to validate one's perceptions. Many of the people who made up one's world are gone, and changes in living conditions can lead to a sense of unreality. There are also losses of cognitive ability to make and maintain connections between experiences, past and present. Yet the self can be, and indeed is, preserved.

Erikson talked about confusion between "I" and "you." In my own recent research with very old respondents, I have found it enlightening to distinguish between the two aspects of self first proposed by William James and George Herbert Mead: the "I" and the "me." The "I" would be the self as observer, the core self, while the "me" is the part of the self that the "I" observes. An example of perceived continuity of "I" would be a statement that one was the same person one had always been: the sense that one had not changed essentially. An example of perceived continuity of "me" would be that one had the same attributes as before: that one's characteristics and traits had not changed, that one still liked the same things or did the same things. It is the perception of continuity of the "I" that Tobin's book is most about. He points out that this perception is so necessary that it can involve what David Gutmann has called "magic mastery," the distortion of reality to fit psychological needs.

When, a few years ago, I analyzed the responses of a sample of 150 community-living San Franciscans over 85, I found that three quarters of them said they felt that they *were* the same person they had always been. They didn't think they had really changed much at all. What is more, not one of them felt that he or she had changed in any major or essential way. At the same time, though, two thirds acknowledged that they had changed in such attributes as health, appearance, or activities—the "me" part of the self.

We must remember that almost all of these very old San Franciscans were functioning independently in the community and therefore had not experienced the kind of major changes that would make them feel they were no longer the same person. Although temporary major disruptions like moves or hospitalizations did not prove to be associated with feelings of becoming different, it is possible that major disruptions like no longer being able to maintain oneself would tip the balance. It is residents of extended care facilities who have been among the prime research subjects.

Dr. Tobin has many pointers for professional workers in institutional facilities. But not all his clinical illustrations deal with nursing home residents. He discusses ways in which any caregiver can help maintain the self. Above all, from my point of view, he devotes a lot of thought to the family, to feelings about husbands or wives or parents or children. He talks about what it feels like to see one's husband or wife change into a person one no longer knows. What is more, he gives hope. He goes beyond feelings and concerns to practical advice and suggestions and shows how family members can help prevent or even reverse such changes.

I enjoyed reading this volume. Shelly has done us all a true service by saying what he has. He appeals to theorists, to caregivers, to therapists, to family members, and to policy planners. Most of all, he appeals to those of us who are inexorably growing old ourselves.

Lillian E. Troll, PhD
Professor Emerita
Department of Psychology
Rutgers University
New Brunswick, NJ

Adjunct Professor
Department of Medical Anthropology
University of California, San Francisco

Preface

"*Lucky for me*," said the spry but wizened man of 86 "that you don't grow old real suddenly. It takes a little time to become like me, like an old wine takes time to mature."

So, too, it has taken me time to write this book. When I began my studies of aging as a graduate student almost 40 years ago, I was too young to comprehend some psychological aspects of the oldest old years.

Most very old persons in the interviews I read or personally interviewed talked as if they accepted their deaths. But, I asked myself, how can a person of any age accept her or his death? It must be denial!

Then, after chatting with decrepit and shrunken 90 year olds, I was befuddled because they talked of how they were still the same persons they had always been. How, I asked myself, can that be? They surely don't look the same. Most can barely move around. All but a few of the very old women are widowed. How can the 92-year old-petite, white-haired lady still believe she is a coquette of 21? When asked about her current self, she brought out a flattering picture taken when she was 21 and said, "That's me, but maybe I changed just a bit."

Too many seemed to feel satisfied with their lives. How could it be, especially with no sex life? This was certainly a sensible question to ask in my late twenties. Feeling satisfied made sense for those who glowingly reminisced about their earliest life. It seemed paradoxical, however, when those who reported the most wretched earliest years and then endured the hardships of the Great Depression said that their lives had been very good.

As they reminisced and reconstructed their pasts, I often could not tell if they were talking about the past or reliving the past. At that time, as a budding clinical psychologist, I had to ask myself whether it made a difference. Obsessing about this distinction, I vacillated in my interpretation because to live in the past is sick, its psychopathological. But their reminiscence did not seem sick. Rather, it seemed natural for these very old people to reconstruct their past vividly and dramatically as if reliving their past.

Strange to me also was the feeling that suspiciousness and distrustfulness of others, which I very well knew from my textbooks and instructors were signs of pathological paranoia, appeared to be particularly helpful for them.

I could not put it all together. There was obviously something different about the psychology of the very old. I could not, however, integrate the discrete elements into a sensible framework. What was figure and what was ground? What was cause and what was effect? What was primary and what was secondary? I addressed some of these kinds of questions in my 1991 book *Personhood in Advanced Old Age: Implications for Practice* (Springer). Since then some of my ideas have become clearer, more crystallized, especially with help from how Colleen Johnson and Barbara Barer (1997) have interpreted findings from their *85+ Study*. Still, the impetus for this book has come from readers and reviewers of my *Personhood* book who have said that my formulations are sensible and meaningful. Some asked me questions that I did not address in *Personhood*. Others wished that I had used more examples. Still others asked when I planned to write a next edition, especially my publisher Ursula Springer. This book, however, is not a second edition of *Personhood*. Whereas it is an expanded version, it is also a reorganized one that includes more content and many more examples.

As before, however, the explicit focus remains on ordinary people in their oldest years and is neither on the most productive nor the most creative. Understanding ordinary very old people forms essential knowledge for practitioners, as well as being particularly useful for our students, our family members and, indeed, for ourselves. This knowledge is now contained in a different sequence. Whereas, for example, the second chapter in *Personhood* was on interventions with individuals, now interventions are considered within sequential sections on Facilitory Processes, Benefits of Survivorship, and When Care is Needed. The discussion of facilitory processes, in turn, has not only been expanded, but I also have divided the processes into two sets of psychological processes or, if you will, adaptive coping mechanisms that differ in taking into account the demands of reality. Among the many other changes is the incorporation of a married couple, Marilyn and Jack Sampson, who are used illustratively throughout this volume to make the experience of aging when very old more intelligible, more vivid, and more immediate.

My current formulations for how the self is preserved in the oldest years, as just noted, began with questions that elderly respondents challenged me to ask myself decades ago. I was first introduced to oldest old people by reading interviews gathered for the Kansas City Study of Adult Life, the first large scale study designed to understand aging from the middle through the oldest years. My mentors, Bernice L. Neugarten and Robert J. Havighurst of the Committee on Human Development at the University of Chicago, encouraged me to absorb the heterogeneity among our respondents and to understand each person as an individual so that scores on social and psychological dimensions, as well as relationships among scores, reflected something real about people. Concurrently, I was being mentored at Drexel Home for the Aged by Jerome Grunes, a psychoanalyst, consultant to the Drexel Home for the Aged, and dear friend. Here, too, I had to understand each resident I interviewed as a clinician before making any generalization about aging and very old people. These simultaneous clinical experiences and social science research excursions raised more questions than gave me answers regarding viable generalization about commonalities among very old persons.

Given the obvious differences among individuals, how can we say they are alike on any characteristic? Can all we say is that everybody differs from everybody else? Emerging from these earliest puzzlements, however, were some kernels of insights. Somehow despite all the losses associated with advanced aging, both the losses of others and the losses in functioning, people are able to retain a sense of self. But how can they do so? What psychological mechanisms are employed to retain a sense of the continuity of the self? Are some psychological processes more prevalent than others? Or are there idiosyncratic psychological processes used to assure a preservation of the self?

I worked with Bernice Neugarten and Bob Havighurst, as well as with other doctoral students, on developing an age-appropriate measure of well-being, a measure of life satisfaction that captured more than mood or morale, whether happy or sad. Most of our oldest respondents enjoyed their lives, but what they enjoyed were activities that were more narrow, more limited in focus than earlier in life. Then too, respondents were determined to carry on despite adversity and were looking forward to something in the future. For some respondents it was a wedding in a few months, for others it was a family visitor next week, and still for others it was going to church this Sunday.

Additionally, it was common to express a congruence between expected and achieved life goals. Indeed, our oldest respondents, comprising a cohort born in the late 1800s, usually felt that they achieved more than they expected. Moreover, most felt themselves to be valued persons in the way they had been earlier in life. We also considered their mood, which was often reflected in becoming tearful when talking about losses, especially of the deaths of spouses and parents and sometimes of children. So mood or happiness became for us only one of five components of our life satisfaction measures that were useful for sorting out older people so that we could investigate attributes associated with feelings of well-being. From developing measures of life satisfaction, I began to appreciate how the psychology of the very old years differs from the psychology of the younger years. We, for example, would surely not consider a young adult to have good well-being if enjoyment of activities was so constricted, if future enjoyment was limited to a few days or a few months, if expected goals were already achieved, or if self-esteem was predicated as much on the past as on the present.

We then used the life satisfaction measure to develop patterns of aging. Some people exhibited an openness to life and had high life satisfaction, others were constricted with somewhat lower life satisfaction, and still others were passive and dependent people with moderate life satisfaction. Although we used cross-sectional data rather than longitudinal data gathered over many years, like from the young adult years to the oldest years, it was our assumption that basic or core personality remains relatively stable.

What became known was that, albeit there is diversity among community-dwelling very old people, there was a ubiquitous resiliency and a capacity to preserve identity when enduring age-associated assaults that were likely to corrode the self. Were, however, Drexel Home for the Aged residents similar? These very old individuals suffered more losses and were also living in nursing homes. To be sure, their life satisfaction was not as high as community-dwelling elderly people, but they used similar processes to maintain well-being and to be themselves. But other lessons were learned. Sometimes they had to distort their interaction with others to maintain a persistence of self. When the gentle resident of 83 who described herself as always loving and kind to all the other residents was asked to give an example for her self-description, she said, "I make no trouble for anyone. I don't complain like others do when the coffee is too cold."

Additional lessons were learned. Jerry Grunes taught me how to listen to residents who were in acute crises and how assisting them to reminisce and revitalize memories of their earliest life helped them to reintegrate. In recapturing their earliest recollections of family life, they became able to regain a sense of self that had become fractionated when in acute crisis. He also contrasted his therapy based on the usefulness of reconstructions of the past to the therapy of Alvin Goldfarb, who was then the psychoanalytic consultant at the Hebrew Home in New York City, who focused on "overinflating beliefs" in mastery.

Jerome Hammerman, the Executive Director of Drexel Home for Aged, was also my teacher. Because he understood the frustrations of living in a nursing home, he felt that it was appropriate and even expected that residents would "bitch about living here." It was the passive, noncomplainers who bothered him.

Complaining, beneficial distortions, use of the past, and beliefs in control of the environment—all became useful to understanding what Morton A. Lieberman and I called "the unique psychology of the very old" 2 decades later in our 1983 book *The Experience of Old Age* based on findings from studies that focused on the relocation of older persons. My work with Mort, a wonderful colleague, began in 1963 following my doctoral studies and a clinical psychology internship. I was indeed fortunate when he asked me to join him on his National Institutes of Health-funded project to study adaptation to stress in old age. The stress Mort selected to study was institutionalization, and we began to follow elderly individuals from before to after relocation to long-term care facilities using control groups comprised of similar persons not being relocated. In four separate investigations with over 600 respondents, we determined how environments of poorer quality hasten death and the lethality of passivity and of the inability to transform the relocation situation into one perceived as under personal control. Put the other way, we found that adaptation is facilitated when undergoing the stress of relocation by assertiveness, even nastiness, and is also facilitated by magical coping in which an involuntary relocation is transformed into a voluntary relocation and in which a formerly undersirable relocation setting is transformed into a desirable, or even ideal, setting. As reported in our earlier (Tobin and Lieberman, 1976) book *Last Home for the Aged*, older persons not undergoing the stress of relocation, those in control groups, who were passive did not have their deaths hastened as did those undergoing the stress of relocation.

But we investigated much more with upward of 15 Committee on Human Development doctoral students. Some of our former students' findings were particularly important in identifying aspects of a unique psychology of very old people. Briefly, Barbara Turner affirmed the importance of assertiveness. James Gorney showed that introspection on feelings lessens with age. Arthur Rosner's data revealed how the stability of the self-picture is maintained by blending the past with the present. Virginia Revere found that when older people reconstruct their past, they are more likely to dramatize persons from their early life than are people in their middle years.

Then, with a modest understanding of normative adaptative processed among community-dwelling aged persons and facilitory adaptative processes for very old persons when in crisis, I began a series of studies of services for elderly people with doctoral students in the School of Social Service Administration at the University of Chicago. In the 15 years from 1967 through 1982 before I came to Albany, I continued clinical work at Drexel Home for the Aged as a consultant, but my learning about the preservation of the self came largely from my social work doctoral students. Jordan Kosberg taught me more about nursing home environments. Studies of nutrition programs, including Dan Thompson's study, sensitized me to how older people with the most deprivation in their earliest years can feel that the oldest years could be their best years because of so few expectations from life. Regina Kulys showed me that about 5% of persons 65 and over who have concerns about their future are those without family supports; the other, more than 9 of 10, said that because of event uncertainty and timing of events uncertainty (that "anything can happen at any time"), it is best not to worry. And Mary Schlesinger found that emotional security increases to the extent that the most "responsible other" adult child can be perceived as likely to act in their best interest if a crisis were to occur and also the extent that services for elderly people are known by this child. Then came Lucy Steinitz, Ellen Netting, Jane Thebault, and especially Jim Ellor who identified an important omission in my thinking: Religious beliefs inculcated early in life are very important to the well-being of the very old. Particularly salient are beliefs in God's blessings of a long life as a divine reward for service and a hereafter filled with reunions with departed loved ones, a belief held by three of four Americans independent of education.

More recently, for the past 15 years at the University at Albany, I have read about 400 interviews of very old individuals that have been gathered by my master of social work students for an assignment in my class "The Latter Half of Life." These interviews have aided me in fleshing out the preservation of the self in advanced old age. Meanwhile, I continued clinical work as a member of a hospital-based geriatric consultant team led by Michael Wolff, an internist. Also, I edited *The Gerontologist*, the leading applied journal in the field, which was like going back to graduate school for a refresher course. Reading 1,600 manuscripts submitted over a 4-year period provided a breather from writing and also added breadth to my thinking. But during this time, I also studied nonnormative aging because of having unfinished business as the life course nears its end. One group was composed of elderly productive visual artists, another of older mothers caring at home for adult offspring with mental retardation. This large investigation of perpetual parents with Gregory Smith and Elise (Mickey) Fullmer and enhanced by Phil McCallion's practice experiences, and made possible by funding from the National Institute on Aging, used in-depth interviews by clinicians to provide an illuminating contrast to their normatively aging peers who perceive their life tasks as completed and with no unfinished business as the course of life draws to a close.

My many different experiences and collaborative work with others spread over most of my adult life has led me to being comfortable in making generalizations on adaptation among the oldest old people. Then too, through illness in my family, I had to ask how adaptation when experiencing age-associated losses in the oldest years differs from adaptation when illness causes disability and nearness to death that is premature, as before one's time, which is not so for people in their late eighties, nineties, and increasingly, when past 100.

For the maturation of my ideas I am indebted to all my former students, colleagues, and my mentors, especially to the pioneer in adult development and aging Bernice Neugarten and to the ever insightful geropsychoanalyst Jerry Grunes. Then, too, I am indebted to cherished colleagues, particularly to Mort Lieberman, Bert Cohler, Lillian Troll, and Ron Toseland. For the preparation of this book, I am most grateful to my secretary, B. J. Kelly, who worked with me through several drafts. Yet it would be extremely remiss of me if I did not acknowledge the thousands of older persons who have informed my thinking, most having been interviewed by skilled interviewers or students but also many by myself, including those I interviewed as a therapist.

PART ONE

A Life Cycle Perspective

If the task of the earliest years is to become oneself and the task of the adult years is to fulfill the self, then the task of the oldest years is to preserve the self when age-associated assaults can corrode the self. How the self is preserved in the everyday lives of ordinary very old people forms essential content of this book. The use of ordinary is purposeful. Most people are ordinary but not in a pejorative sense because we ordinary people are important to ourselves, to our families, to our friends, and to our communities. We may not make it to the front page of The New York Times or to the cover of Time magazine or have a transitory comment made to us on the evening news, but our lives can be no less meaningful and fulfilling than those who do.

We may, however, know extraordinary older individuals who transcend illnesses and losses to remain productive and creative throughout their eighties and nineties, and even beyond 100; and if we personally do not know any of these exceptional people, we certainly have read about them. The newspaper carried a story the other day about the couple, he at 82 and she a relative youngster of 74, who decided that it was now time to set their sailboat on a course to Hawaii. Stories of businessmen and women who are still working past 90 have become commonplace. Then there is Grandma Moses who began painting late in life and continued past 100. But these are not most people.

Our parents, our grandparents and, increasingly, our great grandparents are quite unlikely to be among those we perceived as extraordinary. Yet, we may know that the oldest members of our families are exceptional, even extraordinary, because of how they persist in being themselves in the final years of their lives despite illness and losses that assault their personhood. They may be neither productive nor creative by conventional definitions. Still, how they manage to be themselves, to maintain control of their lives, to resolutely carry on in an ever contracting personal and interpersonal world and to obtain gratification despite illnesses and losses that can easily overwhelm the human spirit, cannot but help make them admirable and indeed special to us. Most have long ago accomplished their major life goals of raising children and making a living and now have no critical unfinished business as their life cycles become completed. Then, when they contemplate their past lives, their current circumstances, and their limited futures, it is likely that they accept their death with equanimity. It is these ordinary people who are the primary focus here; ordinary people who invariably are admired by us and sometimes with whom we are in awe because of how a resiliency we never imagined they possessed is there for all to see as they live their daily lives.

This first section contains two chapters, one entitled Preserving the Self When Nearing the End: An Overview and the other entitled Pathways to the Oldest Years. The former chapter provides the ground plan for the remainder of the book, whereas the latter chapter encompasses two kinds of historic changes: first, the emergence of a large group, or cohort, of very old people; and second, the vicissitudes over time in typical, or normative, lives from the middle years until advanced old age. A specific focus is on stability and change over the course of life.

Readers will note that the "oldest years," the "oldest old years," and "extreme age" are used interchangeably. So too are "the very old," the "old-old," "the oldest old" and the "extreme aged" people. As will be discussed in chapter 2, data are analyzed by demographers to identify this cohort; that is, demographers use data gathered on individuals to approximate the age when disabilities accelerate among those living to and beyond 65. Seventy years of age was the demarcation for the "frail year" in the 1960s when I began my studies of aging and clinical work with elderly persons. It then became 75 by the mid-1970s when Bernice L. Neugarten (1974) coined the phrase "the oldest old." Soon it leapfrogged to 85 in the early 1980s with "the extreme aged." Using chronologic age to demarcate oldness is only, however, a demographer's rendition of reality and cannot characterize any individual. Put differently, 85 is a proxy for disability that tells us nothing about any individual. Some will suffer age-associated illnesses and losses well before 85, whereas others will be relatively free of these age-associated assaults on the self while living toward, or even beyond, the longevity of our human species, which is 110 years or so.

Many vignettes, all disguised to be anonymous, are used illustratively throughout this volume. Most of these depict individuals 85 or over who are coping with age-associated assaults, but some vignettes will be of individuals less than 85 who are coping with normative assaults associated with age, while others will be of individuals over 85 who have evaded most age-associated assaults. There will also be vignettes of individuals who are aging nonnormatively because they have critical unfinished business such as elderly parents caring at home for adult children with mental retardation and visual artists who continue to seek to be productive and creative through their advanced old age. It is, however, the Sampsons, Marilyn and Jack, who are introduced to readers early in the first chapter, who are continually used illustratively in the chapters that follow. As with other persons depicted in vignettes, the Sampsons are real people. Sometimes their quotes, as well as the quotes of others, however, are not always in the words they actually used but rather have been reconstructions from my recollections of what they said. In taking the liberty to employ nonverbatim quotes, my intent is obviously not to deceive. It is to make the oldest years vivid for readers.

CHAPTER 1

Preserving the Self When Nearing the End: An Overview

$E_{ach\ person\ ages}$ differently and, indeed, people as they age become increasingly different from each other. Yet there are some commonalities among people as they near the end of their lives when very old. Shared is the task of preserving the self when confronted by age-associated deterioration in functioning from illnesses and waning energies, as well as from the deaths of family members and friends. After focusing on preserving the self, the discussion shifts to the processes that facilitate this preservation, specifically adaptive coping mechanisms, use of reminiscence, and religiosity. Next discussed are the benefits of survivorship: the acceptance of death and aging successfully. Then covered is when care is needed. The sequence and content of these brief discussions form a template for the later chapters where there is a fleshing out of content. Here, in this first chapter, the attempt is to provide a panoramic overview of what can be called the unique psychology of the very old. Later, when there are fuller expositions on facilitory processes, benefits of survivorship, and when care is needed, relevant select literature and theory will be introduced, as well as implications for practice.

Preservation of the Self

Remarkable is how the task of preserving the self in the oldest years is achieved by the current cohort of oldest old people. This task occurs in the special context and time of being at the end of the life cycle. For very old people, now considered 85 and over, it is a time when there is an awareness that a life has been lived, when death is approaching, and usually when there is no unfinished business to complete. It is also a time when age-associated assaults, which include physical deterioration and losses of others, corrode the self.

INTEGRALITY

Instructive is the writings of the renown psychoanalyst Erik Erikson. In his original theorizing on the last stage of life in his 1950 book *Childhood and Society,* he postulated that integrity is achieved and despair avoided by accepting life as it has been lived and by investing in the continuity of generations; that is, in investments outside oneself. Later, in 1982, in his advanced old age, Erikson reformulated the last stage of life in his book *The Life Cycle Completed* and wrote that

> . . . integrity in its simplest meaning is, of course, a sense of coherence and wholeness that is, no doubt, at supreme risk under such terminal conditions as a loss of linkages in all three organizing processes; in the soma . . . ; in the psyche, the gradual loss of mnemonic coherence in experience, past and present; and in the ethos, the threat of a sudden and nearly total loss of responsible function in generative interplay. What is demanded here could simply be called "integrality," a tendency to keep things together. (pp. 64–65)

THE AURA OF SURVIVORSHIP

Integrality and preservation of the self is invariably achieved by those community-dwelling very old persons who are able to maintain a modicum of functioning. This achievement, in part, provides very old people with an "aura of survivorship," which is the subtitle of Colleen Johnson and Barbara Barer's 1997 book *Life Beyond 85 Years: The Aura of Survivorship.* Why the aura? What emanations are given off so that those of us who know or interview oldest old persons experience an aura? Maybe it is because we also would like to survive into our late eighties, nineties, and even beyond 100? Of course we wish to become persons of advanced old age and, like the more than one half of those 85 and over now called "the extreme aged" person, to retain sufficient functioning so that we can adequately carry out our activities of daily living. As Ben Franklin said, "All would be long lived but none would grow old."

It is, however, more than a wish to survive intact to a ripe very old age that evokes the experience of an aura of survivorship. One part of the experience is how ordinary people, who have often lived what only can be considered rather mundane lives, have a sense of well-being, of integrality, in spite of the many losses associated with advanced aging. Also a part is how well they are coping in the here-and-now. Another part is how easily we can forget the age of the octogenarian or nonoctogenarian as that person tells a life story. We have been visualizing the person as a younger person living a life, but then as we get up to go, we suddenly come back to reality. We have been talking to a very, very old woman or man and not to a coquette in her courting years or a vigorous tradesman in his most productive years.

Witness the Sampsons, Marilyn and Jack, projecting their auras:

Outliving Friends (and Enemies Too!)

Jack Sampson, who at 87 is barely 5 feet tall, said he was once 5 foot 3. A carpenter before he retired, he is built like a bulldog, with shoulders that are broad and a torso that is thick. A car accident shattered his right leg, and now he walks cautiously with a cane, tilting somewhat to the left. His speech is slightly but detectably slurred from a stroke, and he lost one eye from the occlusion of a retinal blood vessel. When asked how he is doing, he responded, "What can you expect of an old man? I look in the obituaries, and if my name isn't there, I know that it's another day. I play a little cards and we, with my wife who is also no spring chicken at 85, go to the early birds. You get a lot to eat, so it's our meal for the next day too. The kids, they're no spring chickens either. They're doing fine. I guess we did something right. Since we came to Florida, after I retired at 70, we don't see them enough. But so are my grandchildren and my great grandchildren doing fine. But I don't know them like I should. I used to have lottsa friends. I don't anymore. They're all gone now but (said with a twinkle in his one good eye) so are my enemies!"

His "no spring chicken" wife Marilyn, who also has a litany of complaints, infirmities, and illnesses that includes cancer of the colon, has a different perspective:

We've Had a Good Life

"He is always complaining! I don't do this right. I don't do that right. But its always been like that. When he says all his friends are dead, it is like he is blaming me. What did I do? I'm just an old lady. You should hear him go

on about his enemies. You would think he got beat up every day. We've had a good life. It was real bad in the Depression, but we're secure now. Never thought we would be. We can't take trips anymore, but I make sure we do things. Otherwise we would stay home too much and watch TV all the time. Jack doesn't drive at night anymore, so if we have something to do at night, I make sure of a ride. We go to early birds with different friends. I talk to the kids every week." Thinking out loud, she mumbles, *"I guess its better he gets angry. The other way he would be unhappy and sleep all the time. He never slept so much. Me? I doze a lot watching TV. When I was a little girl, I slept the whole night through. My mother had a rough time waking me up to go to school. You should have met her. She was wonderful. We had a special relationship. Even when we didn't have much, she made sure I had what I needed. I liked school. I remember my first school room like it was yesterday. My teacher, Mrs. Burke, thought the world of me."*

PRESERVATION WHILE STRIPPING DOWN

The Sampsons illustrate much of what is known about adaptation in the oldest years. Although there has been a stripping down of activities, primarily because of age-associated deteriorations in health and vigor as well as losses of friends, Jack and Marilyn have preserved their senses of self, their identities. Marilyn still considers herself a person to be admired, readily recalling her first teacher's name, Mrs. Burke, who considered her to be someone special, and she was also special to her mother. Being an admired women is a recurrent theme in the reportage of her life: "When I married Jack, he was so handsome, all my girlfriends were envious of me." Also evident is her characteristic way of managing and directing activities, as reflected in her comment, "I make sure we do things." Later, for example, she said, "I was President of the Sisterhood at our synagogue and always in charge of the rummage sale. I got everyone involved. Jack borrowed a truck, the kids pitched in, and they went around the neighborhood picking up clothes, old toasters, and all kinds of used things." Jack meanwhile is still combative but has mellowed, "I used to be pretty tough. You had to be if you were a Jewish tradesman. I remember every fight I ever had. Now I remember everything. But who am I going to fight with? With my poker players? They would kick me out of the game. With Marilyn? We used to fight, like cats and dogs, mostly over money when I wasn't making a living but not anymore. We take care of each other."

The Sampsons, differ, however, from most of their peers of the same age in still having each other. Marilyn said, "My girlfriends have all become widows." In having each other, it is apparent that they interact in much the same ways they have always interacted. Jack is quick to anger, and Marilyn gets annoyed when the anger is directed at her. She has come to recognize, however, that Jack's anger and blaming of others is good for him because otherwise he would become depressed and withdraw into sleep. They also maintain their traditional division of labor. Marilyn is responsible for maintaining the household, assuring that their apartment is clean and orderly, and that each meal is prepared properly. Jack pays the bills and invests their modest savings. Both relate to their three sons, mostly by telephone, but they travel north periodically for family functions. In common with the four of five elderly persons who age in place, preferring to be near children rather than relocate to a leisure world, they maintain intimacy at a distance with their children, grandchildren, and siblings. Intimacy with old friends also persists until friends die, as is now happening with increasing frequency to the Sampsons as they age in their oldest years. Beyond participating in an interpersonal world that confirms their identities, the Sampson's internal dialogues assure the preservation of self. Jack is heard to ask himself, "If inside I still feel like that young buck of 20, how can I also feel so old?" When Marilyn looks at her gallery of family pictures, she will turn to their wedding photograph and say, "It still looks like me. It looks more like Jack, but it still looks like me."

THE ARTISTS' ESSENCE

Over time there is an apparent stripping down to the core self, but with the retention of the core, the self is preserved and integrality achieved. A stripping to a core has its counterpart in the perceptions of elderly creative individuals. Connie Goldman produced a 1-hour audio tape containing excerpts from interviews with some of the 44 active elderly artists in a 1987-1988 traveling exhibit, Elders of the Tribe, organized by Bernice Steinbaum, a New York City gallery owner. The sculptor Peter Agostini said, "All I am looking for is to get at the essence. In other words, I am only looking for essence." Some talk about stripping down to the pure expression of their visual pursuits. Beatrice Wood, the ceramic potter, said at 93, "I am somewhat detached from the need to express myself which I had once." Knowing herself, and with the knowledge that she is still the same person that she had always been, there is a lessening of introspection and a lessened need to discover herself. This is the self-wisdom of very old people. Wood continued "I

don't think about my age. I am happier now. It's only the outer cover-
ing that ages. The essence of the soul or whatever is the person never
ages. I know I'm over 90, but inside I'm still 16 or 17. I know a lot, but
little of the universe. . . . It is a blessing to be 90. You know what is right
or wrong. You don't waste time." Expressing the essence of oneself is a
common theme. Sally Michaels, the painter, puts it, "When you're older
you want to say what you want to say, unlike the young who want to
jump on the bandwagon."

Collaboration for focusing on the essence of one's work comes
from Dean Simonton's (1989) study of the last works of 172 classical
composers. He found that last works, as compared to earlier works,
were "brief, relatively simple in melodic structure, but profound
enough to acquire a lasting place in the concert hall" (p. 45). The less
emotion that Simonton inferred from the brevity and simplification of
structures was interpreted by him to be an expression of resignation or
even contentment as death approached. A different interpretation, consistent with statements by the visual artists, is that the movement
toward concise and simplified versions of earlier works reflects the
successful capturing by these composers of the essence of their earlier
works. This capturing of the essence in sound does not necessarily tell
us that death has become acceptable to them. It does, however, tell us
that the self has been preserved. It is indeed the preservation of the self
that is the adaptative challenge in the latter years.

The next chapter, Pathways to the Oldest Years, includes a discussion of a construct related to self-preservation; that is, stability of
personality. Evidence and practice wisdom indicate a persistence of
the self. Self-preservation, however, has a motivational aspect that is
more compelling than does stability of personality.

Facilitory Processes: A Unique Psychology

Eight kinds of coping that preserve the self will be considered,
and they are divided into two clusters of four each based on their relationship to reality. The four more rational coping mechanisms are
engaging in some meaningful activities that affirm the core self; control in the here-and-now; contractions of the environment, future time,
and relationships to make life more manageable; and downward social
comparisons in which one's functional status is compared to peers
who function less well or who have died. The second set of less rational mechanisms encompasses magical mastery wherein there is some

degree of ignoring reality; aggressiveness under stress that while counteracting lethal passivity also includes a component of nastiness; functional paranoia in which blame of others reduces feelings of vulnerability; and acceptance into consciousness of previously repressed material if helpful in defining the core self. Although considered separately, the coping mechanisms are often, if not usually, intertwined and inseparable.

To be oneself it is necessary to be involved in some meaningful activity or activities in everyday life. Playing cards and eating with friends are activities the Sampsons have always pursued and enjoyed. Still able to carry out these activities, while unable to travel and carry out other activities, provides for a persistence of the self. Common among very old people is to hear a sentence that begins, "If I can still . . ." A woman in her nineties said, "I will still be me if I can go to church to play bingo."

Bingo

"Bingo. Its what I do. I play bingo at church. I go to church to play bingo. I go with my sister. Sometimes her daughter comes." So answered Grace Gotowsky when asked how she spends her time. "I don't do much else of anything. But every Tuesday night I play bingo. My kids ask me how much I won. I say I won a wonderful time every time. If I ever win I yell bingo so loud that everybody can hear it. Bingo! Bingo! I yell just like that!"

CONTROL

Able to maintain meaningful activities when very old relates to being in control of one's life. Marilyn controls their daily routine including with whom they will spend time and where they will go for early birds. She also is not hesitant to be subtly manipulative and often is quite controlling. Jack being able to drive is especially important to his sense of control. For both of them being in control provides feelings that they are in control of their lives, and that their lives are controllable. These are the most human of beliefs in a world where anything can happen at any time. Control takes many forms.

Still a Saint

Mrs. Connors was well known in her neighborhood for her generosity to others. When my student Christie moved into her new house, Mrs. Connors asked a grandchild to bring over a pot of soup because of her difficulty in walking, which also caused her to curtail her many volunteer activities.

Christie then asked a friend about Mrs. Connors. Her friend said that she was always doing for others, and added that Christie better call her immediately because Mrs. Connors expects others to acknowledge her assistance. After some further discussion, Christie and her friend decided that every neighborhood needs a "saint" even if obeisance is the price to be paid. Its a small price, they agreed, if it keeps Mrs. Connors happy and in control of her shrinking world.

CONTRACTIONS

Contractions of the personal environment, time, and interactions with others to make life manageable are visible in the lives of the Sampsons. They have a small negotiable apartment, future time is limited, and they now have a smaller interpersonal world. So, too, has Mike Foster witnessed contractions.

Making Changes

Mike Foster is a collector. His house is filled with artifacts that others might consider junk. To Mike, however, each object is precious. People bring him things he might find interesting, and in the past he would seek out collectibles at auctions and lawn and estate sales. Lately, however, he has slowed down and has made some changes. With his eyesight failing, he and his woman friend shifted around the overflowing things in his living room so that he would not stumble and trip over anything precious. They also organized a kitchen countertop so that he would know the place of his many medicines. Time became foreshortened as he planned excursions for only the near future, which he looked forward to with great anticipation. Visiting friends who were also collectors were curtailed, "Making changes. That's what life is all about. There was a time I wasn't a collector. Now I'm still a collector, but I've changed so that its easier for me."

DOWNWARD SOCIAL COMPARISONS

Helpful is the use of what has been called "downward social comparisons." Simply put, the evaluation of functional status is enhanced by comparisons to peers whose health is worse or to friends who have died. Indeed Johnson and Barer in their *85+ Study* found that when interviewed again 5 years later, their respondents reported their health as better than they previously had reported because of illness or death of age peers. Jack, who chuckles with glee because he has outlived his enemies, could not have done so in his middle years when his enemies were still alive.

MAGICAL MASTERY

There often are magical qualities to the sense of control. Jack, for example, is not capable of driving without the possibility of an accident at any moment, but he neither admits this possibility to himself nor to others. David Gutmann (1964, 1987) found that magical mastery is normative for older persons, as contrasted to passive mastery in the middle years and active mastery in the younger adult years.

AGGRESSIVENESS

Aggressiveness when under stress is not evident at this time in the Sampson's lives. Yet it is essential. Magical coping and aggressiveness were predictors of intact survivorship in our four relocation studies of the elderly (Lieberman & Tobin, 1983; Tobin & Lieberman, 1976). Each separately predicted positive outcomes to the stress of relocation. Regarding magical coping, those who were able to transform involuntary relocation to an unwelcomed place into a volitional relocational to a rather ideal place fared well. And those who were more aggressive, even nasty, were more likely to survive intactly after the relocation.

The necessity to keep going and not to give in comes across loud and clear in a poem by Langston Hughes (1926):

*Mother to Son**

Well, son, I'll tell you:
Life for me ain't been no crystal stair.
It's had tacks in it,
And splinters,
And boards torn up,
And places with no carpet on the floor—
Bare.
But all the time
I'se been a-climbin' on,
And reachin' landin's,
And turnin' corners,
And sometimes goin' in the dark
Where there ain't been no light.
So boy, don't you turn back.

---

* From *Collected Poems* by Langston Hughes. Copyright © 1994 by the Estate of Langston Hughes. Reprinted by permission of Alfred A. Knopf, Inc.

Don't you set down on the steps
'Cause you finds it's kinder hard.
Don't you fall now—
For I'se still goin', honey,
I'se still climbin',
And life for me ain't been no crystal stair.

Crystal stair refers to the staircase on which Bojangles Robinson danced in the early movies. Often this tap dancer who appeared in Shirley Temple movies was the only African-American who approached being successful in the popular media.

FUNCTIONAL PARANOIA

Functional paranoia reduces a sense of vulnerability. Robert Butler, psychoanalyst, Pulitzer Prize winner, and first Director of the National Institute on Aging, described this kind of distrustful behavior that is functional for elderly persons (Perlin & Butler, 1963). It is a relatively mild kind of paranoia when contrasted with paranoia that contains psychotic persecutory elements. Still, for Jack and many others, distrust, suspiciousness, and blaming others can take on an angry quality that certainly can be aggravating for others. The paranoia is functional for Jack, as it is for others, because it reduces his sense of vulnerability; his responsibility for his deterioration. Certainly it is better to blame others than oneself and become depressed.

ACCEPTANCE OF PREVIOUSLY REPRESSED MATERIAL

This acceptance is helpful if it defines the core self. The psychoanalysts Norman Zinberg and Irving Kaufman (1963) have written, "The older patient is less likely to kid himself." An illustration:

It Was My Fault

 "I always blamed my brother." So began the narrative of the Drexel Home for the Aged resident that Jerome Grunes brought with him to his lecture in Bernice Neugarten's class on adult development and aging. Mr. Klein, who never married, said that all his life he had been telling himself that it was because he never found the right girl. Now at 79, he told a different story. "My older brother was a winner, and I was a loser. I couldn't compete with him. So I didn't try. I never felt good enough. I never felt that any girl I wanted would find me good enough." When asked when he came to this realization, he said, "Two years ago."*

REMINISCENCE

Reminiscence can serve to reinforce a core self when current everyday life does not provide evidence for the self concept. Marilyn's adulation by her first teacher Mrs. Burke provides evidence for her specialness now. A man in his late eighties whose core self concept was constructed around making business deals regaled the interviewer with many successful deals he made in buying and selling property. When asked to describe himself as he is now, although he has not made a deal in the past 25 years, said jokingly, "Just call me let's make a deal." Women are likely to define themselves as nurturant mothers even though their children in their fifties and sixties, and sometimes seventies, are obviously no longer being nurtured by them. When asked for current evidence that supports the here-and-now self-picture, validating evidence is as likely to be from the past as the present, as the past becomes interchangeable with the present (Lieberman & Tobin, 1983). Also, the past is made vivid with parents and others made bigger than life to reinforce the self (Revere & Tobin, 1980/81).

RELIGIOSITY

Religiosity takes a different form in advanced old age. The belief that living beyond four score and ten, 70 years of age, is a reward for service is not important in the middle years. It does, however, provide a sense of self-worth in the latest years. Another belief inculcated early that matters later in life is the belief in the hereafter that contains reunions with departed loved ones. Marilyn is looking forward to seeing her departed beloved mother. Then we have Frank:

Why Uncle Charley?

Frank is one of the more than three of four Americans who believe in a hereafter. In heaven he expects to not only meet his Maker but everyone he lost. "Lately I've been dreaming of Uncle Charley. Why? I can't figure it out. I was never close to him, my mother's brother. He was a somber guy. Never joked. Never laughed. I like a good joke. I've had it nice. I think maybe I'm a lot like Charley. I could have enjoyed life more. Maybe I want to tell him that."

A UNIQUE PSYCHOLOGY

When we witness these processes among very old people, they seem natural and even healthy. Would these processes, however, seem natural and healthy if used by younger persons? Would we not be concerned if the person in her or his young or middle adult years produced a photograph taken decades earlier when responding to the query, "Have you changed much as you have aged?" If activities were as limited as among very old people? If meager control meant so much? If functional status was measured by "downward social comparisons?" If contractions were essential to make life manageable? If magical mastery was necessary to preserve integrality? If aggression under stress was mandatory to ward off lethal passivity? If there were feelings of vulnerability that made paranoia functional? If to sustain the self, previously repressed content was evoked? If they used their past to validate their current self concept rather than structure and perceive current life as validations? If they were looking forward to reunions in the hereafter? Also, we must consider how death becomes acceptable when very old. Surely death would not be as acceptable!

The Benefits of Survivorship

ACCEPTANCE OF DEATH

Acceptance of one's personal finitude is facilitated by religious beliefs, but even among those without facilitory religious beliefs, death becomes acceptable when life's tasks are perceived as completed, when there is no unfinished business at the end of the life cycle. The fears of death among younger people are from concerns with a premature death, with life being cut short when there is much to be accomplished. Those, in turn, in their middle years with a terminal illness who know their foreshortened life span will end their lives prematurely are preoccupied with death. To be very old, however, is to recognize that nearing the completion of the life cycle is the appropriate time for the end of life.

Recall Jack Sampson's joking about reading the obituaries to see if he had another day to live. At another time he said, "I've seen it all. I've done it all. Now all I want is for my children to be happy. Every day is an added day. I just don't want to linger. Too much pain, and I don't want to have Alzheimer's at the end. It would be too hard on Marilyn." Jack fears nonbeing less than the process of dying that could include intractable pain and persistent confusion. His fears of the process of dying more than death itself is common among persons of advanced old age who not only fear pain and confusion but also dying alone and becoming immobile. Marilyn has similar fears of the process of dying, but her fears of death are more focused on Jack, whom she believes will die before her and leave her a lonely widow.

The Sampsons are aging normatively, but there are others who age nonnormatively because their life goals are not yet completed as the life cycle nears its end. In contrast to the Sampsons, whose life goals have been completed, some persons of advanced old age have unfinished business, individuals who still wish to be productive, such as active visual artists, who cannot accept their approaching deaths.

Never Say Die

The renowned painter Balthus (Balthazar Klossowskij Count de Rola) at 85 mentioned to his interviewer, Ted Morgan of The New York Times Magazine, during lunch that Makino, a "Japanese wiseman," was writing a book on vegetables at the age of 96, which he deliberately left unfinished as a way of staying alive. (January 9, 1994, pp. 36–41).

Another Japanese man of wisdom, Hokasai, the greatest of Japanese woodcutters, on his deathbed at 94 said, "I am just beginning to learn my craft." Visual artists in advanced old age are more likely to say something like, "I am just beginning to see the essence of my vision." Sometimes the unfinished business relates less to one's vocation than to one's avocation. "I would like time," said the 87-year-old Mrs. Stevens "to reread all of Edith Wharton." Or witness the alert Mr. Brown at 103: "C-Span is wonderful. I keep up with all that's happening. I still have a lot to learn about how politics and our government works."

There is a different kind of unfinished business for Mrs. Angel, who cares at home for her daughter with mental retardation:

To Never Grow Old

Mrs. Angel at 96 says about her severely retarded daughter Amy, who is 50, "She is still a child." Although she considers herself a very religious convert to Catholicism, when asked about death she said, "I don't know. I never went through it or thought about it. There is nothing I can say about it." She is also not ready to think about future plans: "I'll think about that <u>in due time</u>." The interviewer wrote, "She is very busy performing as much as she can until she can no longer do so." She is now having trouble doing so

because she can neither bathe nor dress herself, broke a hip 2 years ago and now uses a cane, and has a pacemaker. Although she has begun to feel "old," she says that she is still in late middle age.

Oldest old people with unfinished business are different. Death is not acceptable, and age-associated losses are less acceptable to them than to others. They may deplore their loss of control, and if they have retained religious beliefs that are invaluable to those with finished business, these beliefs are not very usable for acceptance of death and feelings of well being.

AGING SUCCESSFULLY

The preservation of the self can permit those who are very old to maintain feelings of well-being. When young, happiness may be an indicator of well-being. When very old, however, happiness or current mood is an insufficient reflection of well-being. Jack is very unhappy about his loss of vigor. Marilyn becomes sad when talking about the wonderful trips they enjoyed the several years after Jack retired, and she usually becomes tearful when talking about her departed mother. But both are satisfied with their lives, with their current activities; and with resolve and fortitude, they are determined to carry on. For them, there is a congruence between what they had hoped to achieve in life and what they have achieved. This congruence between expected and achieved life goals is revealed when they reflect on their financial security from Jack's pension, Social Security, and their few investments. They even have some discretionary money to give gifts to grandchildren on special occasions. When they talk about those terribly difficult years rearing three young children during the Great Depression, now is indeed a very good time.

Well-being can be enhanced when acute crises cause depression and confusion. Psychoanalysts Alvin Goldfarb and Jerome Grunes have developed different therapeutic approaches dating back to more than 3 decades ago. Whereas Goldfarb (1959) focused on inflating beliefs in mastery, Grunes (1982) emphasized recapturing earliest recollections. Reconstructive psychotherapy has also been found useful for very old persons who are capable of insight. Therapists, however, are likely to use different processes with very old patients; for example, touching more because very old patients or clients often feel untouchable due to physical deterioration and using reminiscence to elicit examples of successes in past life. Because of how therapeutic encounters with oldest old persons evoke feelings of dependency and death, it is sensible to ask: Why do clinicians choose to treat the oldest of old person?

When Care Is Needed

Receiving care at home is three times as common as care in nursing homes. Whereas 5% of those 65 and over reside in nursing homes, about 15% who have similar difficulties in the activities of daily living remain at home. The Sampsons reflect the normative pattern of spouse-caring when elderly wives care for their dependent husbands. Thereafter it is typical for women to become widowed for an average of 7 years before their deaths because women typically marry men 4.5 years older than they, and genetically women apparently live 2.5 years longer than men. It is thus common for elderly widowed mothers to live alone and later be cared for by their children, who are likely themselves to be 65 or over. Then, during the last years of life, hospitalizations and life in nursing homes are common. Although, as noted, 5% of elderly persons reside in nursing homes, to live to 65 is associated with as high as a one of two probability of spending part of the next and final years of life living in a nursing home, typically entering a nursing home in the 9th decade of life. Also warranting discussion is the dreaded Alzheimer's disease, which is becoming more frequent as people live longer lives.

FAMILY CARE AT HOME

Marilyn is caring for Jack, whose health status is not unlike those who reside in nursing homes. He has difficulty with most activities of daily life that are necessary for self-care: with getting about, bathing, and dressing himself. Marilyn, too, has difficulties in those tasks but can manage appreciably better. Sometimes spouse-caring is sufficient for remaining at home, even when the deficits are greater than Jack's:

Taking Each Day As It Comes

 "I take each day as it comes." At 87 it was apparent that although Tom was wheelchair bound, he had been a man of much physical prowess. "As long as I can move around the house, I'm okay." Following his stroke, he no

longer goes upstairs to the second floor of his two-story ranch house where his bedroom was once located. A bed has been placed in the living room, confining him to the first floor. Still, as he said, "Everything I need is down here." It is obvious, however, that Tom is dependent on his wife Martha for his daily needs. "Thank God for Martha. I'm taken care of. Meals? They're the least of it. She has to help me dress and onto the toilet. She has to make sure the aide bathes me right and all the other things."

Tom is able to preserve his selfhood because of Martha and also because of his determination not to give in to his disability. To be sure his world has contracted to a small first floor, but he retains sufficient feelings of being in control to assure a sense of continuity and wholeness. He looks forward to watching all the ballgames on television and the stream of visits by siblings, children, and grandchildren. He refuses to feel sorry for himself and avoids blaming himself for his poor dietary habits that may have led to a high cholesterol level eventuating in his stroke. Reminiscences and religion are important parts of his life:

"We like to sit around and remember all the good times we've had. We went to all the dances when we were young. Bad times too. We got through them. We can laugh now, but I can tell you it wasn't funny then. A piece of bread and some beans was sometimes a good meal. Now if I don't have a steak and potatoes I feel cheated." Also, religion is important to them. They consider themselves reborn Christians, and they believe that their prayers helped Tom's recovery. Together they watch television evangelists on Sunday morning. "It is the best part of the week."

It is different for Tillie:

A No Good Life

"Life used to be good. Before I broke my hip, I went to the senior center at the church every day. I can't anymore. I have a walker, but it's too hard. I just sit here. An aide comes every day. Sometimes friends come, but I know they're itching to get away. My daughters stop, but they don't stay long either. They have their own lives. They make sure I'm okay and go away. Its a no good life."

Tillie, now 81, became a widow early, at 46, 35 years ago. She then went to work for the first time, having married at 17 and thereafter was busy raising two daughters and three sons. Her daughters stayed in town, but her sons left. She worked in a school lunchroom, which she enjoyed immensely and did not want to retire. When she retired at 65, she began attending the local senior center, where she made many friends, participated in many activities, and ate lunch every day. She also became more involved at church, where the center was located. Then, a year ago she slipped on the ice and broke her hip, and life has never been the same. There is nothing she can do at home to replace the center and church activities. She does not feel in control of her life and has few things to look forward to. Memories of better times cannot sustain her. So Tillie is frustrated, bitter and angry, and rather depressed.

Tillie lives alone, whereas many older persons who are disabled and dependent live with their children. Mr. Livingston, an African-American, who atypically outlived his wife, lives with one of his daughters:

Caring For Our Nasty Dad

The group I was leading for family caregivers included two sisters, one of whom made a home for their severely diabetic father who had lost both legs to the disease. "It is difficult," said Meg, "especially when he yells at me. Its hard on my husband too." Then she looked around at the other caregivers as if she were ashamed of having expressed any anger toward her father. After I assured her that it's permissible to be angry, his sister Molly spoke up: "He is a tough one. He's always been hard on us, especially on us daughters. It's strange. He lives with Meg, but I'm the good one. Its hard caring for our dad when he's being nasty. I would be a lot angrier if I were her." I asked to describe behaviors that are bothersome. Meg answered: "He thinks he can still do everything. He can't. I don't want to tell him, but I have to tell him or I don't know what will happen. He can hurt himself." Then it was Molly's turn, again. "Don't forget Meg. The other day we were complaining. Is it all right to say bitching?" After I assured her that it was permissible to say bitching, she continued, "We were saying that it drives us crazy to hear the same stories over and over. He worked on the railroad, and we've heard about it all our lives. That's not as bad as when he tells Meg that he saved her from a bad marriage. She was going with a guy who drank a little too much and dad kicked him out of the house. He tells that story all the time."

Illustrated by this family is how the processes that help their father preserve his self disturbs them. Indeed, the constancy of his basic personality is troublesome to his daughters because he has always been a demanding and controlling father. Controlling his daughters, however, provides him with feelings of being in control. His nasty disposition, in turn, aids him in staving off depression from his illness and incapacities, and blaming Meg for her shortcomings is his way of dealing with anger, which in being externalized obviates its internalization.

It is, however, his daughters who internalize their anger. They may be angry at their father, but they are also angry at themselves. Later in the session they could talk about how their anger has been turned inward. Meg said: "I get angry at myself for getting angry at him. Then there are other times when I get angry at myself because I'm not doing enough. Maybe if I did some things differently it would be different. I remember when he was a real man." "The real man" allusion could not be ignored. I asked her what she meant. "Did I say that? I must have. Let's see, maybe I feel ashamed that he can't walk and do what he used to do." When I asked Meg why she should be ashamed,

Molly spoke up. "You put her on a hot wire. I know what she wants to say. We want to make dad whole again but we can't."

So, too, there is anger turned inward from feelings of inadequacy, in this instance from the irrational fantasy that if they truly were good and obedient daughters, they could make their father whole again and give him two nice legs to walk on. This turning in of anger on themselves is common among caregivers for perceived inadequacies in caregiving, as is anger toward their dependent care receivers for provoking feelings of inadequacies. Anger and frustrations also are generated from exaggerated beliefs in control and mobilization when reflected, for example, in functional paranoia that preserve the self in normative advanced old age, as well, of course, as by the characterologic behaviors that reflect the persistent self.

IN HOSPITALS AND NURSING HOMES

Hospitals can be disorienting to persons of any age, and they can be dangerous places, too. Jack developed an available bladder infection as he was recovering from his leg surgery. The causes of hospital iatrogenesis are many when iatrogenesis in its narrow meaning of inadvertent adverse effects from treatments by physicians is expanded to the diversity of hospital practices, diagnostic procedures, and therapeutic interventions. Patients, for example, may be labeled with Alzheimer's disease when they are only temporarily confused from being in an unfamiliar place or from one drug or the interaction of many medications or from "sundowning". Sundowning refers to confusion that occurs as the sun goes down among hospitalized patients who usually are receiving some kind of soporific, sleep-inducing, medication.

When nursing home care is necessary to assure survival, it is difficult to preserve the self and to use the psychological processes and beliefs that facilitate preservation of the self. Yet, our longitudinal studies of older people relocated to long-term care facilities has shown that people can and do retain their self-pictures. How the adverse effects of this and other crises can be resisted is evident in Ronnie Wacker's report of our findings in the magazine *Science 85*:

> Everybody in the old age home loved Mary Frances. In her seventies she was cheerful, undemanding, cooperative. She went out of her way to help other residents in the little Midwestern home, sewing for a woman whose fingers were stiff with arthritis, writing letters for another whose eyesight was failing. She kept up with a large circle of friends outside the institution and was a regular at the kaffeeklatch. Although

a hip operation had left her with a slight limp, and arthritis had settled in her knees, she rarely complained. When the operators of the home announced that they would have to close and the 45 residents would be relocated to a larger, more impersonal institution, she took the news better than most patients. "I'm not happy about it," she told an interviewer, "but I'm sure it will work out for the best. There will be things in the new place we'll like better than here."

Shortly after the move Mary Frances was bedridden and listless. In 6 months she was dead.

After relocation, she lapsed into what psychologists call the first-month syndrome, a common institutional malady caused by a change of environment. She sank into deep depression; she began to complain about the pain in her arthritic knees. For patients who can adjust to new surroundings, the depression lifts, and the frequent complaints of minor pains gradually cease. For Mary Frances, they did not. Her depression deepened into apathy. Some days she wouldn't leave her bed. She seemed never to recover her old spirit and finally, one gray day as unpromising as the previous one, she died.

Harry was something else again. The day he entered his old age home at 81 he complained to a social worker about the racial makeup of the staff. A few weeks later, he drove a volunteer aide out of his room in tears, accusing her of having stolen his false teeth, "You probably hocked 'em!" he shouted at her.

He boasted to everyone around him that he had beaten up his top sergeant in the army 60 years earlier," and "I could do it gain if I wanted to, by God!" He refused to bathe regularly and carried so strong a scent of urine that other patients shrank from him in the halls. He proudly attributed this avoidance to their fear of his physical strength.

A bachelor, he was persuaded to enter the home by his only relative, a young woman. She convinced him that he needed close medical attention because of a serious heart condition and emphysema. She helped him move in and at first visited him frequently. But then they had a disagreement over politics, and he ordered her to leave and never come back. She continued to call, but he refused to speak to her.

Eight years after being taken to the home, despite his heart condition and worsening emphysema, Harry roared on, ignoring or feuding with his fellow patients and abusing members, who whispered to each other that he was "just too mean to die."

Why did Harry, ill, suspicious, and hostile, apparently thrive in an environment similar to that which felled Mary Frances, originally far healthier and more hopeful? Two University of Chicago psychologists, Morton Lieberman and Sheldon Tobin, became interested in questions like this 21 years ago, when a study they were doing on stress and elderly persons turned up mortality results that surprised them. With disturbing consistency, the "wrong" old people were dying. The surly and paranoid survived, while the cheerful, cooperative, seemingly mentally healthy succumbed. (p. 64)

Whereas it was expected that the move would limit aged individuals' abilities to maintain a coherent and consistent self-image, they instead showed a remarkable self-image stability; a stability that is comparable to that which is maintained by elderly persons who are not undergoing such upheavals. But adaptation when living among nonfamily caregivers is always difficult. Too often nonfamily caregivers do not appreciate the inner experience of a persistent identity. Bumagin and Hirn in their 1979 book, *Aging is a Family Affair*, provide a poignant example by reproducing the following poem, which was found among the effects of a patient who had died in the Oxford University Geriatric Service Facility in England. The author is unknown.

What Do You See?

What do you see, nurses? What do you see-
Are you thinking, when you are looking at me;
A crabbit old woman, not very wise.
Uncertain of habit, with faraway eyes.
Who dribbles her food, and makes no reply,
When you say in a loud voice, "I do wish you'd try."
Who seems not to notice the things that you do.
And forever is losing a stocking or shoe;
Who unresisting or not lets you do as you will.
When bathing and feeding the long day to fill.
Is that what you are thinking, is that what you see?
THEN OPEN YOUR EYES, NURSES,
YOU ARE NOT LOOKING AT ME.
I'll tell you who I am, as I sit here so still,
As I rise at your bidding, as I eat at your will.
I'm a small child of 10, with a father and mother,
Brothers and sisters, who love one another,
A young girl of 16, with wings on her feet,
Dreaming that soon now a lover she'll meet,
A bride soon at 20, my heart gives a leap,
Remembering the vows that I promised to keep;
At 25 now, I have young of my own,
Who need me to build a secure happy home;
A woman of 30, my young now grow fast,
Bound to each other, with ties that should last;
At 40 my young sons now grow and will be all gone,
But my man stays beside me, to see I don't mourn;
At 50, once more babies play round my knee,
Again we know children, my loved one and me.
Dark days are upon me, my husband is dead.
I look at the future, I shudder with dread.
For my young are all busy, rearing young of their own,

And I think of the years, and the love that I've known.
I'm an old woman now, and nature is cruel.
It's her jest, to make old age look like a fool.
The body it crumbles, grace and vigor depart,
There is now a stone, where I once had a heart.
But inside this old carcass, a young girl still dwells,
And now and again, my battered heart swells;
I remember the joy, I remember the pain,
And I'm loving and living life all over again.
I think of the years, all too few-gone too fast,
And accept the stark fact that the nothing can last.
So open your eyes, nurses open and see
Not a Crabbit Old Women. Look Closer-see ME.

Just as the woman who wrote this poem retained her identity, so, too, did the respondents in our relocation studies, although, to be sure, their identities were threatened by the relocation.

THE DESELFING ALZHEIMER'S DISEASE

Our relocation studies in the 1960s and 1970s were undertaken when there was less prevalence of Alzheimer's disease. Now about two of three residents of nursing homes are victims of senile dementia, and their awareness of the loss of self can indeed be devastating.

Alzheimer's disease is an insidious disease that begins with a modest deterioration in intellectual functioning and ends in as many as 10 years later with total confusion, bizarre behaviors, and a vegetative state. Because a definitive diagnosis can only be made at postmortem, other causes for a progressive and inexorable deterioration in intellectual functioning must be ruled out before making a provisional diagnosis of this terrible affliction. The rising prevalence of this disease (apparently one of three persons 90 and over will have Alzheimer's disease) has sometimes made health professionals overreact to confusion in older people, particularly if there is a treatable condition such as malnutrition thyroid dysfunction, or vitamin B12 deficiency.

When all other causes have been ruled out, and the elderly person is diagnosed as having Alzheimer's disease, the lengthy period of deterioration begins. A deselfing process has started that leads to a person who is no longer himself or herself. The essential task for this family is the same as it is for families of all elderly people; that is, to help the victim be herself or himself as much as possible.

CHAPTER 2

Pathways to the Oldest Years

O*urs is an aging* society in which the oldest segment continues to increase as individuals age in the latter half of their lives to become persons who are very old. To be considered is the emergence of the cohort of oldest old persons and also pathways traversed over time by this cohort to become the oldest of the old people. Thus, in this context, pathways refer both to societal changes over time that account for the emergence of a cohort who are living toward the genetic limit of the human life span and to normative, or typical, changes in people's lives as they age from midlife to their oldest years.

The Emergence of the Extreme Aged

The nomenclature "advanced old age," "the oldest old," and the "extreme aged" is rooted in the demography of aging. Using data gathered in the 1960s, the United States Administration on Aging declared not 65 but rather 70 as the beginning of the frail years; and frail elderly persons, those 70 and over, were targeted for services. Then, in the 1970s, Bernice Neugarten (1974) used national data on disabilities to make a distinction between the "young-old" and the "old-old," with the old-old years beginning at 75. By the 1980s, national data showed the acceleration of disabilities to begin at 85 and thus the cohort 85 and over became the extreme aged group. Colleen Johnson simply called her investigation *The 85+ Study*. From 70 to 85 in 25 years is truly a great leap forward. And now from 65, society's demarcation of oldness, to 85 years of age is a remarkable 2 full decades, when designated as old but not yet of extreme old age.

To use 65 now for oldness, in its essential meaning of deterioration and frailty, is of course nonsensical. There are simply too many people over 65 who remain in good health. It certainly was different early in the century when Bismarck in Germany announced that individuals who reached 65 would be provided a modest stipend to enjoy their later years. Bismarck did not have to worry about bankrupting his treasury because it was rather uncommon to live much beyond 65. But now that 12% or more of populations of advanced technological societies are 65 and over, there is indeed concern about costs for retirement income and for health care. The cause for alarm is exacerbated by the awareness that when the baby boomers, those born after World War II when soldiers returned home and began their families, reach 65 that society's costs will rise dramatically. The estimate is that in the year 2010, persons 65 and over will comprise 20% to 25% of our population, with a significant percentage who are 85 and over.

The dramatic increase in those 85 and over is most evident since 1940. In each decade after 1940 the population 85 and over has increased more than 50%, a growth rate well beyond the rate for the total population of the age group defined as 65 and over. Whereas the proportion of those 85 and over within the total population of those aged 65 and over remained constant at 4% between 1900 and 1940, the proportion has increased steadily since 1940 to reach nearly 9% in 1980, and Census Bureau projections suggest that the 85 and over segment will double by the year 2000 to reach as much as 15% of the total group over 65.

Statistics for average life expectancies provide another perspective. In 1900, life expectancy at birth was 49.1 years for females and 49.6 for males; and at age 65, 12 more years for females and 11.4 for males. By 1940, life expectancy at birth for females was 65.3 years for females and 60.9 for males; and at age 65, 13.4 years for females and 11.9 for males. By 1990, life expectancy at birth was 78.6 for females and 71.8 for males; and at 65, 18.8 for females and 15.2 for males. Stated another way, females reaching 65 could expect to live to 77 in 1900, to 78.4 in 1940, and to 83.8 in 1990; an increase of 1.4 years from 1900 to 1940 but 5.4 years from 1940 to 1990. Correspondingly, a man reaching 65 in 1900 could expect to live to 76.4, to 76.9 in 1940, and to 80.2 in 1990; an increase of .5 years from 1900 to 1940 but 3.3 years from 1940 to 1990. (See the excellent 1996 book by Leonard Hayflick, *How and Why We Age*, for these and other statistics on aging.)

HUMAN LONGEVITY (110 YEARS OR SO)

The variety of statistics reveal that more individuals are living toward the limit of the human life span. Our life span, the longevity of *homo sapiens*, is estimated to be 110 to 115 years or so. Some individuals in antiquity have lived this long or even longer, but they were only a few among many. Eating yogurt, as much as we may wish, does not assure living beyond our longevity. Elders in the Caucuses who claimed to live 150 years and more, unfortunately, were found to be greatly exaggerating their age. When asked how old they were when they experienced a historic event, such as a flooding of their village, their calculated ages could be a third of what they claimed. The man who said he was 150 in 1970, for example, would report that he was at prepuberty in 1930 when the great flood occurred, making him closer to 50 than 150.

Population statistics alone do not suggest 110 years or so for longevity. George Sacher (1978) in his investigation of mammalian longevity showed that life span is predicted by the ratio of brain weight to body weight, as well as the ratio of the cephalic (thinking) part of the brain to the rest of the brain. The interpretation he gave to his findings was that the cybernetic, or integrative, capacity of the central nervous system permits retention of viability while organs decline in functioning. Homeostasis is lessened but life continues.

BUT NOT FREE OF CHRONIC DISEASES

As more older persons live out their life spans, they are not free of chronic diseases. The younger old years may be golden for many, but the older old years can indeed be tarnished. A distinction between being old in years but not feeling old and living a long life has a counterpart in the differences between the active life span and the average life span. If now the active life span approaches 85, the average life span, the time when death occurs, is beyond 85; and the mathematical difference between the active life span and the average life span gives the duration of the average years of disability preceding death, when experiencing oldness because of deterioration. These years of preterminal disability may be lessened when cures are found for the leading causes of death, for cardiovascular disease and cancer. The average life span, it has been estimated, may increase by about 2 years if cancer were cured and about 12 years if cardiovascular disease were cured. The difference in added years is because cancer patients are now being kept alive rather long, whereas cardiovascular disease often is lethal in younger years. Yet, disability cannot be expected to vanish. Cures for musculoskeletal deterioration and for Alzheimer's disease are not forecasted for the near future. Philip Katzman (1987) has estimated that one of three persons who are 90 and over are, and will be, victims of Alzheimer's disease. Living longer, therefore, does not mean avoiding growing old and not experiencing preterminal disabilities. Yet, many more individuals will not have a specific disease that causes death as they live to be centenarians and live out the human life span but rather will die of nonspecific old age, of an exhaustion of vitality. Still, they may experience a preterminal period of disability and deterioration.

Pathways

Whether there will be more or less preterminal disability in the future is unknown. Even if one third of persons 90 and over are afflicted with Alzheimer's disease, for example, many will die in an early stage with little disability, and as many as two thirds of those 90 and over are likely to escape this dreadful affliction. These two thirds may or may not have crippling musculoskeletal disease. Many, however, will have impairments from their genetic weaknesses, and still others will have impairments from dysfunctional life styles and environmental forces such as pollution. Yet, before a possible preterminal phase, those who live toward the end of the human life span can expect to have several years of dependency-free active life in their oldest years, in their years of advanced age. Slightly more than one half of persons 85 and over have no incapacities in their activities of daily living.

THE YOUNGER OLD YEARS

Working backward, preceding the possibly dependency-free years of advanced age are the many younger old years of the active life span that are beyond 65. But 65 may cease to be a demarcation for the beginning of the younger old years. Sixty-five years of age, as noted earlier, once had meaning because of how few survived beyond this age; and if they survived, they were likely to be frail. Because 65 was a good proxy for frailty, it became a reasonable retirement age, but now most people are in good health at 65 and are capable of continuing to work. Being able to work, it must be recognized, is not, however, the same as wishing to continue working, which explains why more than one half of the work force retires before 65. Put another way, most are physically and mentally capable of working but choose not to continue working at their jobs. If, therefore, the young-old years are considered to begin at retirement, they normatively begin before 65. From a public policy perspective, federal entitlements of Social Security and Medicare are provided at 65 because people are veterans of life then and not because they are frail and cannot work. Put differently, we have come to accept that our life cycle will include, and moreover that we deserve, a reasonably lengthy period approximating the popularized golden years of later life. A critical public policy issue is how to provide reasonably priced health insurance to those who retire early and are not eligible for Medicare.

In their landmark book *Successful Aging*, John Rowe and Robert Kahn (1998) rely heavily on knowledge gained from 1,350 individuals 70 to 79 who were followed for 8 years as part of the MacArthur Foundation Study. Their focus, in my lexicon, is more on the current younger old. Components of successful aging for them are threefold: avoiding disease, maintaining high cognitive and physical functioning, and engagement with life. Rowe and Kahn are particularly concerned with the promotion of functioning and observe that "usual aging" entails substantial risk for disease and disability, much of which can be reduced by life style choices. To be sure, many persons in their oldest of years can avoid debilitating disease, maintain functioning, and continue highly engaged in life. Yet ordinary people are usually unable to avoid those serious kinds of losses that necessitate psychological adaptive processes in their oldest years if integrality is to be maintained and the self preserved. In one sense, my focus, as well as Johnson and Barer's, is on what's next. That is, what are likely to be the adaptive processes after Rowe and Kahn's earlier successful aging?

MIDDLE AGE

Still working backward, preceding the young old years are the years of middle age. Assuming that by 50, children have been launched, there can be half of a lifetime ahead from the years of the empty nest to death at the end of the life cycle. The "latter half of life" has thus become the focus for research by gerontologic social scientists and also circumscribes the boundaries for geriatric practitioners, as well as for policymakers as, for example, in discussions of "older workers."

The middle and young-old years anticipate and are preparatory for later adaptation. Advanced old age, said one respondent, as noted in the Preface, fortunately does not occur suddenly. It occurs after a lifetime of living. Stability of the self is always important. Similarly important is being in control in everyday life, as well as self-determination and using reconstructions of the past to meet current adaptive needs. If there is a midlife crisis, it comes from the awareness that major family and career goals, Freud's *Liebe und Arbeiten*, have not been achieved by late middle age. There is no evidence, however, that this awareness causes any kind of upheaval, a midlife crisis characterized by inner conflict and anguish. Bernice Neugarten and Nancy Datan (1974) found only a mild interiority in which there is some introspection on what has been achieved, an awareness of bodily changes, an identification with parents, and a tendency on birthdays to not only count how many years lived but also how many years left to live. It is also normative to feel generative because most people feel that children have been launched successfully, career goals achieved, and leisure pursuits meaningful. The accrued sense of generativity therefore reflects the typical feelings of satisfaction experienced sometimes in the middle to young-old years from having achieved major life goals, particularly for Erikson in having been a productive person, primarily in producing offspring successfully but also more broadly defined in making a difference because of one's efforts and actions.

A MIDLIFE CRISIS?

For the current cohort of oldest old people, generativity became rather easy to accomplish. The woman who was 85 in 1990 was born in 1905 and raised with expectations that if her husband worked hard, they could afford a family. After marriage and bearing children, life may have been fine, evoking rising expectations of a splendid future. Then, while rearing her children, the Great Depression occurred, which wreaked havoc with her great expectations. As the economy improved, life became better than expected. Very old people talk about the terrible years during the Great Depression but not about a midlife crisis.

I Couldn't Afford One

 When asked if she had a midlife crisis, Mrs. Tortelli at 80 laughed and said, "I couldn't afford one." She then talked about a midlife crisis as a modern invention, peculiar to the affluent, especially to men who can afford to dis-

card their wives and seek a young playmate. "We just had enough to make ends meet. And my husband? He couldn't afford to get rid of the old girl even if he wanted to. I'm joking. He didn't want to get rid of me. We were just beginning to enjoy life when the kids were on their own."

The good feelings from having weathered difficult times in their middle years is a harbinger of the feelings of satisfaction in their advanced years from achieving a congruence between expected and achieved life goals. The feelings of success in midlife with what has been accomplished is accompanied by what George Vaillant (1977) and David Karp (1985) have characterized as an increased mellowness. When children left home leaving behind an empty nest, there was likely to be a mixture of loss and relief, with only some parents experiencing a great loss. Most report a new intimacy with their spouses following the empty nest.

Most oldest old women also weathered menopause without adverse effects. Bernice Neugarten, Vivian Wood, Ruth Kraines, and Barbara Loomis (1963) found that women reported being apprehensive before menopause but afterward that menopause was not very difficult and had little affect on them. Some even reported that it was a relief.

Retirement, too, may have been anticipated with apprehension, but all investigators have reported successful adjustment afterward. The myth that retirement is lethal is spawned by younger persons in professions of high status who cannot yet see how retirement could ever be a welcomed event.

Some individuals do, of course, have difficulty coping with these typical life events. The oldest old men often report how difficult it was to give up work and to develop a new way to relate to their wives all day long. Those who found retirement most difficult were likely to be professionals who could not replace the feelings of esteem and power achieved on the job. Of all the occupational groups with which I am familiar, it is judges who have the most difficulty retiring. Regarding the empty nest and menopause, some women report having become depressed. Apparently, college-educated women who never worked but remained home to rear children, and did so with great success, have difficulties when their last child leaves home.

The generation before the current cohort of oldest old people, however, had exceedingly more difficulties with these life events. When marriages were less complementary, men obtained their identities from work and women from being Hausfraus (traditional housewives). Those now in their advanced years may minimize the stressfulness of life transitions; men in the stressfulness of retirement and women in the stressfulness of menopause and the empty nest, but they are quite cognizant of how different it was for their parents. Usually said by very old persons is that their fathers' self-esteem was entirely from work and their mothers' from nurturance of children.

Stability with Change

How much did they change during these years? Some geron-tologists emphasize change, others stability. Obviously people change as adaptive demands change throughout life. Being a parent to a newborn is different, as we all know, from being a parent to a teenager or, as is the case for the oldest old persons, to being a parent of a child who is also old, beyond 65. People also are affected by unexpected events, by historic events such as the Great Depression and World War II, and by off-time events such as the death of a spouse or, most dev-astatingly, a child's death. It is the rare oldest old respondent that does not report an off-time, "accidental" event that occurred in their family. Indeed it is the accidental, nonnormative events that affect people the most. Yet, at the same time that changes are described, stability is also reported. Simply put, what people enjoy, what "turns them on," gen-erally persists, as do their dispositions, values, and beliefs. There is surely stability of enduring personality traits that change in expression as life unfolds. The competitive man may be competititve throughout life but he expresses it quite differently at 20, 46, and 80.

PERSISTENCE OF THE SELF

A synthesis of evidence for, and theorizing about, stability and change through the young-old years necessitates encompassing the persistence of the self or identity. Persistence of the self is not a new idea. Cicero, in 44 B.C., wrote his essay De Senectute (On Old Age) when he was 62, a rather advanced age 2000 years ago. In this dia-logue, two younger men pose their questions to Marcus Procius Cato, the wise elder of 84:

> Scipio, aged 35, opens the conversation by saying to Cato: "I have never noticed that you find it wearisome to be old. That is very different from most other old men, who claim to find their age a heavier burden than Mount Etna itself." Cato responds, "A person who lacks the means within himself to live a good and happy life will find any period of his

existence wearisome. But rely for life's blessings on your own resources, and you will not take a gloomy view of any of the inevitable consequences of nature's laws. Everyone hopes to attain an advanced age; yet when it comes they all complain! . . . Old Age, they protest, crept up on them more rapidly than they had expected. Who was to blame for their mistaken forecast? For age does not steal upon adults any faster than adulthood steals upon children . . . I follow and obey nature as a divine being. Now since she has planned all the earlier divisions of our lives excellently, she is not likely to make a bad playwright's mistake of skimping the last act. And a last act was inevitable. There had to be a time of withering, of readiness to fall, like the ripeness which comes to the fruits of the trees and of the earth. But a wise man will face the prospect with resignation, for resistance against nature is as pointless as the battles of the giants against the gods." (pp. 214–215)

The difference between those who are wise and those who are unwise is suggested here and elsewhere by Cicero to be a personality disposition; that is, a characteristic inculcated early in life that persists throughout life.

CONTINUITY AS A MOTIVE

In more recent times, in 1945, Paul Lecky attributed to self-consistency the primacy of human motives. Regarding the gerontologic literature, the anthropologist Sharon Kaufman, (1987) interpreted her interviews of older persons to reflect the persistence of the self. In turn, the sociologist Robert Atchley (1989) developed his continuity theory to encompass both internal and external continuity. According to Atchley, each kind of continuity in aging has motivational aspects. People attempt to be the same persons they have always been when confronting life's vicissitudes and also to use the same coping mechanism they have always employed.

Psychologists are likely to quote William James, the philosopher who is considered to be the first modern day psychologist. Toward the end of his chapter on habit in the *Principles of Psychology*, (1982) he wrote:

Already at the age of 25 you see the professional mannerism settling down on the young commercial traveller, on the young doctor, on the young minister, on the young counsellor-at-law. You see the little lines of cleavage running through the character, the tricks of thought, the prejudices, the ways of the 'shop,' in a word, from which the man can by-and-by no more escape than his coat sleeve can suddenly fall into a new set of folds. . . . In most of us, by the age of 30, the character has set like plaster, and will never soften again. (pp. 125–126).

Psychologists of more recent vintage are likely to discuss two refinements when discussing this quote. First, character is considered broader than temperament in being the complex mixture of all learned habits as is found when adapting to social roles. Second, temperament is now referred to as personality traits that persist from early socialization onward and are distinguished from states that refer to transitory behaviors and to momentary feelings such as elation and sadness. Character is more akin to the self, whereas personality traits have a more specific connotation. Yet both have been said to be "set in plaster."

Traits are subsumed in all definitions of personality, as in Gordon Allport's (1961) definition: "The dynamic organization within the individual of those psychophysical systems that determine his characteristic behavior and thought." Whereas this particular definition would be acceptable to the diversity of theorists of personality, theorists differ on their conceptualizations of psychophysical systems. Freud's structural model of ego, id, and superego may have receded into the background, but common to all believers in personality theory is the persistence of basic personality that is expressed in enduring traits. Recall also Freud's repetition compulsion.

THE PERSISTENCE OF TRAITS

Paul Costa and Robert McCrae(1984, 1997) have provided the most compelling data for the persistence of personality traits in the latter half of life. Following people longitudinally from their middle years through their young-old years, they found remarkable stability in the traits of neuroticism, extraversion-introversion, and openness to experience, agreeableness, and conscientiousness. Stability is assessed by following a sample over time and then determining the extent that individuals remain in the same position on the scale relative to others in the sample. If persons in the sample are sorted out the same way over time, stability is high. Data for identifying stability are provided by self-administered questionnaires that contain statements that require respondents, for example, to reveal their preferred activities and relationships with others.

The five dimensions support good common sense. They are very observable ways in which individuals vary from one another, as has been found not only in older adults but also in children and college students; in men and women; in observations, as well as self-reports; and in Americans, Germans, and Chinese. The five dimensions, not unexpectedly, were found by Costa and McCrae to sort people the same way over time by trait inventories that were administered in two intervals that averaged 20 years apart. Individuals who tend to be guilty, for example, continue this tendency as compared to those who tend not to be guilty about their actions; and people who are more extraverted than introverted remain at the extraverted end of the scale from 50 to 70. Stability is characteristic of normative community samples, but there are changes for groups so that college students are somewhat higher in neuroticism, extraversion, and openness to experience, and lower in agreeableness and conscientiousness than are older adults. Besides levels on these traits changing with age, they may change as a result of psychopathology and, on the other hand, as a result of psychotherapy but, additionally, from catastrophic stress and in dementias such as Alzheimer's disease.

CHANGE WITH STABILITY

Stability, whether conceptualized as a set of basic personality traits or the experience of an inner self, refers to a core that is developed in the early years of life that persists through the oldest years. Recently, however, some developmental psychologists (Baltes, 1993; Ryff, 1993) have focused on more external aspects of the self such as who older people are now, who they were, who they would like to be, and who they would not like to be. A focus on these external and more manifest aspects of the self concept encourages describing people as changing as they age and indeed considering multiple selves and new selves when very old. The two views, however, are not incompatible. Whereas a core self persists, not only do representations of the core self vary but also assessments of our selves.

Obviously stability does not mean that people do not change. Costa and McCrae address this concern by arguing that whereas dispositions remain constant, the life structures of individuals change as they move from adolescence to maturity to retirement. Certainly, the expression of enduring traits change with adaptive demands. Charlotte Buhler (1968), one of the earliest students of the latter half of life, made an analogy to how biologists relate genotype to phenotype. Genotype is what is in our genes, but the expression of our basic make-up is shaped by environmental factors. Identical twins may have a gene making them especially susceptible to developing cancer of the colon, but one twin may develop colon cancer whereas the other may not because of the kinds of food in the diet. Similarly, our basic personality traits (analogized to genotype) may endure, but their expression (their phenotype) may change depending on situations and life experiences. (In my sixties, I am still genotypically competitive, but now rather than compete with peers intellectually, I am more likely to exhibit my competitiveness in doubles on the tennis court. And I hope to continue competitive tennis through my eighties but maybe a little slower.)

Change occurs in response to events, not only to normative events in the life cycle and to historic events experienced by a cohort but also to accidental events. Normative events discussed earlier include the empty nest, menopause, and retirement. These events cause a modification in social roles,sometimes within the same role as in the career of parenthood and sometimes through acquisition of new roles and relinquishing old roles. Very old men from a social role perspective are no longer employed workers, but from a psychological perspective their identities may incorporate their occupation. The 87-year-old judge in the nursing home who retired 15 years ago would be insulted if not referred to as "judge." The woman of 92 still considers herself to be a housewife. The exit from a personally meaningful social role does not mean that it is not part of one's identity.

THE PERCEPTION OF SAMENESS

As the rights and responsibilities inherent to social roles change, so do manifest behaviors. Indeed it is these behavioral changes that cause most gerontologists to declare more instability them stability, more discontinuity than continuity in the latter half of life. Obviously people change. Their behavior, encompassing their thoughts, feelings, and actions, change as their social roles and preoccupation change throughout the life course. Oldest old people are not unaware that social roles and preoccupations have changed throughout their lives, and that advanced old age is another, and the last, season of their life. Yet they also perceive a persistence of their selves. Maya Angelou (1978), the renowned, African-American poet, put it this way in her poem "On Aging"*:

When you see me sitting quietly,
Like a sack left on the shelf,
Don't think I need your chattering.
I'm listening to myself.
Hold! Stop! Don't pity me!

---

* From *And Still I Rise* by Maya Angelou. Copyright (c) 1978 by Maya Angelou. Reprinted by permission of Random House, Inc.

Hold! Stop your sympathy!
Understanding if you got it,
Otherwise I'll do without it!

When my bones are stiff and aching
And my feet won't climb the stair,
I will only ask one favor;
Don't bring me no rocking chair.
When you see me walking, stumbling.
Don't study and get it wrong
'Cause tired don't mean lazy
And every goodbye ain't gone.
I'm the same person I was back then,
A little less hair, a little less chin,
A lot less lungs and much less wind.
But ain't I lucky I can still breathe in.

Some older persons go to great lengths to communicate the persistence of the self:

I've Always Been Like That

"Even when I was a little girl, I liked pretty things," said the 88 year old widow Mrs. Swift who was living in an apartment in a senior housing complex. She was dressed immaculately and had her hair and nails done up for the interview. "I may be the oldest one here (although she was not the oldest resident), but you would never know it. I take care of myself and dress right." Throughout the interview, she interspersed comments on her appearance and dress. "I remember my first day at school. My mother bought me the prettiest dress. I remember brushing my hair. Everyone commented on how nice I looked." Later in the interview she said, "Eddie (her husband) knew I liked pretty things and always bought them for me. He knew how much I appreciated nice things. I've always been like that. He was a dear."

HISTORICAL EVENTS

Major historic events have also occurred. For the oldest old the most critical historic events have been the Great Depression and World War II. Whereas persons of advanced old age could not evade the effects of the Great Depression, residual effects differ among them. Glen Elder (1974) had longitudinal data that made it possible to follow people from the time they were rearing children during the Great Depression through their young-old years. The group that manifested the most significant residual effects from their experiences during the

Great Depression were middle class women whose family income had dropped dramatically. These woman, as contrasted with middle class men whose family income had dropped dramatically and with lower class men and women, were better able to adapt later in their young-old years. According to Elder, they were able to use their inner resources, which were accrued from their early socialization, to meet the challenges of deteriorating family life and to hold the family together. Raised to be passive and dependent housewives, when circumstances made it imperative to aggressively mobilize themselves, they did so. If it were necessary, they moved in with parents against the wishes of out-of-work husbands, and many went to work, also usually against the wishes of their husbands. In evolving to more aggressive people, they became better prepared for coping with later illness and widowhood. Mrs. Sampson tells it as it was:

Times Were Real Hard

 "You can't imagine how bad it was. Jack lost his job. We couldn't make ends meet. We had to move away from our friends, give up our apartment, move in with my parents. It was tough on Jack. Later, he got a job. It didn't pay well. So I went to work, and we moved to a larger apartment a few blocks away so the kids could go to the same school. We took our parents with us so we could afford a larger place. It was still sort of crazy. Seven of us sharing a bathroom. Can you imagine? My going to work hurt Jack. We had no other choice. You know in those days women weren't supposed to work. I believed it too. I kept telling him its okay. Other wives are doing it too. I thought he'd never get over it. He did finally. I did too. Then I liked it. I didn't tell him, but I got a checking account for me just in case of a rainy day. I worked downtown and would stop on the way home to pick up day-old bread, day-old cookies. My kids," now said laughing, "still think fig bars, you know the cookie, are supposed to be hard, and that bananas should be eaten when they are a little black. Oh my, I have so many memories. A big favorite was mashed potatoes with a soft boiled egg on top. Sid, the middle one (child) thought that was the greatest meal. You would never know it now. He eats very well now. But every time he comes to visit, we remember mashed potatoes with an egg on the top."

Later Mrs. Sampson returned to opening her own bank account. Until then she had neither a savings or checking account. Jack paid all the bills and gave her a weekly household allowance. "It changed my life. I didn't know it at the time. I felt more a person. I let Jack take care of all our bills. Now that he is retired, it's like it's his work, his job. Let me tell you. I know everything that comes in and goes out. You better believe it."

Another way to view historic changes is how events and periods in the life cycle have changed over time. At the turn of the century, as noted earlier, there was no empty nest. Childbirth was spread out over many years, with widowhood occurring for women when at least one child was still at home. Pity the youngest daughter still at home who had no choice but to care for her mother and never to marry. The never-married caretaker of mother is sometimes found among the current oldest old group. Most can recall a maiden aunt in their family who never left home.

My Aunt Sadie

Mrs. Sherman at 87 loved to talk about Sadie, her aunt who never married. "She treated me even better than my mother. She brought me books. If she didn't, nobody would, and I would never have become a school teacher." Aunt Sadie, her mother's sister, was the second youngest of nine children and the youngest daughter. When her father died, she was still living at home, and she was appointed the one to stay at home and care for her mother as her mother aged. "Later," Mrs. Sherman said, "Sadie told me that she put on a brave front. She would like to have married and have children. But she had no alternative but to care for her mother. So I became like her child. Why me? I don't know. We lived next door. It was lucky for me that I had Aunt Sadie, but it was not lucky for her."

There were many Aunt Sadie's early in this century. The empty nest, like the midlife crisis, is a latter day invention as families have fewer children and parents live longer. Persons of advanced age are indeed quite aware of these changes over historic time.

Then, too, the timing of life events has changed. The age of marriage has gone up, the duration of the years of birthing has gone down, the empty nest occurs earlier, retirement is also earlier, and the years after the empty nest and after retirement until infirmity and then death have become longer. Correspondingly, when a life event should occur it has changed over historic time. Each generation has a sense of what is on time or off time for each life event. Some oldest old people are likely to say "I was right on time. I got married at 18 and began my family." Others say, "I did things differently. I waited until my thirties to get married and raise a family." What, however, has persisted to be normative is widowhood for women. Women on the average experience 7 years of widowhood because they marry men on the average who are 4.5 years older and genetically live about 2.5 years longer. I advise my female students to marry men who are at the very least two and one half years younger than they.

Independent of whether on time or off time for normative life cycle events, it is the rare oldest old person who does not report an unexpected event. Some scholars of later life, such as Robert Galatzer-Levy and Bertram Cohler (1993) have observed that the most ubiquitous findings of studies of aging are discontinuities from chance factors: "Longitudinal studies from early childhood, through middle age and into later life have produced two remarkable findings. First, discontinuity rather than continuity best characterizes lives over time. Second, chance factors are far more important than previously recognized as a means for organizing personal experience" (p. 215).

CHANCE EVENTS

Kenneth Gergen (1977) has made chance factors, which he calls "aleatory events," the centerpiece of adaptive changes in adulthood and old age. A son may have been killed in World War II, an unexpected pregnancy may have occurred at 40 when the youngest child was then 15, a husband may have taken a job far away from their home, or he may have died suddenly when she was 50 and she had to take over the family business. Each chance event leaves its mark, and each can be recalled with great vividness 20, 40, and even 60 years later. Listen to Jack Sampson:

No Way to Know

 "Who can ever say what will happen? I was lucky when Mickey talked me into starting our own shop. It was risky, and I had a good job working for someone I liked. Mickey and I enjoyed working as a team, but we didn't have the ready cash to go on our own. It was in the early '50s and I only had it good after the war started, when I wasn't drafted and did defense work. So for 10 years it was good, but those Depression years before were too hard. He kept pushing, and when he landed a big job, too big for the two of us, we plunged in. We didn't want to take any of the men from our boss. He was too good to us. We scrambled and found some others. One of them, Carl, stayed with me until I retired. You remember I retired because of another thing you cannot predict. That accident. So Mickey was like an accident. A good accident. If we never became friends, I never would have had my own business. I would have worked for someone else all my life. I would have done okay but not good. How I could have sent my kids to good colleges, and they kept going to school after college, I don't know 'till this day. When they went to college, I was just starting the business and Marilyn had to work. Later, by the time the business was a big success, they were through with school. The timing wasn't perfect, but we're fixed now. So you try to predict. I can't. There ain't no way to know what's going to happen."

INTRINSIC CHANGES TRANSCENDING EVENTS

Stability and change as discussed up to now has included the persistence of the self and of personality traits but with their changing expression during the latter half of life; as well as the obvious changes from anticipated, historic, and chance events. Not yet sufficiently covered are possible developmental changes, intrinsic changes that transcend external events and pressures. Are there systematic changes from internal pressures independent of events?

Erikson's Generativity versus Stagnation is postulated to be a developmental change because it is intrinsic in being provoked by internal psychic forces and not by external events. The crisis is from an awareness in later adulthood or during the young-old years of what should have been accomplished by this time in the life span. Mellowness or interiority, as noted earlier, in addition to being intrinsic to generativity, are offered as descriptions of the developmental outcome. Whatever words are used to communicate developmental changes, all infer change for the better. Indeed, an essential criterion for a developmental change is something better than there was earlier.

Development for biologists is the growth and differentiation of organisms that leads to the mature form, whereas aging is postmature irreversible deterioration leading to death. Development, however, is conceptualized by social scientists as occurring in the postmature years when, for example, Erikson's sense of generativity can be achieved. Therefore, while postmaturation deterioration is observed by biologists, social scientists recognize the transcendence of deterioration after maturity found in the differentiation of human development.

A different kind of developmental change has been proposed by David Gutmann (1987): the release of opposite-sex motives in midlife that have been repressed during the child-rearing years. According to Gutmann, the parental imperative period necessitates this repression to assure the differentiation between mothers and fathers that is essential for family functioning and child rearing. The freeing of opposite sex, androgynous motives, aggression in women and passivity in men, does not mean that women or men lose their same-sex motives but, rather, that opposite-sex motives become added, making for fuller, enriched human beings. An obvious assumption in this theory is that if opposite-sex motives are to be released in persons regardless of gender after the parental imperative, that repression began early in life, when they were being reared. This assumption is certainly more true for older cohorts than for younger cohorts who have been reared with very different expectations for girls than for boys. There is clearly a historic trend toward less differentiation. Certainly, persons who are now of advanced old age were reared with encouragement to act like girls should act, and like boys should act reinforcing repression of androgynous motives.

Androgynous changes preceding the oldest old years can be assumed for those now of advanced old age. Yet, for those women who become less passive and more assertive during the Great Depression to assure integrity of the family, androgynous changes probably occurred before the end of the parental imperative. Older women, particularly from working class families, relate their becoming more assertive to going to work, to widowhood, and to being influenced by children and grandchildren. Some simply say, "I learned to speak my mind." Yet, many in the oldest old cohorts, as well as cohorts after them, have remained the passive and dependent women they were raised to become.

The oldest men, in turn, do discuss slowing down, becoming less aggressive and more mellow, especially in the years preceding retirement. Indeed, Gutmann's projective data gathered decades ago from American men and also from men in traditional cultures like the Druids in Israel, revealed a shift toward passivity and dependency in the middle years; and because the men he studied would now be in the oldest cohort, it is a valid assumption that they experienced an androgynous release of previously repressed motives. When androgynous change has occurred successfully, the change can be considered developmental in nature. Although new elements are added to the self, as well as to the intrapsychic structure of one's personality, the change cannot, however, be interpreted as a transformation. Rather, the core self and the core personality is retained but modified and embellished. Let us again turn to the Sampsons.

What Were We Like?

"When our youngest left home," said Jack Sampson, "I was starting my business. The other two were in college. It was strange not having kids around. We didn't know what to do with each other without the kids around. It's different now. We take care of each other. It's like we had to get acquainted again. It took a while. It was sort of tense. I guess I didn't relax until I knew the kids would be okay, could make a living."

Marilyn Sampson puts it differently. "I had a hard time. I would make too much for dinner but there was only two of us. We had nothing to talk about. I noticed that Jack would come home late. I didn't want to fight, so I would just heat up dinner. Sometimes I would eat, and he would eat by him-self and read the paper. Slowly we got back together, and it was better between us. In many ways, we were more comfortable with each other." Later she added, *"At some point I decided there were things I wanted to do for myself. I took up Mah Jong, and then when the synagogue moved, we did too. I rented a marvelous apartment, threw out old furniture, and bought the best we could afford. I told Jack that with no kids to scratch the furniture, I was going to treat myself. Before I knew it, I was worrying less about the kids. I never stop worrying about them. I did worry less at some time and took care of myself better. Until you asked about it, I never thought about it. Or maybe I did but can't remember."*

Becoming "Old"

As changes are experienced in living through the younger old active life span years, people are certainly aware of becoming older but not necessarily of becoming old. To be "old," is a statement of mind that can occur at any age. The football player feels old at 30. The Olympic gymnast can feel old at 20. The 15 year old can feel old when talking to her 10-year-old sister. And certainly illness preceding advanced old age causes feelings of oldness. Chronologic age, how-ever, does exact its toll. Even without disabling diseases, people in their late eighties, nineties, and one hundreds are likely to say, "I'm old now." When nearing the end of the life cycle with attendant wan-ing energies, it is difficult to escape the self-appellation of "old." Still, some who are chronologically of extreme age say, "You are as old as you feel and I do not feel old yet."

Transcending how oldness is experienced in advanced old age is the shared understanding that life has its vicissitudes, that changes have occurred, and that "I am still me." Reflections, in turn, on events from one's past life are filtered through the screen of cur-rent adaptive needs. What is recalled, and how it is recalled, as will be discussed in the chapter on reminiscence, may tell us more of how current adaptive challenges are being met than of how events were experienced when they occurred. Although each person has lived a unique life and has an idiosyncratic personal narrative, there are adaptive processes and beliefs normative to the current cohort of persons in advanced old age. Considered in the next part are succes-sive chapters on normative adaptive coping, on reconstructions of the past, and on religiosity.

The Ever Changing Personal Narrative

But recall is fickle. The personal narrative is continually changing. As life stories are told and retold, the events may be the same, but the elaborations change to meet adaptative needs. The man who was wedded to his job in his early career may tell the story of the stressful interview he underwent when hired last year at age 26 by elaborating on his sweating palms and collar. At 40, now a close friend of his boss, and now he himself in charge of administrating stressful interviews, he may elaborate on how easy his boss was on him compared to how hard he is on new recruits. Then, at 60, he may laugh about the silly games they played. This metamorphosis of the reconstructions of the past may not be in consciousness, with little awareness that elaborations on events have changed over time. Childhood memories may retain their vividness while changing with the seasons of life. What may be recollected may also change depending on current life situations. The modifications of reminiscence will continue until death at the end of the life cycle, unless Alzheimer's disease in a late stage causes an inability to recall the distant past.

Apparently, however, as the oldest old years draw near, there may be a reviewing of life from the awareness of the nearness of death. As will be discussed in chapter 4, which focuses on reminiscence in advanced old age, after completing the creation of an acceptable life story, there is less introspection on the meaningfulness of life as it has been lived. Concurrently, the past is made vivid and dramatic, and often mythicized, to enhance the reality of the current self.

PART TWO

Facilitory Processes

The three kinds of processes for preserving the self in advanced old age will be discussed in sequential chapters: adaptive coping mechanisms in chapter 3, reconstructions of reminiscence in chapter 4, and religiosity in chapter 5.

Some adaptive coping mechanisms used by very old persons, such as control and assertiveness, are important, independent of age, when confronting adversity and stress. A life-threatening illness in the younger years can be resisted longer by personal feelings of being in control and by assertiveness, but elderly persons are particularly vulnerable to passivity that can be lethal when there is a weakened biologic substrata. Paranoia, however, is not likely to be functional in young people, nor are they likely to accept into consciousness previously repressed content as do very old people when the content helps to define the core self. In all, eight mechanisms will be considered.

Regarding reminiscence, very old persons blend the past with the present to maintain the self picture and make the past vivid to affirm the core self. Younger persons facing a premature death are less able to turn to the past when knowing that a foreshortened future has thwarted life goals. When, however, goals have been accomplished by the end of the life cycle, the past becomes useful for validation of the self and for validating a life lived as it should have been lived. If a full life span has not been lived, the past cannot provide the same kind of meaningfulness to life.

Two kinds of religious beliefs are salient to the very old: God's bless-ings of a long life as a divine reward for service and a hereafter filled with reunions with departed loved ones. To live beyond the biblical three score and ten, 70 years of age, provides believers with a specialness in the eyes of their god. A life curtailed before old age does not allow this belief, a belief inculcated when young that becomes salient when old, to be useful for feelings of spe-cialness. The belief in reunions in the hereafter is less meaningful when fac-ing a premature death because wished-for reunions with loved ones are likely to be with people who will outlive them and thus be left behind after their death. It is their departed loved ones, usually parents and often spouses that have gone to their Maker years ago, that the religious very old look forward to seeing in their next life.

CHAPTER 3

Adaptive Coping

In all, eight mechanisms will be considered. As noted earlier, these eight mechanisms comprise two sets of four each. The four more rational coping mechanisms are engaging in meaningful activities that reaffirm the core self; control in the here-and-now; contractions of the environment, time, and relationships to make everyday life more manageable; and downward social comparison in which comparisons with aged peers and persons now dead permit favorable assessments of health. The second set of four mechanisms that have less rational elements encompasses magical mastery in which there is some degree of ignoring reality; aggression, when there is stress, that counteracts lethal passivity and includes a hostile component; functional paranoia in which blaming of others attenuates feelings of vulnerability; and acceptance into consciousness of previously repressed material if helpful in defining the self.

The division of coping mechanisms into these two types, and further distinctions within the types, however, is somewhat artificial. Realistic control in the here-and-now, for example, can be considered to have an irrational quality because of the reinforcement of the belief in the controllability of the world. This kind of covert magical thinking that we all use to cope with a world that is essentially uncontrollable is, however, different from manifest magical mastery, where there is some degree of a disregard of reality. Elia Femia, Steven Zarit, and Boo Johansson (1997), for example, grouped the two types together under the rubric "mastery" in their study of predictors of change in activities of daily living among the oldest old. In referring to my writings in *Personhood in Advanced Old Age* (1991), they additionally consider aggressiveness under stress as a reflection of high mastery. They wrote, "This process of mastery can involve both a defiance against lethal passivity and a cognitive illusion of mastery whereby individuals possess any overinflated sense of mastery that confronts the stress" (p. P296). Although distinctions among mechanisms may be artificial, it is heuristic to discuss each separately because, in part, each has a different implication for practice.

The set of adaptive processes can be divided in other ways than by relationships with reality. Colleen Johnson and Barbara Barer (1997) in their report on the *85+ Study* make a primary distinction between managing daily routines and discourses on self and time. Managing daily routines, which includes changing the physical environment, regulating time, and reordering what makes a good day while adjusting to incapacities, I have included in the more rational processes of meaningful activities, control in the here-and-now, and contracting the environment, time, and interactions with others. In turn, discourses on self and time, which include downward social comparisons and disengaging from roles and others while recognizing a limited future, I have also included in all four of the more rational facilitory processes. Note, therefore, that all the Johnson and Barer processes are of the more rational type, reflecting the yield from interviews developed from the perspective of social anthropology. Their superb analyses of their data reveal how very old people adapt in everyday life. Because, however, of my psychodynamic orientation and clinical experience, I have generated the set of four less rational facilitory processes. Still, we share the observation that the adaptive processes used by very old people defend against anxiety, but whereas Johnson and Barer emphasize how withdrawal, detachment, and disengagement contain anxiety and agitation, I emphasize how a range of more to less rational processes preserve a core self, containing anxiety that would come from a loss of self and a dissolution of integrality.

Meaningful Activities

The Sampsons do much less than they did just a few years earlier. Marilyn is acutely aware of the changes in their activities:

The Days Are Much the Same

"We used to do a lot more. Especially if you have arthritis like I do, its hard to move around, but we manage. Everyday is too much the same, but it's okay for now. I get up, make sure Jack takes his pills at breakfast, talk to friends, eat a little for lunch, sometimes play cards in the afternoon, except on Wednesday when I play in the evening. If we're going to an early bird, I have to take the time to bathe and dress. Jack has to fasten my brassiere. With my arthritis I can't reach back anymore. At night we watch TV. Sometimes the routine is broken up. There are doctor appointments, going to my hairdresser, my girlfriends come by. What else? The kids fly down in the winter to visit, Susie comes, my brother comes, and my sister and her husband. Then a few times a year we go back north. Once in a while we still go on a junket to Freeport to gamble."

Jack talks about driving; and like others, says "As long as I can. . . ." (in this instance, driving) I will still be me.

I Can Still Drive!

"When I lost my eye, I thought I would never drive again. I was so depressed I thought I would never get over it. I adjusted to not being able to see at night, but to not drive during the day, to shop and to dinner, was too much. The eye doctor at first didn't say a word about driving with one eye. Then when my kids said it would be okay if I drove during the day on familiar routes, I asked the doctor what he thought. He said it was up to me. He didn't want to say to do it. I think he was concerned about his insurance, about his liability if he told me I could drive. But when I told him how I planned to drive, he didn't stop me. I have this big Lincoln Continental that's safe and easy to drive. I drive slow and watch myself. Its like a miracle. With only one eye I can still drive."

The stripping down to meaningful activities is central to the Paul Baltes and Martha Baltes (1990) process model of successful aging, the model of selective optimization with compensation (SOC). The first component of selection appears to have a more volitional quality than the adaptive mechanism among very old people that I have referred to as maintaining meaningful activities. Although narrowing down among very old people is from a combination of what is still possible to do with what is personally meaningful, conscious processes are more pronounced in the Baltes and Baltes model, as reflected in their example of the old marathon runner who maintains the goal of winning by competing with older men in easier races (selection), varying footwear (compensation), and using a special diet and vitamins to increase fitness (optimization). This process is more applicable to younger old persons than to the very old ones who find it harder when stripping down to compensate and optimize; and, therefore, may rely more on less reality-oriented adaptive mechanisms. Still, what is critical to preservation of the self and to integrality is to be involved in activities that are meaningful.

Always a Horsewoman

The elegant Mrs. Sandra Westcott told the student interviewer, "Just call me Sandy. Everyone does." Sandy at 80 was described by the student as "more preppy looking than even me!" Impeccably dressed, replete with fine leather riding boots, Sandy exuded an ambiance of complete comfort with herself and her life style. Her husband died suddenly of a heart attack 6 years ago, and 2 years later she slipped on the ice and broke her hip. She pensively said, "My husband's death was hard to take but maybe even harder was giving up riding." She could not, however, give up her horses. Each day, "rain or shine, sleet or snow," she tends to her thoroughbreds on her large, exemplary breeding farm, and described in vivid, lengthy detail care for her horses. When another student broke in to ask whether she was intimidated by Sandy, the presenter answered, "The horsey stuff got a little boring but I was wowed by how she switched from riding. When we walked over to the barn and she gave one of her favorites a little rub, she was like a little girl. I never saw anything like it."

Sally also illustrates how involvement in meaningful activities provides for control, just as does Jack's driving and Marilyn's daily routine.

Control

Control is as American as apple pie. Ours is a society that values independence, self-sufficiency, and self-reliance; autonomy has recently become the appropriate *linqua france* for gerontologists. Whatever terminology is used, the message is the same: Life has no meaning if you are not in control. The maintenance of control to preserve the self is manifested in as many different ways as there are persons of advanced old age as each person strives to maintain, or to regain control, in her or his own way.

When You Have Slept in the Same Bed

Mrs. Wexler, an obese 81-year-old widow, was placing herself in danger by persisting in living in a third-floor apartment. Her physician insisted that she move because walking up the stairs even once a day was taxing her

already weakened heart. She left her apartment a few times a day to shop and to participate in activities in the community with her friends. When asked why she would not move, she said to the interviewer, who was 43, "Honey, when you slept in the same bed with your husband for half a century, you don't change it easily." She then communicated that it was better to die in her own bed in familiar surroundings than relocate and be miserable, and added, "If I want to risk it, it's my business. Ain't a little exercise always good for you? And I know better than my doctor what's good for me and what my heart can take. It's only a few steps and he makes it a big thing, like it's the Taj Mahal or something." Although the interviewer feared for Mrs. Wexler's health, she was sufficiently perceptive not to interfere in any way with Mrs. Wexler's rationalization for the health-producing stair-climbing that was interpreted by Mrs. Wexler in a later interview as "Only a little exercise. You need it too. I saw how you couldn't catch your breath when you got up here."

Mrs. Wexler succinctly communicates the importance of controlling what is personally meaningful. There is no way that everything can be controlled, nor is it essential to control everything. Essential is to control something that has personal significance so that the external world is perceived as mastered and controllable. With these perceptions or beliefs, the continuity of the self can be assured. Without these beliefs, we are at the mercy of external forces in a chaotic, unpredictable world that has us in its control. We cannot be ourselves in this kind of world where we are at the mercy of unknown forces. Sometimes very little is controlled. The small amount that is controlled to be in control is quite evident in studies of elderly persons in nursing homes. Judith Rodin and Ellen Langer (Langer & Rodin, 1976; Rodin & Langer, 1977) showed that giving residents in nursing homes as little as a plant to watch over or the choice of where to have visitors prolongs life.

LOCUS OF CONTROL

Until recently social scientists employed measures of locus of control to determine where individuals are on a continuum from an internal to an external locus of control. The optimum has been assumed to be an internal locus of control where one's fate is completely in one's own hands. Internal control is diminished when perceiving luck or fate as determining what happens, which has been considered as an external locus of control. There is, however, a serious concern regarding this continuum because luck and fate do matter. Maybe very young people can expect that the future can all be from their own doing, but the experiences of age teach that life is unpredictable, that great news can occur suddenly, and that bad things can happen to good people. If there is anything like wisdom that accrues with age, it is the awareness that anything can happen at any time. So it is possible to have a sense of control and still believe that not all is under personal control, that luck and fate do matter. Certainly, it is common for the more than 9 of 10 Americans who report having a personal relationship with their God to believe that one's fate is ultimately in the hands of the Lord. Because the Lord helps those who help themselves, control can be exerted by being a good person in the eyes of God and by religious activities and practices. Prayers are believed by religious persons to make a difference because prayers of those who are observant can, or will, be answered by their God.

EFFICACY

Rather than a locus of control continuum from beliefs in internal, personal control to being externally controlled, the cognitive psychologist Albert Bandura (1977) has advocated apprising the extent of efficacy, which refers to self-appraisals of personal influence. You can, for example, ask if plans made, generally come out as expected and thereby avoid the extent of beliefs in luck and fate. The Sampsons believe that luck and fate have played a role in living long and surviving together as a couple while friends and family members have become widowed. Yet they also know that they are efficacious, that when they make plans, even though only shortly into the future, that their plans usually come to fruition.

The importance of feeling efficacious when there is a loss of control is illustrated by Norman Cousins, the former editor of the *Saturday Review of Literature*. When told he had a progressive, incurable neurologic disease of unknown etiology, he left the hospital, went to a hotel and watched old comedy films all day and through the night, particularly Marx Brothers' films. Slowly he went into remission, attributing his recovery to displacing gloom with humor. Clearly, he retained control in this controversial case that most medical experts consider to reflect a self-correcting medical condition. Yet it may be that restoring feelings of being in control and efficacy were curative through some unidentified biologic mechanism, possibly by bolstering his autoimmune system.

PRIMARY AND SECONDARY CONTROL

Questioning the meaningfulness of locus of control has also led investigators and theorists to make a distinction between primary and secondary control. Primary control is direct action. If my students want top grades, they must study hard. They can, however, decide to change their expectations, referred to as secondary control, and study less to obtain less than top grades. As people age, they change their expectations, shifting the balance from primary to secondary control, as did Sally the horsewoman.

DOMAINS OF LIFE

Although it surely may be our wish to have complete control, every domain of life cannot be controlled. For Sally to be herself, control must be in relationship to her thoroughbreds. Other domains are less critical. She can no longer enjoy wonderful trips to exotic places with her husband, which she thinks about often as she contemplates mementos from all over the world that fill her house. What is most meaningful for Sandy to control now is her everyday care for her horses. In retaining control in a domain of her own choosing, a domain that is within her to control, she has shifted to secondary control by modifying her expectations. Modifications within and among domains, however, are not only produced by incapacities. The Sampsons can control where they will go for their early bird dinners, but they no longer can control their adult children as they did when their children were growing up.

Sometimes lamenting their inability to direct the lives of their children now that they are in their eighties and their children in their late fifties and sixties, they have grown accustomed to what they can and cannot control. Always important for them, as it is for others of their age, is to be in control of the activities of daily living, especially of mobility and of personal care. Other domains in which control is sought vary over time and also with circumstances and from personal inclinations. For the oldest of visual artists, control in producing artworks retains importance. For elderly mothers caring at home for offspring with mental retardation, the maintenance of caregiving until their last breaths can never be relinquished.

It is not necessary, therefore, to control as much as has been controlled in the past, but it is necessary to control something that reaffirms essential aspects of the self. Observing the stripping away of that which is unessential to the core self, Johnson and her associates have referred to "outliving conventional concerns." Marilyn Sampson no longer must attend religious services to be seen by her friends as an observant person. Jack Sampson no longer needs to be a breadwinner to feel important to his family. In knowing who they are, each has attained a self-wisdom.

Contractions

Contractions in the living environment, in time, and interpersonal relations make life more manageable.

Looking Forward to the Next Meal

 The student chose to interview Elsie, who, at 93, was the oldest resident in her parents' board and care home. Elsie slept throughout the day but always joined the others at the dinner table, where she appeared very happy with her life. When asked about her earlier life, she answered in her characteristic way, "Nice life. What else? Got married. Had children. Husband died. Came here." When asked if she would elaborate, Elsie said, "I like to eat. I look forward to the next meal." To the query on her current affects, she said, "I already told you. My next meal." This interview was very frustrating for the student. Because, however, the student knew that Elsie's son visited her on Sundays, she asked Elsie if she looked forward to his visits. Elsie simply answered "Okay." But she did so without any affect. The student added, "Her son Ed is a little man, over 70, who comes and sits with his mother. They talk little. I just assumed she enjoyed it a lot, but I guess all she looks forward to is her next meal."

Elsie lives in a manageable world. Her physical environment has been simplified. Time is very foreshortened. Interpersonal relations are sparse. Of course, Elsie is an extreme example of contractions. A more modest contraction of the physical environment occurs when furniture is rearranged so that there is a sturdy piece of furniture to grasp when walking. Housekeeping is made easier by removing extraneous objects while keeping those mementoes that have special meaningfulness.

It is in daily routines that contractions of time become apparent. As noted by Johnson and Barer, very old individuals "orchestrate their day around the scheduling of meals, the times for taking medications, exercise, grooming, television, and for some prayer." Mornings tend to be more active times than afternoons. Mornings are used for grooming and household chores, whereas afternoons are for more passive activities, including napping. The day may be broken up by a noon meal at a senior center and socializing afterwards. Evenings are usually spent at home.

Contractions in interpersonal relations must be considered in relation to friends and family. There is a diminution of socialization that occurs with friends from waning energies and from disabilities and also from deaths of friends. There may, however, be more contact with children. Nearly one half of Johnson and Barer's respondents had weekly contact with their children. Only one of eight grandchildren, however, provided instrumental assistance. Lillian Troll (1994), using Johnson and Barer's interview data, reported that the oldest generation emphasize their children more than grandchildren. As grandchildren reach adulthood, they become more independent from their own parents, who are then freed up to spend more time with their own parents. These middle generation children of the very old are likely to be old enough to have retired and thus may have more time for their very old parents. The net effect of the change in social interaction is, therefore, likely to be a contraction in which there is less socialization with friends and more visiting or telephone conversations with children. The one half of the oldest generation who have children but whose children do not visit weekly are likely to talk to them weekly by phone, indicating intimacy at a distance.

Downward Social Comparisons

Johnson and Barer found that the primary way their elderly respondents reconstructed the meanings of their health symptoms was by comparisons to others. A typical response was "My health is good for my age." This positive comparison is derived not only from contrasting one's health with the health status of peers but also from comments made by physicians and others that reinforces the contrast. Then, too, often heard was "I am a healthy person because I still have my mind." The high prevalence of senile dementia makes this kind of statement rather ubiquitous among the oldest old cohort. Following a general question about health, Johnson and Barer's respondents were asked to compare their health with their aged peers. The investigators reported:

> Most respondents gave favorable and even glowing evaluation of themselves in comparisons to others their age. This process of positive social comparison is a well-known coping technique that uses a distinct reference

point to others their age. "I am healthy for my age, because I am healthier than my friends." Even more telling is the conclusion, "I am healthy because I'm alive. All my peers are dead." Moreover, no matter how disabled a respondent may be, he or she usually knows someone else who is in worse shape.

"I see people younger than me who are in worse shape,"

"I think I'm excellent for my age. The lady who lives across the street is 12 to 14 years younger, and she can't walk."

Those with limited mobility or even those confined to their beds or wheelchairs can usually find someone worse off than themselves, who can be used as a source from which to make a positive comparison.

"I'm much better than some. Many are bedfast, but I can get around in a wheelchair."

"I'm better off than many people I know. Others need help to get to the bathroom."

"I'm better off because I can breathe lying down." (p. 151)

Sometimes student interviewers were quite confused when reporting on their respondents because of positive evaluations.

The 100-Year-Old Man

 My student Katie won the prize for interviewing the oldest person, Mr. Prentice, the 100-year-old man. Mr. Prentice told her that he had some ailments but was never really sick, "not one day in my life." This, however, was not so because later he told her that when he was in his fifties, he fell off a ladder when cleaning a gutter on his house and broke a leg, a wrist, and some ribs. The minor ailment was a bout with cancer. He readily acknowledged that whereas he could barely see or hear and has trouble moving around, his mental faculties were fine. "My mind is clear as a bell. Okay for a 100-year-old man? Not many can say that!" Katie said she "played along" and said, "Not many can say anything at 100. There aren't many around to say it." They both chuckled.

In addition to illustrating the beneficial use of downward social comparisons, Mr. Pearson illustrates the suppression of thoughts about past and present medical conditions. The accident 50 years ago and the bout with cancer are minimized as they are only casually mentioned with little affect. There is a magical quality to the dismissal of ill health, which, along with others who are very old, allows him to transcend the infirmities of age. Transcendence is assured when able to maintain a modicum of self-caring and by downward social comparisons, which for Mr. Pearson are with those now deceased and also using what doctors and friends say to him, "Not bad to be alive and kicking at 100."

Magical Mastery

It is human to believe more is controllable than actually can be controlled. By harboring this belief, the external world becomes manageable, and internal equilibrium assured. At times, particularly when unavoidable calamities occur, however, distortions of reality are useful in maintaining beliefs in one's ability to control external forces. Shelley Taylor (1989) found that in her studies of breast cancer patients it is common to maintain an illusion of mastery of the disease, and that these cognitive illustrations were associated with better adaptation and even with longer survival. An example of an older person:

She Can't Do It But I Don't Stop Her

 Jackie, an accomplished executive secretary in her fifties, applied for the half-time job when I became Editor-in-Chief of The Gerontologist. She and her sister, both of whom never married and were living at their lifelong home with their mother, decided to each work half time so that they could share the caring for their elderly mother, who was becoming more frail each day. One winter day after reading some of my writings on exaggerated control, Jackie said, "That's my mother! She walks around the house turning down all the radiators, but she doesn't have the strength anymore. And you know who is going to have all the troubles when she topples over and breaks a hip?" So I asked if she stops her mother from turning off the radiators. "Are you crazy," she answered, "that's what my mother does."

Although fearful that her mother would topple over and break a hip, Jackie understood the consequences of changing her mother's irrational behavior that provides her feelings of being in control. Jackie laughed and added, "You don't know my mother! If I stopped her, she would break my neck. Better for her to break her hip than for her to break my neck!"

Jackie's mother only manifests a modicum of irrationality in her effort to retain being in control. Others are more irrational. Shellie Taylor has vividly portrayed the irrationality of feeling in control when afflicted with breast cancer. For these women, cognitive illusions that provide feelings of control of outcomes to their desperate states apparently can prolong life. Ingesting, for example, the latest disproved remedy affords the illusion of control that somehow can be life sustaining, at least for a while as deterioration and death is valiantly resisted.

MAGICAL MASTERY IN TREATMENT

Alvin Goldfarb, the psychoanalyst and disciple of Salvor Rado, who made mastery a keystone of his theory of psychoanalysts, recognized external control for retaining a sense of internal control and intrapsychic integrity when confronted with acute disorganizing distress in later life. In 1959 Goldfarb wrote:

> Treatment efforts may therefore be directed toward augmenting the patient's ability to master problems . . . or toward inflating his belief that he can and does master current problems (p. 386). . . . Because of interest displayed in him, the person comes to believe that he has won, charmed, tricked, or otherwise gained the social advantage. The receipt of medicine, assistance in environmental manipulation or acceptable advice with acceptable ranges if often taken as a token or symbol of having gained the therapist as ally, friend, or protector and, simultaneously, as proof of having triumphed over, or having dominated him. This sense of triumph, of having won the therapist's powers and of owning them, may be carried out of each session; a parent figure has been incorporated (p. 393). . . . To encourage acceptance of limitations and disability is to foster self-recrimination and loss of self-respect; it encourages . . . regarding oneself as crippled and weak. . . . (p. 394)

Goldfarb would illustrate how a little control goes a long way by discussing his patient who had hands gnarled by arthritis whose joy in life was crocheting. When she felt that she could no longer crochet, she became deeply depressed. Goldfarb's treatment consisted of encouraging and then insisting that she resume her favorite activity, praising her for her splendidly crocheted sweater, even though it was unwearable. Continuing to crochet made her feel in control of her life, and her depression gradually lifted.

Jerome Grunes, my mentor and a psychoanalyst who was consultant to the Drexel Home for the Aged, also understood the importance of inflating beliefs in mastery as a way of treating depression in very old people:

The Infamous Diva

 Miss Petosky had been a famous and infamous diva of an internationally renowned opera company. Now, at 92, she was a resident in the Drexel Home for the Aged, and all she had left were her memories. To sustain herself, Miss Petosky was writing her memoirs. Whereas her written words were unintelligible, her verbal stories were wonderful. In her youth she had many lovers, and at one time had three lovers, all famous men, in three different cities. But she had cycles. She would go from a fulfilling immersion

in writing her memoirs to becoming suicidally depressed saying, "Nobody wants to read about an old lady's life." Grunes at these times would bring his many trainees, mostly men, to Miss Petosky's room, prepping them beforehand to express adulation for Miss Petosky. This was not difficult because her stories were always interesting and filled with modestly told, but sexually revealing, anecdotes. After silently reading Miss Petosky's scratchy unintelligible writing, he would put his arms around her and praise her for her excellent memoirs. Following his gestures and words, Miss Petosky's depression would lift before our eyes, and she would return to writing; that is, until the next time she became depressed.

MAGICAL MASTERY IN EVERYDAY LIFE

The ignoring of reality in inflated beliefs of control has, as noted earlier, a counterpart in how we inflate our importance to others. Not only do teenagers exaggerate their importance to peers, but workers who are laid off in their forties and fifties are often shocked in disbelief when realizing how of little importance they were to their companies. These are modest disregards of reality when contrasted to the gross denial that often facilitates adaptation. It is helpful for rape victims not to recall the assault too soon because it cannot adequately be coped with until there is distance from the attack. Distortions and denial were signs of an impoverished ego when I was taught about ego functioning a few decades ago because ego strength necessitated the acceptance of reality. Signs of ego strength have changed so that now "healthy denial" has supplanted acceptance of reality. Too much rejection of reality, on the other hand, is to live in a fantasy world devoid of gratifications from current activities and relationships. But how much avoidance of reality should be considered pathologic? Is it pathologic to revitalize and mythicize deceased mothers and fathers and husbands and wives? Is it pathologic to transform the involuntary relocation to a nursing home into a relocation that is voluntary and under one's control? Then, too, what may be pathologic when young may not be pathologic when in advanced old age. The overinflating of beliefs in control would be pathologic for the youth who has both the capacity and the opportunity to master the current environment without gross exaggerations of potency. But would it be similarly pathologic for the 95 year old who lacks the physical capacity and the meaningful others that are essential for mastering the environment in ways that have formerly assured the preservation of the self to distort reality by inflating beliefs in mastery? Recall Harry, the feisty veteran of the Boar War, an isolate all his life, who must distort the motives of the women in the nursing home to be himself. Although they turn away from him because he smells terribly of urine, he must believe that they turn away in fear of him.

But inflated beliefs in control are helpful to very old persons in any setting. David Gutmann (1964, 1987) found that magical mastery is the norm in old age, whereas in the young adult years it is normative to exert active mastery and in the middle years passive mastery. Magical mastery was particularly evidenced by telling idiosyncratic stories when presented with Thematic Apperception Test (TAT) pictures depicting scenes of either one person or two or more persons interacting. I learned about these idiosyncratic stories early in my training to become a clinical psychologist:

Is He Jewish?

 I presented a TAT card to a woman in her eighties and asked her, as this test requires, to tell a story to the card that depicts a young lad contemplating his violin. Whereas the typical respondent begins the story by saying the violin belongs to the boy, this elderly woman in a Jewish home for aged persons immediately asked: "Is this boy Jewish?" In turn, I asked, "Does it make a difference?" She replied emphatically, "Sure!" She then concluded that he was Jewish and proceeded to tell a story about how he became another Heifitz. Had she concluded he was not Jewish, she certainly would have told a very different story.

Aggressiveness

Assertiveness reflects the mobilization necessary to withstand stress. Its obverse, passivity, is lethal because of physical vulnerability. Slight imbalances can overtax biologic systems with little residual hemostatic capacity, leading to a rapidly accelerating downward course.

The passive Mary Francis, as described by Ronnie Wacker in *Science 85* and quoted in chapter 1, succumbed to the stress of relocation with a hastening of her death, whereas feisty Harry survived the severe stressor and adapted to his new home. Passivity, however, was not lethal for older persons not undergoing the stress of relocation. Respondents in our comparison groups, as discussed in the 1976 Tobin and Lieberman book *Last Home for the Aged*, who were passive but not relocated did not have their deaths hastened. Their passivity, however, must be alleviated when they confront severe stress, or otherwise they will not be sufficiently mobilized to withstand the adaptive pressures and can succumb with a hastening of death. The hastening of death when becoming passive also occurs among younger healthier people in voodoo death. Believing that death will ensue if hexed causes the demise of the believer. The biologic mechanisms may be unclear, but the phenomenon is startling in its clarity as the formerly vigorous individual who sinks into apathy withers away. Also, it is still common for elderly widowed men to die soon after their wives' deaths. Listen to Jack Sampson:

He Was Going Downhill

"When Max Sweet lost his wife Sarah he started to act like a goner. He could take care of himself but didn't want to anymore." When Jack saw Max at the grocery store, he said to himself that Max only looks like a ghost of himself. He had lost a great deal of weight, and his face looked long and drawn. Jack described Mr. Sweet as having a nice round face when Sarah was alive. He then added, " His daughter came to stay with him awhile, and he pepped up, and he now plays cards with the boys. That old wives' tale that old husbands fade away when their wives die is true. I know it from experience."

What appears to be passivity is sometimes a deviant kind of mobilization. A student interviewed a homebound woman whose appearance suggested listlessness and apathy:

The Rich and Famous Lady

Mrs. Bates is an 80-year-old very obese woman who is not only homebound because she is afraid of negotiating the steep stairs but lives in a small space in her large, decaying house. Her days are spent in her kitchen where her television keeps her company, and she now sleeps on the downstairs couch. An episode of syncope following a change in "heart pills" has induced her to avoid any moving around.

When asked about her current life and her past experiences, she gave succinct answers, rushing through the interview with little elaboration and with very flat affect. She kept asking, "When will this be over." Among her sparse answers was a comment that her only child, a son, lives far away, and although he phones her about once a month, he has not visited in "3 or 4 years." She also said that the senior center provides her with a hot lunch each weekday and, by careful planning, she stretches this meal throughout the day and through weekends.

Only when the formal interview was completed did Mrs. Bates reveal herself, "You asked me what I do all day and I said I watch TV, but you didn't ask what I watch. I watch Lifestyles of the Rich and Famous. If you don't watch it, you don't know what you're missing." She quickly became animated, no longer the apathetically, depressed homebound isolated obese widow. "Now she was," according to the student, "talking a mile a minute" as she elaborated on an almost bibliographic accounting of everyone who was ever featured on the television program. The interviewer, who had never watched the program, sat spellbound and began to realize that Mrs. Bates was not an inert vacuous lady. It then emerged that the meals-on-wheels people linger to hear her animated, gossipy reports, and also that she has a network of friends who chat daily on the phone about the latest people featured on the program.

Mrs. Bates, labeled by us "The Rich and Famous Lady," is obviously neither rich nor famous. She may be considered by some to be living in a dream world with only vicarious thrills. But regardless of her reasons for immersion in the world of the rich and famous, her mind is active. She feels in control of her life, as well as of others, and also feels satisfied with her current circumstances. When it comes to evaluating the lives of others, we must be cautious in our judgments and recognize the old adage: "Different strokes for different folks."

When anger reflects mobilization under duress, it is functional for very old people. The ubiquitous observation in nursing homes is that the nasty ones live on and on, whereas the good ones die young. It is, however, dysfunctional for younger persons not under duress to be continually angry because anger can cause physical damage, particularly to the cardiovascular system. It also is hard on caregivers, whether staff of nursing homes or family members, to tolerate the nastiness, grouchiness, and bitchiness of the persons in their charge, just as it is difficult tolerating the paranoid behaviors that are functional when very old.

GENDER DIFFERENCES

Not unexpectedly there are gender differences in what is essential to control and how assertiveness is expressed. The Sampsons manifest these differences. Marilyn controls their social life, whereas Jack household finances and his care. Marilyn's assertiveness is usually direct but often is more subtly manipulative, whereas Jack is feisty and can be argumentative. Their differences in assertiveness resemble the gender differentiation Barbara Turner found when assessing psychological characteristics for their association with institutional adaptation in studies of relocation stress with Morton Lieberman. Turner, one of our exceptional doctoral students, assessed nine characteristics of older persons while awaiting admission to enter nursing homes to determine whether preadmission characteristics predicted adaptation upon entering and living in the homes. Selection of characteristics was based on hypothesized relationships between the congruence of the characteristic and successful institutional adaptation. Turner wrote regarding assertiveness: "In a setting in which residents are physically or mentally incapacitated or both, the aggressive resident is best able to meet her or his needs because she or he is able to assert herself or himself." The other eight characteristics were status drive, distrust of others, authoritarian, nonempathy, activity-passivity, other directed body image, extrapunitive, and nonintropunitive.

For each characteristic, 5-point scales were developed where the highest level on each was scored a 5. She found that assertiveness was indeed important, if not essential, for successful adaptation to the stress of relocation and, on the other hand, that passivity can be lethal. In developing the scales, she discovered, however, that she had to modify the high end of the assertiveness scale to accommodate differences between women and men.

The low end of the assertiveness scale, which was associated with adverse outcomes to the stressor of relocation, was similar for the two genders, with both women and men manifesting helplessness, hopelessness, apathy, and compliance. The following are Turner's descriptions of guidelines for scoring very high assertiveness (scored 5) and high assertiveness (scored 4), first for women and then for men.

For women, very high assertiveness was scored when the respondent takes over; is a leader; may pop off unrestrainedly at every opportunity, has a never-say-die attitude, and is a formidable opponent; may manipulate people but in an active, commandeering, openly assertive way, as well as being belligerent and pushy; is an iron-willed dictator who compels deference; is instantly prepared to fight for her rights in almost any situation. In turn, high assertiveness was scored when the respondent is very goal directed in certain areas of life; she may be tough and argumentative, but is occasionally unsure of herself and withdraws; she is somewhat domineering; or tends to assume leadership roles and actively assumes responsibility in social situations but is not as intrusive/dominant as a highly assertive woman; or a mild, unobtrusive front covers her ability to assume control of people and social situations so that she is strongly directive and powerful without seeming to be so.

For men, very high assertiveness was scored when the respondent is verbally aggressive or is quarrelsome as well as maintaining a masculine-aggressive pose; he is forceful and may even be physically aggressive or describes self as so when younger; was and still tries to be dominant over others; or is an egotist who takes on organizational responsibilities or relentlessly seeks a limelight. In turn, high assertiveness was scored when the respondent describes himself as quite competitive in his business and took on many organizational activities and responsibilities; often has been a "doer" and still tries to control others; he is occasionally quite irascible, or he may be an egotist who persistently seeks to be the center of attention; although he may express some timidity about crossing others, he will stand up for his rights if need be.

The similarities are obvious. Assertiveness that facilitates adaptation independent of gender consists of a determined toughness. Women, however, are more likely to express their assertiveness through "a mild, unobtrusive front" that "covers her ability to assume control of people and social situations," as Turner describes for high assertive women. Men with the highest level of assertiveness, in turn, may be "verbally aggressive" or "quarrelsome" and "even be physically aggressive." Their high level contains being "occasionally quite irascible," and both levels suggest an egotistical quality with a propensity to be the center of attention and to describe themselves as aggressive in business.

The gender differences are the kind that are to be expected of an old-old cohort reared with sex role differences in attitudes and behaviors around the turn of the century. Women were taught to conceal their aggressiveness; men to be macho and express theirs. The oldest men who become mobilized to confront relocation express aggression openly and are often quite abusive but may have been somewhat mellower after the postparental imperative in their middle years, continuing through their young-old years. Then with stress, if adaptation is to be assured, resume a former combative style. Men who never became mellower, refusing to accept their previously repressed opposite sex motives of passivity and dependency following the postparental imperative, may be considered by some to be less psychologically healthy, but their feistiness and belligerence is helpful to them when there is a need to adapt to stress.

Women will retain their propensity for less overt expressions of aggressiveness, often shying away from direct verbal invectives toward others and certainly from physical attacks. Yet previously subdued aggressiveness may give way to overt expressions of potency and control of others in social situations. Marilyn Sampson now can be more direct in how she expresses her wish and need to control others, "I often did not speak my mind. Now I just do it. When my brother-in-law says something crazy, I just tell him off. No sense being nice if its going to bother you." Whereas earlier in life she would swallow her tongue and suppress her anger, she now is likely to express it directly but always mindful of the social consequences.

Functional Paranoia

Preceding our finding that aggressiveness is beneficial under stress was Robert Butler's (Perlin & Butler, 1963) observation that mild paranoia is associated with survival for community-dwelling older men. Those men who were distrustful and suspicious survived longer than those who were not, even though their initial physical conditions were comparable. Whereas their paranoia was functional for resisting deterioration and death, it cannot be said, as just noted, that the paranoia was functional for those around them. No one wishes to be the object of suspiciousness nor the target of abusive invectives. What is bad for the accused, in this instance, is good for the accuser. Marilyn Sampson recognized that Jack's blaming of others is irksome to her but good for him.

Benign functional paranoia must not be confused with pathologic paranoia that has psychotic elements. In the functional paranoia of old age, the person is oriented to time, to place, and to person. Harry, our feisty Boer War veteran, knew the current date, the nursing home in which he resided, and who he was. He also did not have a delusional system of persecution such as the belief that he was being persecuted because he was a Christ-like person. Nor did he have auditory or visual hallucinations. Neither did he hear voices that were persecutory or who told him to harm others, nor did he see strange, threatening creatures. Still there certainly was an irrationality to his belief that the residents in the home feared him. But nonfunctional, pathologic paranoia does occur that often is reversible.

The Refrigerator Hit Me

 A master of social work student whose field placement was in a senior housing complex asked my advice in class about one of her assigned cases because she felt that her supervisor was not doing enough for her client. The client, Mrs. Bauer, had related an incident in which she believed the door of her refrigerator had "intentionally" hit her on her back. Apparently, Mrs. Bauer had pushed the door to close the refrigerator, but rather than closing, the door

swung back and hit her. She was left with the bizarre thought that the inan-
imate door hit her on purpose. Also strange was that Mrs. Bauer was stuff-
ing newspaper down the toilet but would not share with the student or the
supervisor the reason for stuffing up the toilet. In class, the student voiced
her belief that Mrs. Bauer did so to form a barrier to something she feared
would come out of the toilet.

The student's supervisor insisted that Mrs. Bauer get dressed and leave
her room early in the day without attempting to uncover more of Mrs.
Bauer's paranoid fantasies. The student social worker, who was unhappy
with not knowing more about Mrs. Bauer's fantasy life and possible root
causes, was assigned to assist in this mobilizing effort and to report on
whether the paranoia subsided. The supervisor understood from experience
that paranoid ideation subsides following reengagement in activities and a
cessation of isolation; and, also, that extremely frightening paranoid ideation
is different from the benign functional paranoia reflected in suspiciousness
and distrustfulness in the absence of bizarre paranoid ideation.

The distinction was discussed in class, including why some paranoia is functional. Then, a few weeks later, the student reported that Mrs. Bauer began leaving her room to participate in activities, refusing to discuss the content of her former paranoid ideation, while retaining some suspiciousness and distrustfulness. Rather, she simply thanked the student for helping her. Now that she felt protected, Mrs. Bauer no longer believed that things were coming out of the toilet to attack her, or that she would be attacked by whatever was pushing the refrigerator door. Mrs. Bauer apparently suffered her acute paranoia from one prevalent meaning that paranoia has for the very old who have suffered losses: "If you really cared for me, you would make things better, make me healthier and shield me from harm." Alone in her room and isolated from others, she felt abandoned to all kinds of imagined dangers.

Acceptance into Consciousness

Clinicians have observed that those now old can allow into consciousness some feelings and motives they previously disavowed. Norman Zinberg and Irving Kaufman (1963) noted:

The older patient is far less likely to "kid himself." His awareness of being stirred up by disagreements may be accompanied by a cynical disregard for his own feelings, because he understands himself in a sense too well, but he is more likely to know where the feelings come from and why he is upset. . . . Many feelings which are strongly resisted by younger people are accepted in the aged. The fact that people have destructive and envious urges are often admitted to consciousness without the anxiety and accompanying disorganization that may have occurred if the same feelings had reached awareness earlier in life. They fear the judgment of others less because they see the future as unimportant. (pp. 29–30)

The future judgment of others is a secondary cause for the acceptance of previously repressed material. Rather, as also noted above by Zinberg and Kaufman, the primary cause is a self-understanding. But why with age per se should there be an increase in self-understanding? Is it because self-understanding serves the purpose of preservation of the core self? It is a self-wisdom that is achieved and not a wisdom regarding regularities in the external world. In the seeking and gaining of a wisdom about the self, a making sense of oneself, there is a selective screening out of reality when warranted and, also, an acceptance of previously unwelcomed motives if they are useful for self-definition. Put another way, the task of the very old to maintain a consistency of self when confronted with losses, which occurs within the awareness of having lived a life and with the acceptance of death, is achieved by a purposeful simplification of identity that reaffirms the self. The stripping away of nonessential elements of the self when outliving conventional concerns is accompanied by allowing suppressed or repressed motives into consciousness.

I Never Told Anyone

 My student was eager to discuss her respondent. Mrs. Leahy said, "Call me Genevieve. Everybody does." Thus began the interview that the student said was more like a confession than an interview should be. Genevieve told her that in her forties, when her husband was away for several months working as an engineer in South America, she had an affair with a married neighbor. Genevieve added that she had never told anyone, but now in her eighties, she was having recurrent thoughts about the affair. It was a fleeting affair that never jeopardized her marriage, and she was always in love with her husband of 47 years. It was time to accept this part of her life, and it was safe to tell about it to the student interviewer. The student, however, at first found it hard to believe that she would tell her but not her closest friends. Then another student said that it occurs all the time in therapy because the treatment setting is a safe place. We then discussed why now, 40 years after the indiscretion, Genevieve has a need to recall the affair.

In knowing their essential selves, very old persons attain a self-wisdom. From this process of attainment, they have become less introspective, as if putting to rest any doubts as to who they are. This lessened introspection was evident in our study when we focused on introspection on feelings (Lieberman & Tobin, 1983). Introspection was assessed by using 7-point scales to rate responses to eight questions on personal feelings. Respondents, for example, were asked, "Could you tell me about the times when you feel very lonely?" or "happy," "sad," "proud," and so forth. An association was found between age and unwillingness to introspect on feelings. Apparently, as decreasing biological, and thus psychological, energies become deployed for self-maintenance and a sense of sameness is achieved, there is less introspection on, or certainly a preoccupation with, internal feeling states and a corresponding acceptance of the previously repressed if it simplifies and adds to self-wisdom. Acceptance of the previously repressed into consciousness necessitates a change in the content of reminiscence, a modification of the personal narrative, which will be discussed in the next chapter.

CHAPTER 4

Using Reminiscence

Remembering is inseparable from thinking and consciousness. At times what is now happening conjures up the past, whereas at other times memories spring up spontaneously for no apparent reason. Who has not asked, "Why has *that* popped into my head?" Sometimes memories are comforting; at other times, disturbing. Sometimes they are infrequent; at other times, they rush forth like a torrential storm. Not only is there this kind of variability in each person's recall of the past (intraindividual variability), but also people differ from each other on whatever dimensions are used to describe processes in recollections of the past (interindividual variability). Given the polymorphic nature of reminiscence, can any viable generalization be made?

Cherished Objects

Ubiquitous among the very old are collections of physical objects that researchers have called "cherished objects," especially photographs, but also jewelry, consumer items such as visual art and recreational objects, and religious artifacts. These cherished physical objects are icons for reminiscence that reinforce the continuity of the self. Edmund Sherman (1991) has called memorabilia "reminiscentia," inducers of memory. Indeed, Edmund Sherman and Evelyn Newman (1977–78), in the first study that focused on cherished possessions of elderly persons, found photos to be the most cherished. Later, Mihalyi Csikszentmihalyi and Edward Rochberg-Halton (1981) in their book *The Meaning of Things* reported that photos were grandparents' highest-ranked special objects in a three-generational study. In turn, parents ranked furniture highest, and children ranked stereos highest. Recall the gnarled rather ancient woman who used a photograph of herself as a young pretty woman to show the interviewer that she had not changed very much.

As people change over time, concrete objects that do not change are kept for their personal meanings. The meaningfulness of the possessions that elderly people identify as cherished resides in their legacy. Elderly individuals must choose from a lifetime of objects those possessions they wish to save for themselves as a kind of bequest to themselves. These possessions are, therefore, connections to a person's own historic past. Csikszentmihalyi and Rochberg-Halton wrote that "for an adult, objects serve the purpose of maintaining the continuity of the self as it expands through time." The importance of cherished possessions for such continuity among elderly persons is nowhere more evident than in relocations to long-term care facilities because the leaving behind of cherished possessions heightens feelings of being abandoned.

TIES TO MEANINGFUL OTHERS

Objects may represent ties or bonds with others at a time of life when social losses tend to be greatest." An elderly Jewish widow said, "I still keep my husband's tallis (prayer shawl) as if he will come through the door and run off with it to *shull to daven* (to synagogue to pray)." This comment captures the essence of a cherished possession— a possession for which there is a special fondness. In turn, the special fondness is from the evocation of memories that are meaningful. When a husband of half a century has died, possessions that are reminders of him can indeed be comforting and also assuring of a sense of continuity of the self. These possessions are kept and cherished precisely because of their meaningfulness for one's personal identity.

Recollected people are not, however, restricted to spouses and parents. The recollected person may be a grandparent or even an earlier ancestor: "This cupboard goes way back. I don't know how many generations." Possessions from previous generations provide a sense of coherence and embeddedness in family. So, too, do possessions that serve as triggers to remembrances of the continuity of generations: "See the seashells over there. My daughter, when she was little and we went on vacation, would collect them with me. I loved walking with her on the sandy beach, just like I used to do with my mother." The diverse kinds of cherished possessions—photos, religious items, jewelry, furniture, visual art, and other—can have meanings that span past and future generations: "That's a favorite picture of mine. It shows when my mother and wife were alive and my daughter, the little one, got married." Religious items seem especially useful for spanning the generations. Bibles, prayer books, crucifixes, and menorahs are likely to have been handed down and will, in turn, be handed to further generations. These objects also have a special function because of the importance of religious beliefs among the very old.

What to give to whom—and when—can often be perplexing. Some possessions are bequeathed, to be given during one's lifetime, at confirmations, bar mitzvahs, or weddings. When relocating to a smaller home after adult children have moved, there is a stripping-down of possessions and a likelihood of passing some cherished possessions to children. Usually difficult choices must be made by families regarding what should be given to children at this time and what should be kept after the move to a smaller home. Women are likely to be particularly concerned about the loss of furniture because of the future shortage of space. Men, in turn, may be concerned about adequate space for possessions associated with work and recreation. It is as death approaches in advanced old age that a final sorting-out occurs, and determinations are made regarding who gets what.

As people live longer, however, and are progenitors of four- and five-generation families, giving may be to children for distribution to their lineage. Particularistic relationships may exist with one grandchild and not another (Troll, 1994). Yet, one 83-year-old widow said, "Money I'll divide between my three sons, but the jewelry and art, I don't know. I don't know what all my grandchildren would appreciate." This woman has viable heirs, but apparently many of the very old do not. Whereas almost all of the sample (95%) that Troll studied had living relatives, about one-fourth had no interaction with any of them or just exchanged Christmas cards and had an annual phone call." Still, for these apparently heirless oldest old people, cherished possessions serve as legacies to themselves, as objects for reminiscences that preserve the continuity of the self.

Reworking the Personal Narrative

When mothers are asked to recall the ease or difficulty in birthing their teen-aged children, the reportage reflects current perceptions of parent-child interaction and not how easy or how difficult the delivery actually had been. Current preoccupations indeed color the recall of past events. An easy delivery is likely to be recalled as difficult if the teenager is causing trouble, and a painful delivery as easy if the teenager is not causing trouble.

Long-married couples are aware that their spouses change their life story over time. The husband who was a soldier but never saw action in World War II gets closer to the thick of the battle in the retelling of his wartime experiences. The hardships suffered in his wife's caring for her terminally ill mother recedes in importance as she recalls the loving and caring of her mother for her.

The cause for the recall may seem obvious as when looking at the sunset is a reminder of a late evening picnic on a lake decades earlier. At the same time, there may be a less obvious reason for its recollection.

It Was So Beautiful Then

Sitting alone in her room in the nursing home, the 88-year-old Mrs. Sands likes to watch the sunset and recall a family picnic from more than half a century in the past. It was the last time that the whole family was together because her husband, who earlier had a heart attack, died shortly thereafter. At each recall, this memory becomes elaborated on differently depending on how she felt. When she was living in her own home she would recall how she and her husband laughed as they watched their children roll down the hill. Then, as she waited in the hospital to be relocated to the nursing home, she recalled how her 9-year-old son Charlie could not be found when they started to leave for home, an elaboration reflecting the separation and abandonment felt in the process of becoming a nursing home resident. After admission to the home, she introduced into the recollection her husband's recent heart attack followed by his death, reflecting her feelings that the nursing home is a place of decay and death.

Incorporating current adaptive concerns into reconstructions of the past is only one aspect of how personal histories, now referred more frequently to as personal narratives, are reconstructed to give meaning to life by being organized to be coherent, but not necessarily accurate. In being coherent to the teller, the continuity of the self is preserved. Whereas one of Marilyn Sampson's vivid early memories is how her teacher adored her, Jack Sampson's most vivid memory of childhood is decidedly different:

Like It Was Just Yesterday

"I recall like it was just yesterday. My younger brothers, I had two, were beaten up by bullies when we moved into a new neighborhood. They were like 7 and 9, and I was 12 and big for my age. The Dagos beat them up

because they were Jewish. The Pollacks, Krauts, and all the rest would have ganged up on them, too. It was ordinary in those days. So I told my brothers to walk ahead of me to school and soon three Dago kids who looked about my age started to pick on them. I ran up and asked them instead to start something with me. One kid came forward and before he knew what hit him, I bloodied his nose. He didn't know Jews could hit so hard. We had no trouble, no trouble at all, after that, and later I became good friends with Tony, the Dago I hit."

Jack tells us of his physical prowess that he now laments losing. Still he considers himself macho, even though he has mellowed in his later years. Also in this recollection is his recurrent lifelong theme of distrust of others, here of how the diverse ethnic groups picked on the Jews.

INDUCING MODIFICATIONS

Now in the news is the inducing of modifications in personal narratives rather than in spontaneous modifications. Psychotherapists, including Freud, are being accused of inducing memories of childhood sexual abuse that never occurred. Whereas patients were previously believed to be accurate when reporting traumatic events following the lifting of repression, it is now common to ask whether patients are simply reporting what therapists wish to hear. Inducing false memories is also a concern of the criminal justice system because adult daughters are now vividly recalling sexual abuse by their fathers. Flashback recall of these abuses may be true, but they also may be false, particularly when remembered details conflict with evidence. Does it make a difference to therapy if there is to be no criminal accusations? My students, novitiate therapists, usually ask this question. I believe it does because a false blaming of others diminishes the necessity of taking responsibility for one's own blemishes and actions.

Yet, a false blaming can, paradoxically, be helpful to the very old. By exaggerating the wretchedness of earliest life, including a callous disregard by parents, very old persons can perceive themselves as having transcended their horrendous beginnings and to have made something good out of their lives against the worst of early expectations.

THE ESSENTIAL CORE REMAINS

Whether self-induced or induced by others, reconstructions of events from the past will be distorted in their elaborations to meet current adaptive demands. Yet, when hearing a life story, the essential core self emerges. Details and affects become transformed in retelling, but the persistence of identity causes personal narratives to have an inescapable unique quality reflecting the idiosyncratic self, "the ageless self" in Sharon Kaufman's (1987) interpretation of life story themes of older persons. Bertram Cohler (1982), the perceptive psychologist and psychoanalyst, after reviewing the literature on reminiscing, provided a synthesis in which he argued that memories are not only continually being reorganized, but that a life narrative is created that is not to be judged for its accuracy but rather for its consistency, its coherence, its comprehensiveness, and its intelligibility to the listener or reader. For the very old, the life narrative is most importantly the creation of a self-story that preserves identity.

RECAPTURING AND ORGANIZING THE PAST

When memories cannot be organized to be coherent it bespeaks internal disorganization. I learned this lesson early. Because, as part of my training in clinical psychology, I was to become familiar with the variety of projective techniques, my psychologist supervisor at Drexel Home for the Aged asked me to administer a battery of psychological tests to a depressed woman in her mideighties.

Her Eldest Son Had Died

When I showed Mrs. Davis the first Rorschach card, she became rather agitated and said: "What has this got to do with me?" At that moment, I, too, wondered what the purpose of projective tests were. To be sure, one of the didactic experiences I was to gain was an appreciation of the kinds of projective tests most sensible for very old individuals. Yet, regardless of the nature of her intrapsychic conflicts, it was apparent that this woman was suffering from her deep sorrow. So, I put aside the testing material and simply asked her what was bothering her. A river of tears gushed forth with the telling of the death of her son. Her eldest son had died about 5 years ago, and since then she said, "my life has not been the same. I cannot stop thinking about the beautiful life he never had." As a young clinician, I was befuddled. Death of a child at any age is difficult to accept. Although I wanted to leave the room believing I had nothing to offer this woman, I desperately wanted to help her. To bide my time while thinking about what I should do, I asked her to tell me about her life.

Slowly, in a voice that was barely audible, she began to talk about how wonderful her life was when her children were growing up. Her husband had never made a good living but was dedicated to his family and "to edu-

cation." Her eldest son became a "famous lawyer," her two daughters "married educated men," and her youngest son became "a great professor." When her husband died in his fifties, it was her eldest son who "made sure that I did not want for anything." Although she was proud of her youngest son, he had taken an academic position in another city and then had married out of the faith. Her eldest son had married "a beautiful Jewish girl." She then continued by comparing her eldest son to her father.

Her father had been a caretaker (a shamus) in a small synagogue when she was growing up. Although a learned man, he had little formal education, but because he liked to read the Bible and the Tamlud, he took a job that was below him. Devoted to his family, education was the most important goal for his children. She added, "He was ahead of his time. He wanted my sister and me to be as educated as my brother." She then went into great detail about how he would sit his three children on the couch and discuss with them the portion of the Old Testament that was being read that week in the synagogue. As she talked the depression lifted, and she became rather animated. With a smile on her face, she imitated how he would stroke his beard when formulating a question for even the youngest of the three to answer. He would often say to her, the youngest: "If the question is too hard my little beauty, I will ask it a little differently." And then stroking his beard, he would try to rephrase the question, but it always seemed to come out even harder. And then he would laugh and say that he would save the question for next year.

As she was reconstructing her past, and obviously feeling much better, I kept thinking to myself that she had not said a word about her mother, and that maybe I should ask her about her mother. Concurrently, I was terribly concerned that I had not completed my assignment to gather responses to the Rorschach, but because she was feeling better, I was feeling very conflicted. Anxious and befuddled, I was only half-listening to her reportage.

Quite suddenly she stood up and said "I feel much better now. I have an appointment." "Oh," I said, "and where is your appointment?" She retorted in a rather firm voice, "Every Thursday I have an appointment at the beauty parlor at 10:30. If I'm not there by 20 past, she knows I'm not coming. It is now 10:00 and I must get ready for my appointment." As she walked toward the door she took my arm (which I thought was inappropriate because my training was in psychodynamic therapy), and it was apparent that she wished me to walk her to the elevator. She then thanked me profusely.

My appointment with my testing supervisor was a week away because it was expected that I would need some time to write up the results of the psychological testing and synthesize a written report. I was terribly anxious. Unsure of what to do, I discussed the experience with Grunes, who turned the question back to me. I responded, "The only thing I learned is that I listened to her and she felt better." After many pointed questions by Grunes, it became apparent to me that what she needed was a benevolent person to listen to her. She was able to use me to reconstruct her past and to feel good about herself. Bolstered by the warm memories of her past life, the preoccupation with her son's death receded, and she became less visibly depressed. No conflicts were resolved, and no insights gained. Grunes explained that I was helpful, and that if I saw her weekly, she would most likely be able to contain the depression. When he congratulated me on being such a good listener and being able to see her in the way she had been rather than only in the way she is now, I felt compelled to tell him that the reason I did not interject many questions and simply let her talk was because I kept thinking about how I was not fulfilling the assignment, and I was also preoccupied with what I should be doing. Fortunately, I was also fascinated by the process in which she seemed to become transformed while reconstructing her past. It was this fascination, as well as an ability to appreciate the ambience of intellectual curiosity created by her father, that assisted her in reconstructing the past and making herself vivid to herself.

When later I reflected on what I had learned, it seemed to me that I only needed to listen empathically to Mrs. Davis for her to recapture her earliest memories, reconstruct them in an organized and vivid manner, and thereby contain her depression. Was it this simple? Obviously, I had to be an interested listener who communicated to Mrs. Davis that she was a worthwhile person and deserved to have my attention. But, additionally, I was aware that I was letting myself visualize her as she visualized herself, particularly as she wished me to visual her as she existed in her past. In the later meeting with Grunes to review the therapeutic encounter, he made an interesting observation. He said that his interest in working with very old people came, in large part, from a desire to experience as much as possible how life was for our forebears. So too, did I realize, it is one of my motives in working with the very old.

Concerning his approach, Grunes has written:

> Patient and therapist must work to recover past memories and this work must be an active therapeutic maneuver involving interventions and reconstructions of such memories for the patient. The therapist must permit himself the luxury of regression so that in his own psychic apparatus he can perceive the patient not only as he exists in the present but visualize him as he existed in the past, while conveying to the patient his experiences with such regressive imago. This is the essence of the therapeutic experience. The patient, bewildered and in need of touchstones, can find, with the uncovering and the attempt to reestab-

lish memories from his own life with a nonjudgmental person, a recathexis of his own past and a sufficient organization of the historic sense of self, perhaps less subtly organized but organized nonetheless, to function as a unified personality. . . . It is the recathectic memories reincorporated with the sense of worthwhileness that the patient receives from the therapist. (p. 547)

The Life Review

The conventional wisdom that life is reviewed when facing death at any age provides credence to Robert Butler's (1963) inevitable life review as death approaches at the end of life. When living after facing sudden and imminent death, like tumbling off a boat into icy water or falling off a high cliff, the teller of the event is heard to say, "My whole life passed before me." The quickness of the experience may obviate any kind of lengthy review of life, but the speaker may add, "I swore to live my life differently." as if there was a contemplative review.

Tolstoy, in *Death of Ivan Ilych*, written in 1893, described Ivan Ilych as having a life of comfort and superficiality until a protracted illness forced him to meditate. He then reviewed his life, accepted it as having been completely superficial, and thereby accepted death, freeing him from the tortures he had been experiencing.

As death approaches at any age, memories may be evoked and the past reviewed to make sense of life. Additionally, without imminent death approaching in the middle years, there may be a reviewing of life characterized by introjecting on past accomplishments and time left for accomplishing life goals. This introspection is a forerunner to a possible later life review when therapists can use the resurgence of unresolved conflicts to assist in their resolution. Yet the resolution of conflicts is not inherent to the life review. The essence of the life review is the making of a coherent and acceptable life story. Too often, however, leaders of life history or life events groups assume that conflicts are automatically being resolved in the telling of past events. Resolution of conflicts can occur in these groups, but it is more likely that there is a revitalization of memories. Edmund Sherman (1987), in a careful study of reminiscent groups in which each member was encouraged to consider and to incorporate the feelings accompanying reported events, found greater integration of personal narratives but not a resolution of intrapsychic conflicts.

What has been observed, as discussed earlier, is that those who are very old can now allow into consciousness some feelings and motives they previously disavowed. If unacceptable intrapsychic content can provide a coherence to life as it has been lived, below conscious feelings and motives may emerge when old. Yet, this is not an invariate phenomenon because many older old people do not dredge up unacceptable feelings and motives in developing a coherent life story. Others who could benefit from the release of repressed feelings and motives that would permit or facilitate a coherent life story are unable to allow themselves the freedom to do so.

Although it is possible to use previously repressed material in developing a coherent life story late in life, as well as a continual reorganization of the personal narrative throughout life, there is scant evidence for a naturally occurring life review. Individuals would have to be queried over time through their oldest years in a longitudinal study to determine whether there is a spontaneous review of life as death approaches toward the end of the life cycle. Unfortunately, the conventional wisdom that life passes before you when confronting imminent death is not sufficient evidence for the naturally occurring life review postulated by Butler. For Erik Erikson, a life review is apparently essential if the quest for self-understanding, for self-wisdom, in old age is to be achieved. He used Dr. Isak Borg, a 77-year-old professor and physician in Ingmar Bergman's film *Wild Strawberries* (Erikson, 1978), to illustrate how a sequential review of each life stage allows a grieving for the past and an acceptance of life as it has been lived with all its accomplishments and disappointments. This may be ideal for highly ideational individuals, but for ordinary people there is a quite seamless movement in aging toward self-wisdom without the obsessive kind of life review portrayed so brilliantly by Bergman's Dr. Borg. Still, the life review is an important theoretic contribution that has stimulated research on reminiscence in aging and has encouraged practitioners to better understand the uses of reminiscence by older people and, moreover, to use reconstructions of the past when working with older people or treating them in psychotherapy.

ACCEPTANCE OF LIFE

Regardless of whether Butler's spontaneous life review occurs, we can ask people to review and evaluate their lives and then determine if there is increasing acceptance of life with advancing age. Evidence for increasing acceptance with age was provided by James

Gorney (1968), one of Morton Lieberman's and my doctoral students, who used data from the Last Home for the Aged study (Lieberman & Tobin, 1983). The sample that was composed of both older persons becoming institutionalized in homes for elderly people and persons in control groups not undergoing institutionalization revealed that the older old persons as compared to younger old persons were more likely to accept their lives as it was lived. Respondents were asked to evaluate their lives after a life history interview. From answers to questions such as whether they would want to live life over or change it, their major disappointments, and the happiest events in their lives, Gorney assessed whether there was a resolution to life; that is, resolution was assessed as present when the self was perceived in such a way that the failures and never-to-be recaptured joys of the past, as well as the personal dissolution of the future, could no longer inflict severed narcissistic wounds. Of a group of 44 older old persons who were 80 years of age or over, 57% were assessed as resolved as contrasted to a lesser 32% for a group younger than 80. Although not conclusive, this analysis does provide presumptive evidence for a movement toward acceptance of life as it has been lived.

Accepting Life

Mrs. Turner was an 88-year-old widow whose husband had died about 50 years before. She then supported herself and two small children by giving piano lessons. She was living with her unmarried daughter in a comfortable house owned by one of her grandchildren, but Mrs. Turner's application for admission to an old-age home was necessary because there was no one in her home to tend to her daily needs: her daughter worked all day, and her granddaughter was taking care of a number of young children. In effect Mrs. Turner was a prisoner in her own room during the day since the arthritis, which had disfigured her back and hands, made it extremely difficult for her to negotiate stairs without assistance.

A pleasant, smiling, well-groomed, white-haired lady, Mrs. Turner appeared much younger than her age. She gave the impression of being an emotionally modulated individual, well in control of her emotional responses, yet still capable of sudden spontaneity or unexpected flashes of wit. When asked to describe herself she stated" I can't say intelligent. I can't say stupid. Generous when I can be. Admired by my old friends. Loving my grandchildren and great grandchildren. I have a wonderful family." In her own acerbic style, she conveyed the clear impression that she knew who she was and was quite comfortable with it. She possessed a low level of anxiety and a very high degree of life satisfaction.

Clinical evaluations of personality attributes characterized Mrs. Turner as a woman who clearly asserted herself through external activities and concerns without using hostile aggression to achieve her ends. Moreover, she did not often blame others for her shortcomings, nor did she often evoke guilt feelings in herself through self-castigation. She manifested high trust of other people and exhibited a fair capacity to empathize with the feelings and problems of others.

Mrs. Turner's willingness to provide complex articulation of the past was somewhat limited. Although on occasion she was quite able to provide well-articulated expectations for the future, she did not display the high proficiency clearly exhibited by most other respondents who were categorized as having achieved resolution. This lack of involvement in intense intrapsychic activity was reflected in her verbalizations, which tended to be terse, well thought out and to the point, but not intensely introspective. She appeared to be secure in her own self-knowledge and not going to waste needless words or emotional energy to explore all the complexity of her feelings. This relative unwillingness to engage in introspection is qualitatively different from that observed among older people engaged in a flight from the past. For the latter group, a lack of introspection often seems associated with a denial of feelings and an avoidance of emotional realities. For those who have achieved resolution, however, low introspection may be the product of affective modulation and an attitude of serenity in regard to transitory emotional states.

The achievement of resolution is most clearly illustrated by Mrs. Turner in her responses to the Evaluation of Life Questionnaire and in her lengthy life history. These data indicate that Mrs. Turner regarded her life with a rather philosophic attitude; the good and the bad are both considered and weighed, with no undue remorse, with acceptance, and even with wit. For example, when the interviewer asked the question, "If you were going to live your life over again, what would you change?"

Mrs. Turner's response was to point to the unmade bed in the room and proclaim,"Which I am," meaning that she would soon make her bed. Her gesture and words suggest the fragile use of witty self-depreciation. The interviewer then asked what she would leave unchanged, to which Mrs. Turner replied, "Everything else." She continued to convey her belief that she herself had borne the major responsibility for her life experience, both the periods of satisfaction and the periods of disappointment.

Even when past conflicts were described, and Mrs. Turner did not gloss over them, it is as if they were now being seen through the filter of understanding and tranquility. A good example of this can be found in Mrs. Turner's life history when she described the personality and death of her husband. Very nice. Very good-hearted. He was jealous of me. That was his trouble. If a man spoke to me or anything he would be upset. But otherwise we were very close. I spoke to him about it and said don't you know me better than that. And then he felt ashamed. My marriage went better. Until he had his accident. We were only married a little over 4 years. He had an accident—he was getting out of a car, and a horse and wagon were passing. He was knocked down and hit his head. His brain was damaged, and he was in the hospital 4 years." When asked whether she considered remarrying, she answered, "No sir, I know what I had. But I didn't know what I would get."

In this excerpt Mrs. Turner has not attempted to unrealistically idealize her dead husband, but instead presents what appears to be a relatively balanced picture of him, their relationship together, and the effects of his death. There was a strong sense from her account that this was once an issue for Mrs. Turner, with a multitude of strong emotions attached to it. Now, although still a salient conflict, it is neither distorted nor denied, and emotionally is only a shadow of its former self.

Mrs. Turner appeared neither to flee from her past nor to focus intensely on it. Rather, she seemed to have attained a certain perspective on her life and present situation. She was not apathetic, but tranquil; not pretending that all conflicts had been solved, but serene; not fearing death, but accepting its personal inevitability.

For many individuals who have achieved such resolution, the future is more interesting than the past, not because they deny the quickening approach of death, but because they seem to have made a certain peace with their past and have made most of the necessary psychological preparations for an unexpected stranger at the door. This is what Mrs. Turner meant in her answer to the question, "What do you fear will happen to you as you grow older? She responded: "That's a hard thing to say, I really don't have any fear. I just take what I can get."

Respondents who were like Mrs. Turner in accepting their lives also were less likely to be introspective about their current affects, on why they are happy or unhappy, satisfied or proud. Lesser introspection was not only associated with older chronologic age but also with the resolution style. These very old people who accept their lives are apparently sufficiently secure about their own self-knowledge not to waste needless emotional energy to explore all the complexity of their feelings. It is as if they have put to rest any concerns or preoccupations with how they came to be who they are and how they lived their lives. The survival of the self has been accomplished.

Blending the Past with the Present

Besides using memories to construct a life story, recollections of the past are useful for affirming the diverse content that comprises the current self-picture. Each person has a differentiated self-picture that remains relatively constant after its crystallization in adolescence. The adult years provide activities and interactions with others that can be structured to validate the self-picture and also can be interpreted for their validation of the self-picture. The man whose self-picture contains the perception of being an inquisitive learner can keep up on current events and seek out opportunities to discuss events of the day, as well as interpret conversations to reflect this aspect of his self-image. The woman who perceives herself as a nurturant person will be sure to validate this essential part of her self-picture by giving to others and also by interpreting social interactions as evidence for her nurturance. When, however, current circumstances limit social interactions that neither can be structured nor interpreted to validate the self-picture, evidence from the past becomes particularly useful for the task of self-validation. Indeed, the losses of others and personal physical disabilities of very old age diminish the availability of activities and social interactions that can be structured and interpreted. Then, too, relationships and activities in the past may provide the very best evidence for affirmation of the here-and-now self picture.

I Became The Boss

 Mrs. Greenberg's energy level at 81 was remarkable. She was actively involved in her synagogue and several Jewish philanthropic organizations. "They need me. Sure, I organize things, but I tell it like it is. You can't be wishy-washy if you want to get things done." As she selected the self-descriptive card, "I enjoy being in charge of things," she laughed and said, "That fits me like a glove." Later, however, when asked to give an example in the present for the self-description, she turned to the past."When my husband keeled over from a heart attack when I was only 40, I took over the jewelry business. I had two kids in high school. Sometimes I helped him, but he didn't seem to want me around. He did okay, but I really did well. He was too nice. When I became the boss, I was the boss, and I made the business a great success."

Mrs. Greenberg has current activities and relationships to confirm her self-picture. She chooses instead to focus at times on past events that are most illustrative for who she is. Others who do not have current activities and relationships useful for validating the self picture, as does Mrs. Greenberg, have no choice but to rely on the past.

Nothing to Be in Charge of Now

 Mrs. Levine was a frail, wheelchair-bound resident in Drexel Home for the Aged who still possessed a booming voice. "I can't do anything anymore. I saw an advertisement for a book, Old Age Ain't for Sissies, that describes me. You can't be 80 in a wheelchair and take it laying down." She, too, like Mrs. Greenberg, chose "I like being in charge of things" and when asked to

give a current example, said, "Nothing to be in charge of now. They feed me and take care of me. I always took care of myself. Took care of the family, too. Never let the kids get away with anything. You know my son Buddy, a big success. Always on TV saying good things and doing good for others. He got some fancy degrees. Could have made a lot of money. Maybe I was tough on him but maybe not tough enough. On the day he graduated from law school, already a big shot with the do-gooders, I told him to take care of himself first and to use his head and make a good living."

Mrs. Levine is unable to structure current interactions for self-validation and must rely on her past. She begins by saying she cannot use the present, then talks about the general past when she reigned over her house, follows by focusing on her son, and ends her narrative with a specific incident when she told her now famous but misguided son to make a good living.

A SYSTEMATIC STUDY

To better understand these kinds of observations of use of the past, Morton Lieberman (Lieberman & Tobin, 1982) developed a procedure to elicit self-descriptions that included respondents providing evidence of their self-descriptions. The descriptions were found to remain remarkably constant, but about half of self-descriptions were validated by examples in the past; and, moreover, past and present examples were interchangeable so that for the same self-description it was not uncommon to exchange an example from the present or from the past a few months or 1 year later. That is, the self-description of "I enjoy being in charge of things," at one time can elicit a present example ("I make sure that Jack takes his pills."), at another time, a past example ("I was in charge of the rummage sale at the synagogue.") and at still another time, a statement of the general past ("I have always been in charge of things at home and in the Women's Club at the synagogue.").

The self-descriptions in this investigation of using the past for validation were encompassed in 48 statements in the Lieberman Self-Sort Task such as "I enjoy being in charge of things." The Self-Sort Task consisted of first asking respondents to select from the 48 those statements that describe how they are now and then to provide an example for each statement chosen. The set of statements was based on the interpersonal theory of personality developed by Timothy Leary (1957), the psychologist who later became infamous for his studies of LSD. His theory provided useful categories for developing self-assessments based on consciously perceived attributes. Personality attributes were divided by Leary into 16 categories of interpersonal behavior that can be applied to any unit of observed, self-reported, or self-descriptive behavior. Categories are arranged to form a circle in which adjacent categories are more similar than nonadjacent categories, and categories on opposite sides of the circle are assumed to represent psychological opposites. The 16 categories were then grouped into octanes by pairing categories as follows: success-power, exploitative-narcissism, hostility-punitive, rebellious-distrustful, weakness-masochistic, conformity-trust, collaboration-pure love, and tenderness-generosity. In this scheme, success-power is assumed to be the psychological opposite of weakness-masochistic, with the former reflecting a general trait of dominance and the latter of submissiveness. Likewise, collaboration-pure love is assumed to be the psychological opposite of hostility-punitive, with the former reflecting a general trait of affiliation and the latter of hostility.

Based on Leary's scheme, a set of 48 statements were developed, with each of the octanes represented by six items. For example, for octant success-power, the following three items were constructed for success:

1. People think well of me.
2. I believe I am an important person.
3. I frequently give advice to others.

And the following three for power:

1. I enjoy being in charge of things.
2. I am a good leader.
3. I am somewhat of a dominating or bossy person.

Note that the three items in each set are scaled (Guttman scale) from less to more intensity.

The Self-Sort Task was administered by asking respondents to sort a shuffled deck of cards containing the 48 statements into two piles: "like me now" and "not like me now." Then the respondent was asked to provide an illustration of current interpersonal behavior for those statements in the "like me now" pile. It was expected that most examples would reflect specific current interpersonal characteristics of the self-concept based on feedback or validating experiences derived from these exchanges.

A student, Gloria Edelhart, made assessments of the extent each category was manifested in six different forms of data including a life history interview and responses to Thematic Apperceptive Test cards. The self-descriptions derived from these six tests were compared by computing a single summary score based on a weighting system developed by Leary. Edelhart found that "the self-concept scores on each of the six measures showed a closer correspondence than would be expected by chance ($p=.001$)." Since similar self-concepts were obtained from dissimilar measures, it is reasonable to conclude that the self-sort task yields a meaningful self-concept measure that is not an artifact of a particular type of test data. Not known, of course, is whether a similar consistency across methods of assessing self-descriptions would be characteristic of younger persons. It is possible that the consistency of self-descriptions of very old people are specifically characteristic of them because they likely have accepted alien parts of themselves previously out of consciousness.

The examples respondents provided for each self-descriptive item were categorized into one of five types. A rating of "specific present" was assigned when an example was given from current interaction. For example, to the statement "I enjoy being in charge of things," one respondent said, "I enjoy being in charge of the gift shop (in the home), and I also work in the library."

Given the nature of the task, as well as the importance of reinforcement in ongoing interaction with others, it was assumed that if an example from the present was not available, a specific example from the near past, reflecting a lowered availability of day-to-day reinforcement of self, would be a meaningful way to provide validation for the description selected as "like me now." For example, again for the statement "I enjoy being in charge of things," one respondent gave the example: "Where I worked years ago, they put me in charge of a department, I worked, I did a good job, and people thought well of me."

The "general past" was the rating assigned when a specific example was not given, and the comment made by the respondent referred instead to the description as being a persistent characteristic. For instance, to validate the statement, "I enjoy being in charge of things" a respondent said, "That's how I am, how I've always been." This kind of statement suggests that validation is solely from an internal feeling of conviction.

Sometimes the interpersonal attribute in question was not necessarily possessed but was wished for or strived toward "wish to be" was, therefore, the rating assigned when a comment given to illustrate the item was a wish or hope, reflecting the sense that the respondent may not be certain that the attribute is characteristic of self but wishes that it were. For example, to the statement "I am a good leader" one respondent said, "I'm trying to be," while another said, "I wish I could be that way." In examples such as these, specific self-validating evidence may not exist now, may have existed in the past, or may never have existed at all. Although the respondents might claim certain self-characteristics as their own by their choice of statements on the sorting task, in fact, evidence might not be available to support the claim.

Lastly, a rating of "distortion" was given for examples in which self-validation was based on fantasy, or in which there was confusion, contradiction, or actual distortion between the statement chosen and the example given. For example, to the statement "I enjoy being in charge of things" one person said, "My hair annoys me so, the dandruff. I'm in charge today, they all went out. I'm in charge of everything today." In the absence of more appropriate self-validating data, an individual may become confused, may stretch his imagination to provide a response, or may deny the choice of a particular statement as "like me now."

Several different ratios were computed by Arthur Rosner, then our doctoral student, to assess stability of self-image. The first was a simple percentage of the same items two times. Intervals of 6 months to 1 year revealed that about four of five items were chosen at both times for diverse groups. When socially desirable items were eliminated (17 of the 48), stability was still high. A third stability score was based on shifts in items in octants that also indicated high stability. Further support for the stability of self-image among elderly respondents was found in an analysis of a group of 16 respondents who were administered the self-sort task weekly for 6 weeks beginning after their entrance into the home for the aged. Stability of item selection from week to week remained as high for these 16 as for any other group studied in spite of the immediacy of the disruptive life change! It is apparent that older persons are remarkably capable of retaining a persistent self-image.

The ability of elderly people to maintain a coherent and stable self-image, even in the face of highly adverse life changes, makes the exploration of mechanisms used to maintain such self-stability of singular relevance for understanding the psychology of aging. For a comparison of mechanisms used to validate the self-image at different ages, a group was chosen that was also in transition, but frequently interacts with others. Assessed were 24 high school juniors and seniors, and the distribution of the responses in each category of self-validating evidence at the elderly respondents' baseline (the first interview) was compared to the distribution for these high school juniors and seniors. As expected, whereas the high school students relied almost completely on validating the self-concept by examples from the present, less than one half of respondents in all three samples from older respondents provided validating evidence from the present. In turn, the general past, rarely used for validation by the adolescents, was prominent among the older respondents.

When the effects of environments on the maintenance of self-stability were investigated, contrasts in type of self-validating evidence used by respondents in the three samples revealed differences only in the use of distortion. Those awaiting entrance into institutions and those already institutionalized utilized significantly more distortion than did respondents in the community sample.

The analyses thus indicated, first, that the older respondents used the present for validation appreciably less than adolescents, who rarely used any other mechanism; second, use of the generalized past for validation was ubiquitous among the older group; third, the specific past was used sparingly by all respondents; fourth, wish was rarely used for validation; and fifth, distortion was used by elderly persons in transition. These findings on validating processes suggest that these processes are situationally determined rather than representative of enduring characteristics of people. To pursue this further, the variability in validating processes was examined by making use of the longitudinal data available on the elderly respondents.

Older persons undergoing the life change of relocation were compared to those in more stable environments, the community controls, and the long-term institutionalized. We found that the time 1 and time 2 distributions of the type of validating evidence used were not different for the groups in stable and unstable environments. The comparisons of two distributions at two different times, however, masks the variability of individuals. To circumvent this, percentage changes from time 1 to time 2 for each category of self-validating evidence were computed for each respondent, and then the average change for each category computed. This method of determining variability revealed substantial fluctuations. Respondents in the stressed sample exhibited an average shift of almost 22% in the use of present examples from preadmission to 2 months after admission. Comparable instability was found for the other mechanisms. When changes in mechanisms were computed in each of the eight octanes comprising the Self-Sort Task, all three samples manifested high degrees of instability. Instability is easily understood for those undergoing institutionalization who have lost previous social resources necessary for ongoing feedback, but the reason for the instability of self-validation evidence among other older persons is not so readily apparent. Still, older people clearly rely on a variety of evidence to validate and maintain a stable self-concept, in contrast to the almost exclusive use by younger people of current feedback.

RELATION TO THE SOCIAL WORLD

Evidence that older people use to maintain a coherent self-portrait is noticeably more contingent on the characteristics of their social world than on specific personal characteristics. This is not to suggest that older people, or for that matter younger people, systematically demand of themselves, moment to moment, specific evidence to affirm a sense of self. More likely, in times of reflection, an individual may contemplate various experiences of the day or of the immediate past and evaluate his or her behavior as conforming to or falling short of previously established expectations of self. It is likely that such "internal conversations" are generated by activities in a variety of ongoing roles. It is the reduction of such roles among older people with a consequent lack of opportunities for input that, in part, result in a lack of current evidence to maintain their self-image. A rich illustration of stability of the self-picture with changes in evidence to support the self is provided by Mrs. Apple, who was followed from preadmission through life in a nursing home:

Sameness Using the Past and the Present

Mrs. Apple was first interviewed for the community sample before she began to think about entering a home for the aged and was followed after she made her application and while she was on the waiting list, through admission, and her first year of life in the institution. Although she was seriously affected by losses prior to admission and under a great deal of stress throughout the 3 years of study, she maintained a remarkable degree of self-consistency and self-integrity.

After Mrs. Apple's admission, no major behavioral, physical, or cognitive decrements were noted. Stable functioning, of course, did not preclude subtle psychological changes. We did detect, for example, in her response to the question What are the worst features of your life now? a more receptive attitude toward death: "Why don't He take me? I've lived long enough." There was a change in Mrs. Apple's emotional states. Although she maintained a high level of feelings of well-being (as is apparent from her scores on the ratings of life satisfaction), she also showed increases in anxiety and

*depression. Mrs. Apple became less hopeful and shifted toward a more neg-
ative appraisal of the world. Apparently, her attitude toward the world after
admission reflected a disparagement of institutional life. The clearest example of the general change appeared in the shift from strong disagreement to
strong agreement with the statement "These days a person doesn't really
know who he can count on."*

*Mrs. Apple's response to the time dimension question also revealed this
shift toward hopelessness. To the inquiry "In general, do you find yourself
thinking about the past or the future?" she responded before admission: "I
think about the past. If I think of the past I know what I am thinking about.
But who can tell about the future? No one can!" After admission, she said,
"If people knew what the future might bring, many people might commit
suicide." Mrs. Apple's message might be interpreted as, "If I had only
known what it really would be like to live in a home for the aged, I would
have considered suicide"; or possibly, "If I were to change, to deteriorate as
other old people do before my eyes, it would be better for me to die."*

*Before relocation, Mrs. Apple indicated that she would welcome death if
it would avert physical pain and suffering. In the second interview, however,
after she was in the home but with no evidence of deterioration in physical
status, she indicated that she had no qualifications regarding the benefits of
death. In response to the sentence stem, "To me death is . . ." Mrs. Apple's
addition at first was "a big relief"; after admission, it was "the best thing
that can happen to anybody."*

*It may be that her experience among the home's sick inmates led Mrs.
Apple to believe that her only possible future was to become progressively
more deteriorated. If so, she had indeed become incurable at that point. To
paraphrase Ben Franklin, before admission she was long-lived, but afterward
she was irreversibly and incurably old. Mrs. Apple's concerns with death
and personal vulnerability were associated with actually entering and living in the institution. After relocation, these themes were elaborated to
include a vision of epidemics.*

*To what extent was Mrs. Apple able to maintain a stable self-image when
confronted with such feelings after institutionalization? We compared the
statements she selected on the self-sort task as being like her when she was
living in the community and part of our community sample to those she
selected 3 years later after entering and living in the institution. When living in the community Mrs. Apple selected 26 statements as self-descriptive
(two above average); 2 months after admission to the home, she selected 32
statements. Of the 26 initially chosen statements, 23 (or 88%) were again
selected 3 years later. Because 15 of the statements she initially selected were
among those selected by 75% or more of the respondents, 11 of the 26 statements selected were considered idiosyncratic statements. Of these, 8 (or
73%) were selected again 3 years later. (Mrs. Apple's maintenance of her
self-concept is not only indicated by the percentage of all items and idiosyncratic statements chosen again 3 years later, but by the average shift in
octants, which was 2.9%.)*

The items she selected, as well as those not selected, permit Mrs. Apple to tell us who she is. The 15 social desirability items chosen both times included the following:

People think well of me.
I am a self-respecting person.
I am frank and honest with people.
When necessary I can complain about things that bother me.
I am grateful for what other people do for me.
I am a friendly person.
I am an affectionate and understanding person.

Idiosyncratic items chosen both times reflect the intensity of Mrs. Apple's wish to be engaged and close to others, but not at the expense of her own personal worth. Items such as "I want everyone to like me" and "I love everyone" were selected along with "I can reproach people when necessary" and "I can argue back when I am right about something." Items rejected at both times also reveal the nature of Mrs. Apple's stable affinitive self-image. Not selected either time were items such as: "It is hard for me to trust anyone," "I can be a cold and unfeeling person," "I am critical of other people," and "I frequently get angry with people." The combination of items selected and rejected at both times reveals a stable, complex, and fine-grained image that persisted over 3 years of adversity, including entering and living in an institution.

Contrasting with the stability in her selection of self-descriptive statements is the variability in the processes Mrs. Apple used to maintain her self-image. Mrs. Apple decreased her percentage of examples in the present from 62% to 41% and correspondingly increased the percentage of validating comments classified as being from the general past from 31% to 50%. Also, where initially 7% of her examples were from the specific past, later none were, and although she had used no distortion initially, 9% of her responses were so classified subsequent to relocation.

Four self-concept items chosen by Mrs. Apple at both points in time illustrate variability in the mechanism used for validation.

"I believe I am an important person." Initially the evidence was based on interaction. "I'm important to my family and friends. You should have seen how many New Year's cards I got." Three years later the evidence for the same stem was based on the general past. "I think I'm important to my family, I've always done the best I could for my family, and they appreciate it."

"I can reproach other people when necessary." Initially the evidence was from the general past. "I always explain to them what I think is the best to be done. I don't really scold, I just give my opinion when they want it." Later the evidence was in the present. "If they don't do the right thing, surely, I tell them. Like when somebody said I'm not dressed right, I told them it's my own business."

"I am touchy and easily hurt by others." Initially the evidence was from the specific past. *"If people step on my toes they hurt my feelings. My brother-in-law opened a store and didn't consult me first. I felt hurt for a long time."* Later the evidence was based on a distortion. *"Sure I will. I wouldn't let anybody step on me! I have some kind of feelings! If somebody would say I said something and I didn't, I surely would defend myself."*

"I can be obedient when necessary." Initially the evidence was from the present. *"My son told me I wasn't well enough to come to his home for dinner tonight. I feel bad, but I'm not going."* Later the evidence was from the general past. *"I do. Well, if someone would tell me what is the proper thing to do, I obey."*

Despite marked changes in her inner life, the content of Mrs. Apple's self-image remained remarkably stable. Evidence used to support the self-image suggests the strain inherent in her effort for self-stability. As noted earlier, examples in the present decreased, whereas statements from the general past increased, and for the first time distortions appeared, apparently without reinforcement from the current interpersonal environment. Mrs. Apple relied on her sense of an enduring self-concept. Paralleling the stability of the self indicated by the selection of self-sort items, the interviewer observed that Mrs. Apple remained remarkably the same, and she also adapted successfully, displaying no manifest indications of an adverse reaction to becoming institutionalized. Indeed, her cognitive functioning and sensitivity to her environment improved from preadmission while on the waiting list, and her sense of well-being remained remarkably high. At the manifest behavioral level, all indications showed functioning similar to prestress levels or that even improved.

Mythicizing the Past

After reading a great many of the life reviews we had gathered in the Last Home for the Aged study, Virginia Revere, an experienced clinician who returned for her doctorate, came to a novel conclusion: Older people were mythicizing their past in a way not generally found among younger persons. At that time Barbara Myerhoff (1978) had not yet presented her insightful thoughts on how the life stories of the old are integrated through mythicizing. Revere developed a splendid dissertation to test her hypothesis, which was confirmed and reported in the Revere and Tobin (1980/81) article entitled "Myth and reality: The Older person's relationship to the past." This publication begins:

People have always associated reminiscence with the aged, sometimes positively, as in describing the aged person regaling the young with exciting tales of personal and historic pasts; sometimes negatively when the old are said to be unfortunately preoccupied with the past.

In reviewing the relationship of the older person to his storehouse of memories, several possible alternatives are pertinent. Is the older person merely more involved with his past than persons of other ages—but involved in the same kind of way, or does he relate to his past uniquely? It appeared to the authors that the relationship of the older person to the past was indeed unique, that not only were the elderly more involved with their past, but involved in a way that would not be common to other age groups. The particular involvement expected was based on the assumption that the older person no longer has an adaptational need to see the past realistically. Rather, the need is to see the past in such a way as to achieve some measure of immortality, to see oneself as a hero of a life worth remembering. Stated another way, to see oneself as a hero of a drama worth telling, a drama worth having lived for. As social myth may be defined as a story intended to be believed in order to justify a social institution, individual myth may be defined as a story intended to be believed in order to justify a life. In order to determine whether the past is mythic to a greater degree for the older person, it was necessary to measure aspects of mythicizing in the recollections. We looked for these in terms of greater consistency and certainty in their collections (the myth conveys a simple and unitary message), and in terms of a number of dramatic elements. The primary dimension, however, would be dramatization in which not only would significant others be dramatized but also the whole life story would be made more dramatic. Reconciliation was included because it is not a mythicizing variable, but rather a possible alternative style of reminiscing. (pp. 15–16)

To determine whether older persons would indeed see their pasts as mythical, scales were developed to assess this dimension, and recollections of older persons were contrasted with middle-aged persons on a series of scales developed to assess four dimensions. The first of four dimensions, that of involvement, was assessed to determine if indeed the intensity and type of direct involvement with the memories would be greater for the aged person. This was accomplished by contrasting the amount of affective involvement, the length of the memories, and direct statements by respondents about the importance of their memories. The second dimension was the mythic, in which the earliest memories were analyzed to determine the extent of dramatization, and the entire life story to determine dramatization—whether significant figures would take on heroic proportions, and whether they would be described in culturally relevant rather than personal terms—not "my mother used to take me to a lot of concerts," but, "my mother was a wonderful cook," "my father was the best breadwinner in the world." Scales for the third dimension of consistency/certainty were developed because of the assumption that such a recasting of the past would take place if the individual used the memories to bolster uniqueness. This was accomplished in several ways; assessing, for example, values implicit in recollections of childhood as compared to adolescence and adulthood and evaluating similarities of general description of childhood compared to adolescence and adulthood. The fourth dimension was that of reconciliation, an exploration of whether the use was indeed similar to that described by Butler, specifically, acceptance of life as it was, including the negative events in one's life.

The sample of 35 persons aged 65 to 103 were ambulatory, free of major incapacitating illness, and showed no gross signs of altered brain function. To obtain a sample of middle-aged persons who would be an acceptable match to the older sample, people who would be like the children of this older sample were selected, aged 44 to 55 (mean age 49). The two groups therefore were similar in religious background and were urban but, as expected, were dissimilar in marital status and in education because the older group were largely widowed and less educated. In general, both samples consisted predominantly of Jewish urban females. Given the differences between the two samples, any findings of greater mythicizing among the older people would have to be examined from the perspective of the relationship between mythicizing and education, as well as with other variables, such as social interaction. As will become apparent, these other measures were available for the present sample.

Data were generated from face-to-face interviews of approximately 3 hours each. Three questionnaires were used, the first was a Life Review Questionnaire, which gave participants an opportunity to talk about questions such as, "What was your life like as a child?" "What were your parents like?" "What hardships did you undergo?" The questions were open-ended and divided into reminiscences about childhood, adolescence, and adulthood. This yielded data rich in detail, vividly portraying the lives of our participants. A few examples of early memories will suggest the variety and richness of the data. "I remember a Christmas—my father coming home with an orange for each of us children. We thought this was the most wonderful thing in the world." The respondent elaborated: "A large family—great warmth and affection, but strictness from our parents. I remember putting pennies in a jar from my earnings as a paper boy. We all worked very hard and turned in the money we made every Saturday to our parents." Another recollected, "A next door neighbor girl fell off her tricycle and opened her head. The screaming and blood all over the sidewalk left a lasting, hideous impression." Or, "I never had nobody. The kids at school made fun of the way we were dressed. The teacher was always mad 'cause we never came to school. I never had no more than a couple of years of school all told." Respondents dwelled at length on those aspects of their pasts most meaningful to them, some describing friends as children, or their own children, or vocational adaptations.

The second and third questionnaires provided more structured data, asking respondents to evaluate their lives and make judgments about the role of reminiscence. For example, in the Evaluation of Life Questionnaire, they were asked what kind of life they had, whether they would want to live it over as it was or with changes, what their major disappointments were, and the happiest events in their lives. In the On Memories Questionnaire they responded to such questions as, "How important are your memories to you? Thinking about the past makes me feel. . ." Do you agree or disagree with this statement, "My memories are like spilled milk; one should forget and go on." or "My memories are like money in the bank for a rainy day."

The effort was made to generate scales that would tap data independently for each of the four dimensions: involvement, dramatization, consistency/certainty, and reconciliation. Twenty-three such scales, the Remembered Past Scales, were generated. Each of these scales was rated on a 5-point continuum. Ratings were done in such a way that the highest numbers correspond to those ratings expected for the aged person, contrasted to the middle-aged person, who would be expected to receive lower ratings on all scales. Scales in the dimensions of involvement and dramatization discriminated between the two groups, with the aged group, as predicted, having higher scores than the middle-aged group. In contrast to these two dimensions, scales in the dimensions of reconciliation and consistency/certainty did not discriminate. To determine that the differences in involvement and dramatization were not attributable to characteristics on which the two samples differed, the reminiscence variables were correlated with measures of education, occupation, and social interaction. Neither significant nor appreciable associations were found. Also, because the two groups did not differ on such personal characteristics as personality traits, ego strength, and anxiety, these characteristics cannot have been responsible for the difference in the two samples. When measures of these several characteristics, as well as reminiscing measures that reflect positive affect states (e.g., affirmation of life scales), were examined for their association with involvement and dramatization, again significant and appreciable associations were not found, suggesting that older people who manifest greater mythicizing do not necessarily have better emotional states than those who do not. Yet on the reconciliation scale of positive affirmation of one's life (degree to which significant figures are seen positively) older people scored higher than the middle-aged respondents.

The results of this study suggest that older people were not only more involved in their pasts, but involved in the special way of mythicizing their recollections; in no case was any element or combination of elements of dramatization present in the middle-aged group to the same degree as in the aged group. This is not to imply that all were the same. The rich complexity of human experience was reflected in our interviews. There were variations on the theme, but the theme of dramatizing the past was present in most of our interviews with the aged group. For some, the rhetoric was emphatic but skeletal, "My life? Lousy! Lousy in every way. I never had nothing." Others lovingly retrieved rich, nuanced recollections: "I remember being in the house where the Czar was searching for books. I remember I had been lying on my bed reading. Enthralled in a novel. I hid under the bed." These early memories illustrate the finding that, while a positive view of significant figures was frequent, a generally positive evaluation of the past was not the factor that differentiated the aged group from the middle-aged group. Nor was there a greater degree of reconciliation to the past. Instead, the positive was a way of characterizing individuals dramatically, "My father was the greatest provider." For many the total story was a happy one. This was not, however, true for all, and some portrayed significant figures mythically, but not positively. Above all, memories were recast to make uniqueness vivid. In this sense, the past becomes more real and more poignant. The myth *is* the reality.

MEMORIES ARE MORE VIVID

Occasionally very old people are aware of experiencing this change in their reminiscence:

My Memories Are More Vivid Now

Professor Lerner, who still had an active and fertile mind at 87, asked me if it is still believed that whereas memory fails in advanced aging, remote memory remains constant. He then related how he has noticed how elderly relatives have modified their memories to incorporate current concerns. That is, when happy, the reconstructed event was elaborated upon with pleasantness but when sad, the same event took on a depressive tone. But later in the conversation, he shared his real concern. He has become increasingly aware that early memories have been pushing into consciousness and also that there is a kind of mutability to them so that sometime he felt that his recall of early events was becoming distorted. I assured him that memories are always changing and, also, that there is evidence that they become more vivid. With great relief, he soon discussed his earliest memory that included his mother and then elaborated upon a quite vivid recollection of her.

Apparently, the mutability and vividness of resurgent early memories had greatly disturbed this introspective and perceptive man who could cope with losses in immediate memory but not with the changes in recollections of early memories, which he interpreted as some kind of destructuralization. Unlike many others his age, Professor Lerner is highly introspective, but, in common with most other persons of advanced age, he illustrates the active involvement in memories that are dramatic and vivid but also continually changing as present adaptive affects become incorporated into recollections.

Mythicizing the past when old is not to live in the past but rather to use the past for preservation of the self. Certainly, when older widowed women report talking to their deceased husbands, usually at bedtime, they are aware of the reality that their husbands are no longer alive. When, however, they mythicize their dead husbands, as reported by Helena Lopata (1979) to be quite common, they may be unaware of the transformation. Indeed, an inability to revitalize and mythicize the past when very old seems pathognomonic of a lack of the coherence and wholeness inherent to preserving the self.

CHAPTER 5

Religiosity

Whether one's past life is reviewed extensively or not, reconstructions of the past are used adaptively by very old persons to achieve a self-wisdom that assures the survival of the self. Of significance is that achieving of self-wisdom toward the end of the life course has been conceptualized by some theologians as the culmination of life's spiritual journey. Exploration of the past and the self is perceived as a spiritual quest where the self-knowledge achieved is knowledge of God, according, for example, to gnostic Christians. For existential theologians such as Perry LeFevre (1984), however, the spiritual task is the making of meaning. The making of life meaningful to oneself is a life-long task that takes on different dimensions when age-associated losses occur and as the awareness of nonbeing becomes most real. Beyond sustaining and maintaining oneself, and therefore one's sense of meaning to self and others, is the possibility, it is argued, for new meanings from a reassessment of one's life and goals, and then placing one's life in perspective in preparing for death. The waning of our power toward the end of life can possibly facilitate a reassessment in which conventional values of mastery and control become of less importance; it may facilitate a realization of one's interdependence with others, or one's place in the continuity of generations, of one's uniqueness, and possibly a consciousness of making meaning of one's whole life.

Marilyn Sampson has a personal philosophy, a self-wisdom, that she often shares with others:

You Live With Other People

"I have always known that if you help others, they will be there for you. My mother taught me that. She was always there for me, and I was always there for her. My sister and me, we are like that too. We are devoted to each other. My friends, we help each other. You don't live by yourself. You live with other people. Of course, there are some stinkers. We have helped some people who never think to reciprocate. They haven't learned their lesson yet. They will."

Jack has a quite different philosophy, one that he acquired later in life:

Making It Easier

"Every generation is different. We struggled. Oh, did we struggle. But we made it. We tried to make it easier for our kids. We did make it easier for them. Two are professional, Davie, our oldest, and Sid, the middle one. Howie had a tough time but made it in his father's trade. Then they have made it easier for their kids. I don't know about my great grandchildren. But it seems easier for them. I think that's what its all about. Don't you? Making it easier for the next generation."

From a more pragmatic perspective, however, it is conventional Judeo-Christian practices and beliefs that afford our oldest citizens with comfort and with ways of coping with uncertainties and calamities and facilitate survival of the self. A persistent myth that people become more religious as they age in their later years, however, obscures the reality that religious beliefs inculcated early in life become salient later in life. The belief that a long life is one of God's blessings (Psalms 91:16 and also Proverbs 9:11) and a reward for prior service (Deuteronomy 4:40) is not particularly salient in the adult years, but it surely is salient when very old. Similarly salient is the belief in an afterlife of reunions with departed loved ones. The espousing of these kinds of religious beliefs by older people can indeed be misinterpreted as an increasing religiosity with age when actually they are life-long beliefs that are particularly meaningful and helpful as death is approaching in the last years of life and when enduring age-associated assaults on the self.

Religiosity and Well-Being

The evoking of facilitory religious beliefs is likely to be accompanied by increased participation in formal activities at church or synagogue until disabilities restrict attendance and also in informal practices such as prayer and Bible reading. Increases in both formal and informal religious activities become possible when time becomes available for their pursuits. Widows are perceived to become more religious when in truth they have more time to fill now that their husbands are gone. Church and synagogue have always been important, especially for themselves in their formative years and for their children when they were youngsters. Then, as busy adults, they probably attended services less frequently. When asked, however, about church attendance in surveys, respondents are likely to give inflated responses. Four of five Americans report that they have been to church in the past 2 weeks, which reflects these exaggerated responses that come less from reality and more from an embarrassing sin of omission. This omission can be rectified when old and widowed by going to church. Attendance reinforces one's religiosity to assure God's blessings, enhances a sense of belongingness to the religious community, and also permits socializing with friends and neighbors.

Informal practices at home likewise reinforce one's religiosity and enhance a sense of belongingness to the larger community of one's faith. Prayers, Bible reading, and listening to preachers on the radio or watching them on television, additionally are religious ways of coping with troubles. Beseeching a kindly God is a way of controlling one's fate. Observant people have their prayers answered.

The several discrete functions of informal practices, formal participation, and beliefs coalesce to reinforce the continuity of the self. Memories of confirmations and Bar Mitzvahs, weddings, and funerals emerge into consciousness as religious experiences from earliest life become reconstructed in ways that are often vividly dramatized and mythicized to affirm the eternal self of believers. Adding to memories for the persistence of the self are the religious symbols of crosses or crucifixions on the walls of Christians and mizzuzehs on the doors of those of the Jewish faith.

MENTAL AND PHYSICAL HEALTH

Associations between religiosity and mental health among the aged have been reported (Koenig, 1994), as well as with physical health (Idler, 1987; Idler & Kasl, 1992). A remarkable study that controls for extraneous explanatory variables is the Kark, Shemi, Friedlander, Martin, and Blondheim (1996) investigation in Israel. The association of Jewish religious observance with mortality was studied by comparing religious and secular kibbutzim (a collective farm or settlement) in Israel. This 16-year (1970 through 1985) historic study of mortality in 11 religious with 11 matched secular kibbutzim was controlled for socioeconomic status by the matching procedure. There were lower mortality rates for all major causes of death for all ages in the religious kibbutzim. Because social support, health practices, and other obvious explanatory variables were similar in the two kinds of kibbutzim, the reasons for the differences must be speculative.

The authors offer: "A major possibility is that such a social environment induces less stress, enhances host resistance, and promotes overall well-being and a positive health status" (p. 345). Components of stress reduction may include a coherent world view; a sense of belonging where normative behavior is derived from divine sources, whereas secular autonomy determines the sources are with people; and less worry. Although Orthodox Jews reported more problems, they were less worried by them.

Religion has been found to be of particular importance to African-Americans. The review by Linda Chatters and Robert Taylor (1994) of studies of older-African-Americans, many of which were there own studies, revealed that African-Americans report higher rates of public religious participation than do Whites and are likely to report that religion is more important to them. These findings appear to transcend socioeconomic status. In common, however, with all studies independent of race, no association has been found with age. Instead of becoming more religious with age, people use their religiosity differently. Put another way, religiosity may be more important to very old people. Not because, however, they become more religious, but rather because religious beliefs inculcated earlier in life are particularly useful later in life.

Prevalence in a Secular Society

A Gallup Poll (Gallup & Castelli, 1989) revealed that more than 9 of 10 Americans have never doubted the existence of God and also have a personal relationship with their God. Eight of 10 believe that God still works miracles, and that they will be called before God on judgment day to account for their sins. Seven in 10 know there is an afterlife, and only 16% are sure there is not. Belief in an afterlife is even high among the least actively religious group (58%). Although many religious beliefs decline with educational attainment, beliefs in an afterlife do not. Apparently, but not reported, beliefs in an afterlife are held by more than 7 of 10 persons who are in advanced old age.

Commenting on the importance of religious institutions for elderly people, Erdman Palmore (1980) has written:

> Churches and synagogues deserve special consideration because they are the single most pervasive community institution to which the elderly belong. All the other community institutions considered together, including senior citizen centers, clubs for elders, unions, etc. do not involve as many elders as churches and synagogues. (p. 236)

Among very old people, however, attendance decreases. Some of them are too frail to attend services, whereas others do not have transportation or cannot climb the steps of the church or synagogue. There are some older people who say they "can't afford nice clothing" to go to services, and still others feel that younger members of the congregation have pushed them aside. Although attendance at formal workshops decreases among very old people, personal religious practices, such as reading the Bible, prayer, and watching religious programs on television are often maintained or even increased.

The extent of religious practices and beliefs is sometimes observed in a secular society such as ours that was founded on the separation of church and state. Religious beliefs are private and not to be tampered with, and when public policies go against these beliefs, there is likely to be a groundswell of outrage. To right-to-lifers, abortion clinics are an abomination that violates the deepest of religious beliefs. Older persons are quick to anger when references to God are removed from the Pledge of Allegiance to the Flag at the start of the school day. Persons of the Jewish faith ask, "Why not celebrate both Christmas and Hanukkah at school rather than neither? What's wrong with a Christmas tree and a menorah?" Separation of church and state, however, mandates the display of neither.

SPIRITUAL CRISES

The wish not to intrude on the privacy of beliefs too often becomes an inappropriate ignoring of beliefs. Crises of faith are known to cause mental anguish, but only in 1994 did the American Psychiatric Association include this kind of crises in its lexicon of mental disorders, and thus mandated treatment for spiritual crises by mental health professionals. Clergy are likely, however, to disavow treatment by mental health professionals for their parishioners' crises of faith. When Lucy Steinitz (1980) asked clergy and social workers whether they ever work together on behalf of elderly people, most clergy talked about how they avoid social agencies because practitioners ignore the religious aspects of life. Practitioners, in turn, who believe that guilt causes undue anguish, perceive clergy as inducing guilt and to be avoided by their patients or clients.

Some practitioners adhere to Freud's proclamation that religion is "the opiate of the people." Because religion lulls them to sleep, reinforcing an avoidance of looking inward at how less conscious motives influence behaviors, people must be freed from their religiosity so that insights can be attained regarding motives and their manifestations in dysfunctional behaviors. Whereas Freud's observation may have had truth in Victorian Vienna, and may still be an accurate interpretation for contemporary times, ordinary people obtain extraordinary benefits from their religiosity in advanced old age. Moreover, if religiosity is defined more generically as the making of meaning, which was discussed initially in this chapter, it is impossible to escape the values and beliefs inculcated in the earliest years of life. Psychoanalysis does not eradicate these inescapable personal values and beliefs but rather allows analysands to live more comfortably with them while adapting better to life's vicissitudes. To the extent that the earliest of values and beliefs are components of the basic corpus of the self, their reinforcement at the end of the life cycle preserves the self. The making of meaning at the end of life rather than achieving of new meanings occurs through resurrecting old meanings. The psychoanalyst Erik Erikson returned to the importance of the true love of mother for obtaining ego integrity rather than giving into despair in his eighth and final stage of the human life cycle. Returning to our roots can be conceptualized as the end of a spiritual journey or quest in this chapter on religiosity or in nonspiritual terms as was discussed in the previous chapter on reconstructions of the earliest of memories.

ATTENDING TO RELIGIOUS BELIEFS

Differing values and beliefs between therapists and their patients or clients can limit the effectiveness of treatment. More damaging to the therapeutic encounter may be the ignoring of values and beliefs:

I Prayed to God

As part of the hospital geriatric consultation team, I was asked to interview a 78-year-old patient at rounds who was not eating. The attending psychiatrist told me that Mr. Stone was mourning his daughter's death, which occurred 6 months previously, when according to Mr. Stone, "She flew off the highway while driving home to visit." When we gathered at his bedside, it was obvious that Mr. Stone was quite depressed. I asked about his appetite, and he answered almost inaudibly, "I have none." I came close to Mr. Stone, and when I gently touched him, he did not pull away. We began to talk about how he first lost his appetite when his daughter was killed. His daughter's husband had left her suddenly after a childless marriage of 20 years. Feeling abandoned for a younger woman who could have children, she was despondent and had thoughts of suicide. She did not want to come home because she was always in conflict with her mother, but felt so alone that she decided on the visit. During the interview he said, "I prayed to God for her. It didn't help." My impression was that he believed that his daughter took her own life and to Mr. Stone, suicide is a terrible sin. Cautiously, I raised the hypothetical question, "How would you feel as a good Christian if she did take her own life?" All the shame poured out. "Why," I said, "don't you discuss these feelings with your psychiatrist?" The psychiatrist then began talking to Mr. Stone, and we quietly left Mr. Stone's room.

Until Mr. Stone's crisis of faith was unveiled, he was essentially mute. Later, his psychiatrist reported how his daughter's apparent suicide was being perceived by Mr. Stone as unwarranted punishment by his God for his sins. The bleeding ulcer that brought him into the hospital was also perceived as unwarranted punishment. The message here for us is that the religiosity that is so prevalent among older persons is too often ignored by practitioners in our secular society. Not only is religiosity not sufficiently recognized by practitioners, but it also is not sufficiently recognized by gerontologists in their studies of aging. Whereas the topic of death was once to be avoided, religiosity has become the next topic to be given insufficient attention. Yet, very old people neither shy away from talking about their deaths nor their religiosity. Ignoring what they say, and want to say, is our sin of omission.

Activities of Churches and Synagogues

Religious activities extend beyond going to church, synagogue, or mosque to encompass attendance at sectarian weddings and funerals and also meetings of religious benevolent organizations. Attendance per se provides benefits. Moreover, in my investigation with James Ellor and Susan Anderson-Ray (Tobin, Ellor, & Anderson-Ray, 1986) into the role of religious institutions in aging, we found that programs and services provided by churches and synagogues specifically for elderly persons can be divided into four groups: religious programs, serving as host to community agencies, providing pastoral care programs, and social services. Within each group, programs and services can be organized in an informal or formal manner. Whereas some of the programs are led by trained professionals, others are not. Indeed, many of the people who do the actual work are not clergy or other professionals but lay people, including older adults themselves.

RELIGIOUS PROGRAMS

Religious programs encompass the type of activities that one would most likely anticipate as being provided by churches and synagogues. This includes midweek and weekend worship services that are held in a majority of churches and synagogues. Other types of religious programs include special worship services for seniors, religious study groups, prayer groups, and holiday remembrances such as special programs and food baskets. Further, many churches and synagogues facilitate participation by providing transportation to activities, as well as ramps, large print reading materials, and hearing aids.

HOSTS TO COMMUNITY AGENCIES

Churches and synagogues have become hosts to numerous social service agencies. Possibly the most common of these is agencies that provide midday meals. Often agencies use basements of local churches or synagogues for their lunch programs. In recent years, religious organizations have become conscious of how their buildings often stand empty during the week, seeing their greatest use on weekends. To make better use of the space, other community groups are allowed to sponsor activities in these buildings. The church or synagogue itself generally does not assume responsibility for organizing or managing these programs, and program participants may or may not include members of the congregation. In effect, the agency is simply borrowing the space in the building to provide a service.

PASTORAL CARE

Pastoral care services, which can be provided to individuals, families, or groups, are generally directed toward the members of the congregation and are a part of the general life of the congregation. Pastoral care for individuals includes visitation to the homebound, hospitalized, or nursing home residents; telephone reassurance; home-delivered meals; and assistance with housekeeping. Care can also include general transportation, food distribution programs, and free clothing. As a general rule, clergy and lay leaders (including older adults) provide these services as they are needed. Were clergy and lay leaders to receive a large number of such requests in any given month, they probably would not be able to respond to all of them.

Pastoral care services can also be developed for groups. Many educational activities, discussion groups, and various types of social activities can be considered pastoral care services, as well as some types of support groups and self-help groups. The focus of these group activities may or may not include what could be called "religious concerns," and some advertising may be mounted to attract participants from the community. There is generally no fee. Many of these groups do not have a leader specifically trained to work with the group. Although the array of services move church and synagogue much closer to providing the type of services usually sponsored by social agencies, they are still not considered, however, to be social services by either the church or synagogue or the participants in the programs.

Now becoming more common in congregations is peer counseling. Indeed, elderly peer counselors can make invaluable contributions to other seniors. Sometimes the counseling focuses on specific issues, such as legal or financial issues, but it can be much broader and sometimes include counseling on emotional issues. A variant of peer counseling is self-help groups such as widow-to-widow groups where, through the sharing of experiences, middle-aged and older persons find comfort and are able to successfully reengage in life.

Pastoral care services to individuals in need are often responded to by church and synagogue as would a friend or neighbor. The assistance is usually provided directly and informally when a request is made and generally considered to be informal services that are discontinued when the need for the service subsides. Sometimes, however, pastoral care services are more formally organized.

PROVIDING SOCIAL SERVICES

The fourth group is provision of social services. At times, a church or synagogue may choose to develop a formal social service program in response to a need in its community. Generally this type of program is developed in response to a gap in the local network of services. For example, when there may be a need for inexpensive, in-home supports for older people but very few low-cost home companion or housekeeping services available, church or synagogue may develop these types of services. Alternatively, when services exist in the community that do not adhere to the value systems of the church or synagogue, the religious institution may develop or become involved in developing a service that is provided in a manner that is more consistent with its belief system. Sectarian nursing homes, retirement centers, and senior clubs are all examples of this type of service.

In contrast to pastoral care services, social services tend to be much more formally organized and permanently structured. When clergy become aware of the fact that many families in the community have inadequate food, several types of responses can be developed. On one level, the clergy may choose to provide a bag of groceries to families when they request help, which is clearly a pastoral care service. On another level, a group of clergy may work with others to develop a food pantry that provides food to community residents who meet defined eligibility criteria. The pantry would then be staffed by those who know the basic eligibility criteria, screen applicants, and provide food to eligible individuals. While this service may be provided with the same motive as the pastoral care service, the differences in attitude and structure make it a formal social service program rather than a pastoral care service. Both the provider of the service, church or synagogue, and the program participants would identify this type of program as a service program.

MAKING USE OF CHURCH ACTIVITIES

A full use of church offerings is evidenced by Mrs. Grasso:

It's My Other Family

 The interviewer wrote in her report that Mrs. Grasso reminded her of her grandmother because her life is largely focused on spaghetti and church. A short and quite rotund widow of 80, Mrs. Grasso always has her pot of spaghetti in readiness for the arrival of any of her 6 children, 17 grandchil-

dren, and 4 great grandchildren. As she stirred the pot, she said, "I never know who will come by, so I'm always prepared." When not eating at home, she has lunch at the congregate dining program at her Catholic church, Lady of Sorrow. "It's my other family. I'm there all the time with my friends. I go to Mass, Bible class, find out who is sick so I can call or visit, and talk to my priest and, of course the nuns, to find out all the news.

What else? For lunch, but I told you that already. Let's see, what have I left out? My daughter Natalie, the one who lost her husband, drives me every Sunday, and I make sure that we give a ride to anyone who needs one, and they join us for brunch. I still drive, but Natalie wants to come with us to Mass, so she drives. My biggest worry is that I won't be able to see enough to drive anymore and won't be able to go to church whenever I want to. Before, when I had more energy and could see better to drive, I helped in the food pantry. I don't do that anymore, but others do what I can't do. Our church is like that."

HOMEBOUND ELDERLY PERSONS

The importance of church and synagogue is revealed by homebound elderly persons:

I Did Belong to the Prayer Group

Mrs. Aldrich, 83, was divorced over 20 years ago, has a "weak heart," and lives alone. She has no family nearby and lives in subsidized housing on a limited income. The church is very important to her. She attends a church other than her own because her church does not provide transportation to services. She would prefer to attend her own church, but there is no one who is willing to pick her up and assist her up the stairs. She does not want to blame the church, as she understands that "they are probably very busy." However, she is particularly annoyed at the lay people and considers it terrible that none visits. "No one has called except the pastor. . . . I don't know many people, but I did belong to the prayer group, and they know I'm sick." She feels she could be more active if she could have some assistance with stairs and transportation. However, particularly in the winter, she often is unable to go out for months at a time.

A Jewish woman tells a somewhat similar story:

Abandoned by the Synagogue

Mrs. Shapiro is a 79-year-old woman who moved from New York City to Florida with her husband. Prior to the move, she had been the president of the sisterhood at their synagogue and an important person in the congregation. In Florida, she has been dissatisfied with the rabbi because he does not *treat her with the same respect as the one "back home." She had just begun to develop close friendships when she fell and broke her hip. Now she is unable to leave her home, and her husband is afraid to leave her alone for long periods of time. Thus he, too, has curtailed his activities. Both feel abandoned by the synagogue and the rabbi because they have been neither visited nor even phoned to see how they are doing.*

Mrs. Aldrich and Mrs. Shapiro illustrate how their preservations of selves are corroded when they no longer can participate in formal religious activities and feel separated from, and abandoned by, their religious communities. There are also very old individuals who have aged in one place only to find that their church has changed, and their minister has departed. As one respondent noted, "It seems I'm still the same, but it's changed; you know, church, minister, old friends." She, however, is fortunate because she is able to retain her faith by reading religious magazines and especially the Bible, watching religious programs on television and listening on the radio, and praying privately. She is indeed different from many others who are unable to retain their religious identity if not physically attending services.

Religious Coping

Reading the Bible, watching religious programs on television and praying privately are informal religious activities that illustrate how religion is used to cope with the vicissitudes of life. When older people are asked about their perceptions of how they have coped with stressful events, they often introduce religious coping behaviors. Harold Koenig, Linda George, and Ilene Siegler (1988), for example, found that more religious coping behaviors were spontaneously introduced than nonreligious coping behaviors when elderly respondents were queried about coping with difficult experiences. Nonreligious coping behaviors encompassed focusing attention on other activities, accepting the situation, and seeking support from family and friends. Among religious coping behaviors the most frequent was trust and faith in God, followed by prayer, help and strength from God, church friends, church activity, minister's help, read the Bible, knowing it was the Lord's way, and lived a Christian life. Although this study was conducted in the Bible Belt (the Durham, North Carolina area), religious coping behaviors appear to be quite prevalent throughout the county. Although it has been common to assume that religious coping behaviors are characteristic of those only in the Bible Belt and among African-Americans in general, when elderly people of varied backgrounds are encouraged to tell what has helped them deal with crises, prayer invariably is soon mentioned.

It is the personal, private religious coping activities that dominate rather than the social or group-related dimension. That is, in the Koenig, George, and Siegler study, private prayer, faith or trust in God, and strength derived from God comprised nearly three fourths of the religious coping behaviors mentioned. Thus, the benefits from religious coping are, apparently, less from church and synagogue social activities or from clergy, and apparently more from a sense of control through faith. For those who have little control over their lives or for those in a situation in which they have no control, magical beliefs in control are helpful. Magical beliefs can be nonreligious cognitive illusions of personal powers or religious faith in which the appraisal of danger is diminished ("God would not do that to me.") or the assistance received will help overcome the danger ("God will see me through.").

Valued, cherished, and treasured personal possessions, as discussed in chapter 4 on reminiscence, are particularly important for maintaining continuity with the past. Cherished objects encompass photographs, jewelry, art work, and also religious items. These kinds of personal possessions may assist individuals in maintaining and preserving their identities in the face of events that corrode their sense of self; they may trigger and enhance a life review process; and they may represent ties or bonds with others at a time of life when social losses tend to be greatest. It is quite understandable why religious icons and artifacts are prevalent in the homes of older people, particularly Bibles and prayer books that have given a lifetime of use.

Religious artifacts and coping through prayer and faith, as well as participation in formal and informal activities at church and synagogue, are critical to the preservation of self among most persons who belong to the current cohort of oldest old people. For those who were reared religiously, retention of religiosity is especially meaningful. External religiosity as reflected in practices and internal religiosity as reflected in values and beliefs add somewhat to health and socioeconomic status in influencing their well-being. Those not reared religiously or who were instilled with faith in their adult years do not become religious in their advanced years nor do people become more religious with advancing age. The appraisals of conversions to religiosity or of increased religiosity as death draws near are myths, but they are important myths for true believers whose own religiosity and consequent well-being are enhanced from perceptions that everyone becomes religious when faced with death.

God's Blessings

Three of God's blessings, as noted earlier, are particularly germaine to very old people: a long life as a reward for service, a hereafter where there is a meeting with one's Maker and also reunions with departed loved ones, and relief from unendurable suffering. Whereas these beliefs may be strongly held by elderly respondents, these same respondents may say that they are not very religious. Discussions with interviewers suggest two reasons for this discrepancy. First, the very old respondents are unlikely to be as involved in church and synagogue activities to the extent they were earlier in their lives when they were very young or when they were raising their children. Also, attendance may lessen from functional incapacities and lack of transportation. A second reason is that respondents do not follow all the dictates of their religion. Student interviewers who are Catholic, for example, do not consider themselves to be strongly Catholic when they are pro-choice and believe in abortion.

A LONG LIFE AS A REWARD FOR SERVICE

When the book of Proverbs was written, few people lived to 70, then the demarcation for advanced old age. Infant mortality was high, women died in childbirth, and epidemics wiped out large segments of the populations. Rare were those blessed with old age when the orientation to time and one's life course was appreciably different, when delaying until tomorrow what could be done today was not sensible if death was ubiquitous regardless of age. Now that expectations have become the living out of one's life course, for example, to not only seeing grandchildren but also seeing great grandchildren and even great great grandchildren, delaying gratifications and events, such as marriage and childbearing becomes understandable if people perceive themselves to have many years to live. Then when very old, the self-fulfilling prophecy comes to pass: An anticipated life course has been lived. And having lived a long life, it becomes possible to declare that life has been lived as it should have been lived, as "I have been raised to live my life." If life has been lived as it should have been lived, and given that most Americans believe in a personal relationship with their God, it becomes understandable why so many also feel personally blessed. The Old Testament certainly provides ample support because long life, as discussed previously, is one of God's blessings. Longevity is a reward for prior service as supported by the often quoted "A hoary head is a crown of glory; it is gained in a righteous life" (Proverbs 16:31). Listen to Mrs. Ormsby:

He Wants Me to Live

"You ask me why I think I have lived so long? I don't know." So said the 97-year-old Mr. Ormsby. "I'm ready to go. I've lived beyond my allotted time. But still I'm alive and kicking. With my tired old legs, I don't kick like I did before, but I'm still kicking. Before, when I was a youngster in my eighties, I would say I lived so long because I only smoked good cigars and drank the best whiskey. Now I know that it has something to do with God. He wants me to live. I don't know why. I don't do anything. Maybe because I've been a good Christian, not as good as I should have been, but maybe good enough."

RELIEF OF UNENDURABLE SUFFERING

Another kind of blessing by God is relief from unendurable suffering. A just God does not allow parishioners to suffer from the ravages of bodily afflictions. As stated by the religious Mrs. Kemp:

He Will Take Me

At 93 Mrs. Kemp could barely see and hear. Suffering from metastatic colon cancer, she said, "I know my pain in this world is almost over. It gets so bad that the only way I can stand it is to take pain killers and more pain killers. What kind of way is that to live. I'm not afraid to meet my Lord. He has been good to me, and, if I say so myself, I have been good to him. A good Christian all my life. So I have to ask myself, when will he take me?"

Sometimes being not taken causes a crisis of faith for the observant:

I Feel So Inadequate

At a conference on religion and aging, the Protestant minister raised a vexing concern. "What do I tell my old people who tell me that they have suffered enough? They expected that if they suffered so, their God would stop their suffering. They are ready to die, but God isn't ready for them. One very old lady in a nursing home told me that she is even beginning to lose her faith. What should I tell her? I would like to tell her that soon she will go to her reward. But how soon is soon? I did tell her that God in his infinite wisdom will take her when the time comes. She just closed her eyes and with resignation informed me that my assurance wasn't sufficient, that she didn't want to blaspheme God, but she did feel angry at him."

Others in the group shared her concern. A pastoral counselor echoed her fear that a loss of faith is possible when the suffering becomes unbearable. He then told of a hospitalized patient who asked him to pray for her death because her prayers were not being answered. "I too," he said, "focused on how we must trust God. But I, too, felt, in this instance, that I could not restore her faith."

What is to be said? A loss of faith at the end of the life course is damaging to the human spirit. Whereas the nonreligious can contemplate suicide and stop eating to hasten death, this is not a choice for the observant. They wish to die but cannot hasten their deaths. So they not only suffer physical pain but also mental anguish from questioning God's design for them. Because death is welcomed, their wish is for God's mercy, which is not forthcoming.

AN AFTERLIFE WITH REUNIONS

A merciful God relieves human suffering, and a just God provides the observant with their heavenly reward. A third of God's blessings that is salient to the very old are reunions with departed loved ones in the afterlife.

To Get Back with Susanne

Mr. Poulin, an 87-year-old retired autobody welder of French Canadian descent, lost his wife, Suzanne, 4 years ago. Because they married when he was 17 and Suzanne 16, they had been married 66 years at the time of her death. He maintains a close relationship with his two daughters; both live nearby and visit on weekends. During the week he socializes with cronies in his public housing complex and volunteers with the Little Sisters of the Poor 3 days a week. Still, he feels very lonely when he thinks about Suzanne and "the good times we had together." He then added, "But I have friends here, so I don't get very depressed." Now somewhat choked up, he continued by commenting that he especially enjoys his occasional trips to churches and shrines in Canada. A few minutes later when asked what death means to him, he lightened up, smiled, and answered, "I am ready whenever the good Lord calls me. It will be good to get back with Suzanne and the rest of the family."

Mr. Poulin's picture of the afterlife is obviously not of sitting on a heavenly cloud strumming a harp. Rather, it is of being surrounded by loved ones, and especially for Mr. Poulin, being reunited with his beloved wife of 66 years, Suzanne. Reunions take many forms. A lonely 83-year-old woman who has been widowed for 22 years has a shrine in her living room for her dog Rufus who died 6 months ago, and whom she raised from a puppy. A leash hangs from the shrine, and as she talks, she glances over to the shrine and says, "Whenever I get too lonely, I stroke the leash. I'm looking forward to seeing Rufus again." She never mentioned reunions with her parents or her deceased husband but only with Rufus, her lone companion for the past 8 years.

Possibly the clearest expression of reunions is in African-American spirituals:

> I looked over Jordan
> And what did I see?
> A band of angels
> Comin' after me,
> Comin' for to carry me home.

African Americans are generally reported to be more attached to religion and church than are their Caucasian counterparts. In the 85+ Study, which was carried out in the San Francisco Bay area, African-Americans were more likely than Caucasians to introduce religion and God into discussions of reasons for their longevity. In the study of centenarians in the Georgia Bible Belt, however, both African-Americans and Caucasians introduced religion and God throughout their interviews. Apparently, African-Americans who migrated to California retained the religious beliefs of their rural Southern origin whereas Caucasians who either migrated to or were reared in California have not retained their religious beliefs to the same extent.

The variability in religious beliefs associated with cultural diversity, however, has been insufficiently studied. There are apparent racial and geographic differences in religiosity, as well as ethnic and denominational differences. Still, that three of four Americans believe in a hereafter independent of education is indeed an impressive statistic. As one of my most learned acquaintances said when discussing the cremation of a recently deceased friend, "Why not believe? It doesn't cost anything, and if there is something there, it would be nice. I wouldn't mind seeing my father again." Reunions in an afterlife is a natural segue to the next chapter, which is on the acceptance of death.

PART THREE

Benefits of Survivorship

Adaptive coping, reminiscence, and religiosity facilitate preservation of the self in advanced old age. Preservation of the self per se, however, does not necessarily make death acceptable nor aging successful. Very old people may know and feel that they are still the same persons they have always been but with accompanying fears of their approaching deaths and without satisfactions with their lives. Yet the normative portrait in advanced old age when not dependent on others for daily care is acceptance of death and feelings of life satisfaction. These are the benefits of survivorship to the end of the life cycle for the current cohort of oldest old persons.

CHAPTER 6

Acceptance of Death

What is death for those individuals who anticipate reunions in the afterlife? This question was discussed at length at my presentation to the faculty of the Chicago Institute for Psychoanalysis. Something must persist after death if reunions will occur. Exactly what will persist, however, is elusive. It is better not to ask. The octogenarian Mrs. Schultz has a recurrent dream in which she is a pubescent girl sitting in the kitchen and talking animatedly with her mother, who is baking bread. She is looking forward to a reunion with her mother. But is this the form that the reunion will take? The content of reunions defy reality, but knowing reunions will occur are as real as life itself. Possibly the progenitor of this knowledge is when a mother tells her young child, "I will always be here for you."

Can Death Really Be Accepted?

A belief in reunions may make death acceptable and, also, most very old people lessen in their fear of death, of nonbeing, as the fear of the process of dying increases. Yet I fear death. How is it possible not to fear death, not to fear nonbeing? Because of my awareness that at some future time I will cease to exist on this good earth, I must agree with the existentialist theologian Soren Kierkegaard (1844/1957), who wrote in 1844 that it is not possible for humans to escape from the dread of death. It was he who introduced us to the existential paradox, that of "individuality within finitude." Whereas each of us has an identity that transcends the natural order of species survival, never

119

can we transcend our personal demise. This dualism of the human condition is the price we must pay for being human. According to Kierkegaard, in becoming human, our consciousness creates the dread, the anxiety regarding our nonbeing. It is only human beings that have this peculiar and greatest anxiety.

Older respondents who talked of not fearing death when I began my studies of aging more than 3 decades ago were obviously kidding themselves. They were, it appeared to me then, successfully defending themselves from the deepest and most human of fears. Thirty or so years later, and now in my midsixties, I have begun to understand how death becomes acceptable at the end of the life cycle.

Given my dread of nonbeing, when Lieberman and I launched our longitudinal studies on relocation of elderly persons in the 1960s, we avoided asking elderly respondents about death. Reinforcing our decision was the reluctance of our interviewers to query respondents about their impending deaths. Typical comments made by the interviewers, all professional women in their forties, selected, in part, because of good relationships with their own parents, were, "They will clam up and tell us nothing afterwards." and, "If I have some questions on death at the end of an interview session, they will be so upset that they will never talk to me again." For the interviewers, as well as for us, uncovering attitudes about this dreaded and suppressed topic would be disastrous, we thought, for both respondents and the study. But then we discovered that our respondents invariably introduced the topic of death. Any fears expressed were not of death itself, but rather fears of the process of dying.

Although I was then familiar with Munnichs's seminal work in which he had reported an acceptance of death among elderly persons in the Netherlands, I was skeptical of his results. Johann Munnichs (1966) had written:

> It was extremely surprising to us at the time that there was a great preponderance of confidence and lack of apprehension, though more than half the number of persons interrogated admitted that they did think about the matter. We realized this unexpected result was that if death was awesome in character for only few exceptions, the field of experience during old age must be of a different nature from what is generally supposed. (p. 12)

How, I asked myself, could a person of any age accept his or her death? Our findings, however, confirmed his findings; I had to confront the inescapable truth. Though I can do so intellectually, deep down I still harbor doubt. It probably cannot be otherwise among those of us not of advanced old age. Nevertheless, we can at least make an attempt to understand why it is that toward the end of life elderly persons can accept their nonbeing.

This topic is of concern because of its significance for not only understanding aging but also for social welfare and health policies in an aging society. Daniel Callahan (1987), an ethicist in his middle years, has argued, for example, that because of limited health resources older people must be willing to forego costly life-sustaining medical care. They must be convinced that it is best for future generations and for our society as a whole to acquiesce to rationing so that resources can be deflected to the young. But if death is acceptable at the end of life, it is not costly medical care that is wanted. Rather, it is care that will ease the process of dying. Is this not similar to Cecily Saunder's reasoning when, in 1967, she developed the first modern hospice? Acute medical care, including costly heroic measures, recedes in importance, surpassed by the wish for an easy death.

My interest in the study of the psychology of death among elderly people occurred at a point when the topic was occupying social scientists, mental health experts, physicians, theologians, and humanists. This preoccupation is evidenced today at meetings of national professional and scientific organizations, which are incomplete without a symposium on death and dying. It is also evident in the development of a scientific and professional society devoted exclusively to the subject, the Society for the Study of Thanatology, complete with a journal exclusively given to the exploration of death. The burgeoning social science literature on the topic ranges from investigations of attitudes toward death to inquiries into the social context of dying to broader concerns with how the mortality of human beings constitutes an existential crisis. To many gerontologists old age must be understood in terms of how individuals cope with their approaching death. In his pioneering study, Munnichs succinctly sums up this point of view:

> When we ask ourselves what are the most characteristic features of old age, one difference, compared with other periods of life, stands out most prominently, namely the fact that there is no other period following old age. . . . The experience of death, that is to say, to realize and to know that life comes to an end, and adjustment to this fact, might possibly be considered as the focal point of the mentality of the aged. (p. 4)

My excursion into studying death began with Munnichs's assumption. Older people know their life is nearing an end and must confront the psychological reality of their own finitude. Although social scientists may have long ignored this reality, it is not a topic ignored by elderly people themselves, nor is it a topic that older people dread discussing.

Meanings of Death

Death can hold a variety of meanings for both young and old people. In describing attitudes toward death, the suicidologist Edward Schneidman (1973) observed that death is "the most mysterious, the most threatening, and the most tantalizing of all human phenomena" (p. 3). Death can be feared, yet also accepted; dreaded, but welcomed. Death can mean loss, change, conflict, and suffering, but it can also mean triumph. Each person is challenged to unravel the meaning of death in a highly individualized manner. Attitudes toward life, previous experiences with death, and the specific circumstances surrounding death will shape a person's reaction to a death.

Because human beings are the only creatures known to be aware of their own death, some theorists and theologians have made that awareness the basic principle of human existence. Every culture has developed ways to cope with this knowledge to facilitate and limit the mourning process. Belief systems and rituals are indispensable for dealing with the apparently innate fear of dying, and all cultures provide a system of beliefs to explain death. In some cultures, the meaning revolves around an afterlife. In others, the focus is on living through one's children and the belief that family and social institutions will endure following death. Cultures also define events that are worse than one's personal death. In Oriental societies, for example, loss of face may be more painful than the thought of personal nonexistence. Also, dying to save one's children or dying in defense of one's country has become acceptable for most people in most societies. For the very old, it is not uncommon to wish not to suffer anymore, and therefore death is welcomed.

In our culture, death is most often perceived as a loss. Many years ago, Herman Feifel (1977), in synthesizing his findings from studies of conscious and unconscious attitudes toward death, concluded that the unconscious fear (in his words, "outright aversion") is defended against by limited fear and ambivalent attitudes. This pattern, he maintains, allows "us to maintain communal associations and yet organize our resources to contend with oncoming death" (p. 10).

Ernest Becker (1973), on the other hand, when dying at a young age, focused on the denial of death (the title of his book) through positive illusions and magical coping; for example, through how imposing logic and order onto the world assists in the denial of the randomness of death.

Although death in our culture is perceived as loss, perceptions of what is lost varies among people and especially by place in the life cycle. Cicely Saunder's 35-year-old hospice patient with terminal breast cancer fears her loss of ability to care for her dependent children. The 50-year-old man fears the loss of opportunity to continue plans and projects. Both may also fear the loss of everyday experiences and the loss of body, as well as the grief that will be suffered by family and friends from their deaths. These kinds of losses become of less importance with advancing old age as the concern shifts more to the process of dying. There are concerns about having no control over how they will die, about dying alone, dying in intractable pain and, most recently, dying confused from Alzheimer's disease.

The fear of death itself is often projected onto very old people by those in the middle years. Many years ago, Robert Kastenbaum (1966) conjectured that it is functional to do so because thoughts of an untimely death are especially painful. Whereas people of advanced age are perceived to have lived a full life, death at an early age is perceived as having been cheated of life. Some actually feel that death at a relatively young age is a punishment for not having lived a good life. If, however, one lives to old age, it is often assumed that the person has lived a moral life, and that old age has been given as a divine reward. According to Leonard Simmons (1945), the Hopi believed that kindness, good thoughts, and peace of mind lead to a long life, and among the Berber, deceit is punished by a shorter life. The book of Proverbs notes, "The fear of the Lord prolongs life, but the years of the wicked will be short" (Proverbs 10:27). When Proverbs was written, few people lived to 70. Infant mortality was high, women died in childbirth, and epidemics wiped out large segments of the population. Rare were those blessed with old age. Only recently has a large percentage of our population lived to advanced age. Having lived a long life, it then becomes possible to declare that life has been lived as it should have been lived, as "I have been raised to live my life." Because most Americans believe in an afterlife, it becomes understandable why so many also feel personally blessed.

The Process of Dying

It is not possible to feel blessed with a long life when death is premature; that is, when life is foreshortened in the younger years from lethal illness. Still, Elizabeth Kubler-Ross (1969) has postulated that death can be accepted for those who become aware that their life span is foreshortened, and nonbeing will be soon in coming. She has identified a series of 5 stages independent of age:

Stage 1: Denial. First reactions when aware of impending death may be denial, shock, and disbelief. Denial is a defense that allows an individual time to slowly adjust to the thought of dying.

Stage 2: Anger. After a period of denial, the dying individual often becomes angry and asks, "Why me?" Anger is often directed at family, friends, and caregivers.

Stage 3: Bargaining. In this stage, the patient wants more time and asks for favors to postpone death. The bargaining may be carried out with the physician, family, or more frequently, with God.

Stage 4: Depression. Depression is a signal that the dying person has begun to accept impending death. Illness can no longer be denied, as it causes greater weakness and pain.

Stage 5: Acceptance. If younger people reach this stage, death is accepted. Although essentially devoid of feeling, he or she wishes to be close to loved ones, but verbal communication may be unnecessary.

Observations of many other thanatologists have confirmed the experience of these feelings among young people when they are dying. There is, however, considerable disagreement as to whether all dying individuals experience both the full range of feelings described by Kubler-Ross and the specific sequence of stages she detailed, particularly among older people who can more readily accept their own death. Edwin Shneidman (1973) suggests an alternative for death among young people. He has observed that their feelings can be described as a "hive of affect, in which there is a constant coming and going (of feelings)." He further characterized the emotional stages of the dying when young as a constant interplay between disbelief and hope, and against these as background, a waxing and waning of anguish, terror, acquiescence and surrender, rage and envy, disinterest and ennui, pretense, taunting and daring, and even yearning for death—all in the context of bewilderment and pain (p. 7). According to Shneidman, there is not a single, constant movement through stages but vacillation between acceptance and denial. Kubler-Ross also has cautioned that not all people will experience dying by going through each stage in an orderly fashion.

THE VERY OLD

Is the dying process the same for the oldest old person? Do we see Kubler-Ross' stages or Shneidman's "hive of affect?" Not usually. By the time of advanced old age, Kubler-Ross stages are likely not to be relevant. To ask "Why me?" and respond with rage at one's fate when approaching a timely death late in life is similarly to ignore the reality of impending nonbeing. Dylan Thomas' admonition to "not go easily into that good night" but rather "rage, rage against the dying of the light" is most appropriate when death occurs untimely, whereas it is not as relevant for death late in life for those for whom death has become acceptable with neither depression or a "hive of affect." The concerns among very old people are with how death will occur. It is hoped that death will not occur when alone, with intractible pain, immobile, and with Alzheimer's disease.

BARGAINING IS RATHER TYPICAL

Often a bargain is made directly with God. "If I am good, God will let me live to see the confirmation of my great grandchild. Then I can die in peace." Sometimes bargaining does not include a plea to God:

Sandy's Wedding

Marilyn Sampson is looking forward to her favorite granddaughter's wedding in a few months. "I hope I have the strength to go and enjoy Sandy's wedding. I know that I will not be here for my other granddaughter's wedding. She is only 21. But if I can go to Sandy's wedding, I will not complain." Later she said, "I bought a beautiful dress. I spent way too much. I told myself that if I bought a very expensive dress, I would live to go to the wedding."

Mrs. Sampson survived to attend the wedding and continued her life. Yet it is not uncommon among those of us who work with very old people to have observed how death is delayed until after participation in a welcomed event. Waning residual energies are mobilized for the event and then, afterward, there is a giving in to death.

Death Is Unacceptable if Unfinished Business

New adaptive challenges may cause a previous acceptance of death to become unacceptable during the final stage of life. There are others for whom death is unacceptable toward the end of the life cycle because they are still actively pursuing life goals. Two such groups that I have studied are "perpetual parents" of adult children with mental retardation whom they care for at home and elderly visual artists. Both groups have unfinished business as their life cycles near their end.

A Perpetual Parent

 Mr. Winters is a 77-year-old former chemical engineer who, except for part-time assistance from a paid home health aide, is the primary caregiver for both his 49-year-old profoundly retarded son and his 80-year-old wife, a victim of Alzheimer's disease. Despite his own good health and a charming, erudite, and dapper demeanor, Mr. Winters revealed awareness of his increasing frailty in his comment, "I've become less sure of myself during the past 3 or 4 years, and more often I've been getting feelings of light headedness." When asked if it would be best if other family members after his death were to care for his son after his death, Mr. Winters replied, "It's not fair to place the burden on them." He then commented about residential staff: "If motivated and caring enough, they could learn to care as well as me." When queried about what he enjoys most about caring for his son, Mr. Winters very emotionally replied: "Just having him around, especially now that my wife is bedridden." However, when asked what he enjoys least about caring for his son, Mr. Winters rationale and efficient approach as a former engineer became evident." "He's slow at meals, and consequently, it's late getting him to bed. So, I don't get much sleep at night, but I make up for it with catnaps during the day. You know I often wonder why I can't deal with this better, and that's very irritating to me!" Indeed, the theme of regarding caregiving as a challenging problem waiting to be solved rationally permeated the interview, particularly when he focused on his inability to finalize plans regarding the future living arrangements of his son. Interestingly enough, although specific and comprehensive plans have been finalized regarding the guardianship and financial security of his son, Mr. Winters does not seem able to take the steps necessary to put his son on a waiting list for a group home. When asked what has prevented him from doing so, Mr. Winters replied in a downhearted and puzzled manner: "I don't know! I really don't know! Nothing I guess, I just have to get off my behind!"

Mr. Winters clearly has unfinished business, and although he is aware of his increasing frailty, suppresses thoughts of his death. Instead he focuses on care for his wife and son, both of whom need him. Because nobody can care for them as well as he, he is in a quandry. It is better, he believes, to continue with the status quo, valiantly carrying out his responsibilities and not accepting his own death and contemplating future arrangements for his son, as well as his wife. Recall, too, Mrs. Angel from chapter 1, who, at 96, said that it is not "due time" to consider arrangements for her daughter who is mentally retarded. Although religious, she cannot accept God's blessing of a hereafter with reunions because the reunion she wishes is with her daughter who will outlive her.

For most men, as it is for Mr. Winters, life goals are encompassed by family and occupation, Freud's "Liebe und Arbeiten". Whereas Mr. Winters work goals are achieved, his goals for his family are unfulfilled. For both men and women, there may be unfulfilled family goals; for example, travele ambitions for children.

CREATIVE PEOPLE

Whereas unfinished life goals are likely to be caused by disappointments and losses, they can also be caused by perceptions that time is too short. Artists differ from most by remaining creative throughout life. They do not separate vocational from avocational pursuits. Indeed, as Georges Braque said, "As you become older, art and life become the same". The drive to be creative was expressed loud and clear by 44 active artists over 70 in a traveling exhibit, Elders of the Tribe. Will Barnet said, "No one should ever retire. It's an indignity to retire. I can't understand why anyone would retire. I get itchy fingers. What do you do with your hands? That is, what do you do with your time if you stop creating art?" Louise Nevelson concurred, "I never thought to retire. I don't like vacations. I want to work. I feel alive when I work." Reuben Nakian at 86 echoed these sentiments, "If I don't create something every day I feel I have not done anything. So, if at the end of the day I haven't done anything, I sit down and make a sketch or two, just something." Nakian then added, "I feel like a 12-year-old kid but with more experience, and my bones ache more." To be sure, our bones do ache more with age. But it was Monet who, when crippled with arthritis in his eighties, had the brush tied to his hands. His vision was clear. It was only his body that was deteriorating. Or if sight goes, as it did with Georgia O'Keefe, one turns from painting to pottery.

Many of the 44 artists in the Elders of the Tribe were in their young-old years and in interviews talked on the one hand of an awareness of being older, of being the sum of all the experiences of life, and on the other hand of being the same adult person who had always tried to set up visual problems to solve. They usually added that they will remain this way as long as they remain healthy. Massos Daphnis in his late seventies put it: "Creating, that's what keeps you young. You're always young when you create. Fortunately, I'm in good health. How much I do today I could have done at 30". When asked what he tells young artists, he said, "Do not try to be a star at 30. You have to be mature. You have to have experiences to know yourself. All we paint is who we are." Some say, as did the great Japanese wood-cutter Hokasai on his deathbed at 94, that they are now only beginning to learn their craft. Estaben Vincente in his mid eighties said, "I'm still searching, 'til I die. One thing I will not do is die of boredom."

Still, there are many active and creative old persons who seem to face the end of their life with equanimity. George Burns, on his 91st birthday, after telling reporters that he will play cards in the afternoon and date a pretty girl in the evening, added in whimsical equanimity: "I have made old age popular. Now everyone wants to be old."

The Psychology of Terminal Decline

The process of dying can be approached from the vantage of how death is experienced in the final year of life among the oldest old people. The experience is not of death per se, of nonbeing, but rather of cognitive changes reflecting the inability to maintain integration when disintegration becomes inevitable. The cognitive changes have been referred to as "terminal drop" which should more accurately be called "the phase of terminal cognitive deterioration."

Robert Kleemier reported in 1961 on his observations of intellectual changes in an aged population as early as 2 years prior to death, and since then others have reported similar observations. Morton Lieberman (Lieberman & Tobin, 1983) recalled Kleemier's report when an aide in a nursing home to which he was a consultant was able to predict which residents were experiencing terminal decline. The aide's explanation for her powers was that she was able to pick up their "brain waves," which showed a weakening of their brain preceding death.

THE FIRST EXPLORATION

Ignoring this obviously correct explanation for her powers, Lieberman designed an exploratory study to determine whether systematic changes in ego functions and emotional states occur in elderly persons prior to death and, if they do, to differentiate such changes from changes associated with nonterminal illness. For this exploration, a small group of institutionalized elderly persons was administered brief tests at frequent intervals. Those who died within 1 year of the last testing were compared to those who lived for at least 1 more year.

Fifty people volunteered, from whom 30 were selected after excluding those who had incapacitating physical illnesses, gross neurologic disturbances, or marked psychiatric disorders. Each respondent was tested every 3 to 4 weeks and was paid a small amount of money after each assessment. The results reported were based on those respondents (4 had dropped out or died before a sufficient number of assessments could be made, and one had died 5 months after the 2.5-year study period). All were born in Eastern Europe, and all but 1 migrated to the United States prior to World War I. Most had been (or had been married to) small storekeepers or craftsmen. Educational level was difficult to determine with any precision but seemed equivalent to an eighth-grade education.

Results were reported in terms of comparison between two groups: those close to death (death-near group) and those farther from death (death-far group). The death-near group consisted of eight respondents who died less than 3 months after completing at least five trials on the measures used in this study. The death-far respondents were still living 1 year after they had completed at least 5 trials. For the death-near group, the time from the last trial to death ranged from 2 to 11 weeks, with an average of 5.5 weeks, whereas all the death-far individuals lived at least 52 weeks after completing the last trial.

The death-near respondents showed a pattern of declining performance over time in the size of the Bender-Gestalt reproductions and the complexity of the Draw-a-Person drawings. In contrast, the death-far group indicated a pattern of improving performance over time, apparently a result of practice effects; that is, increasing familiarity with the test. Both groups generally showed similar curves on the estimation of 1 minute and number of affect responses to the stick figure test. On the intensity of activity score, both groups generally showed an increase, but the death-near group reversed the direction after the 40th week, manifesting decreases in the intensity of activity.

Simply stated, these results indicated that death-near and death-far groups could be distinguished by changes in the tasks, reflecting the adequacy of ego functioning but were similar on measures of affect. In addition, the examiners' notes on test behavior (for example, mood) and "critical events" that had occurred in the last testing session, as well as content analysis of responses to the stick figure test, were examined in an attempt to further differentiate the two groups. Overall, this qualitative analysis revealed few consistent differences. These data did indicate, however, that the death-near group made more spontaneous comments about something being wrong or something "going on" or, at times, referring explicitly to the realization that they were going to die. Furthermore, four of the eight in the death-near group gave an increased number of depressive responses to the stick figure test on the trial preceding death compared to earlier trials. Generally, however, depressive content was less characteristic of death-near than death-far respondents; nor did the content analysis of the stick figure test reveal responses indicating increased anxiety or fear.

The scores of each death-near person were examined to determine if changes in performance level occurred at particular points in time. The small number and the degree of response fluctuation from trial to trial prevented a meaningful quantitative analysis. However, inspection of each respondent's set of scores suggested that major shifts of performance of the Bender-Gestalt test could be found as early as 6 to 9 months before death.

Could test score changes have occurred in relationship to illness? A tentative answer to this question was available from analysis of 12 respondents in the death-far group who suffered major illnesses that required hospitalization during the course of the study. Analyses of the performance of death-far individuals who became ill and recovered revealed that illness per se could not explain the decline of performance found in the death-near group.

Before death, respondents showed decreases in level of organization, but changes in affect were not systematically related to approaching death. Possibly the observed psychological changes preceding death are best viewed in terms of the individual's decreased ability to cope adequately with external demands. Perhaps the aged person approaching death experiences upheaval because of currently active disorganizing mental processes, rather than because he or she fears approaching death. The observed psychological disintegration may not be a reaction to the unknown, but may rather represent a general decline of the system preceding death, as reflected in the variety of physiologic and psychological measures. If this interpretation is correct, some frequently reported phenomena in the terminal phase of life become more understandable.

Many observers have commented on the psychological withdrawal of the dying patient and have suggested that the withdrawal is functional because it protects the individual from intense separation anxiety. Our data suggest, however, that withdrawal represents an attempt to cope with the experience of inner disintegration. Individuals approaching death pull away from those around them not because of a narcissistic preoccupation with themselves, but because they are engaged in an attempt to hold themselves together; that is, to reduce the experience of chaos and retain a sense of self.

Because the changes examined in this explanation were primarily alterations in functioning, the task set for the next exploration was the examination of symbolic processes, comparing those nearer and those farther from death to determine if awareness of death played a role in the observed psychological changes. Some marginal evidence from the respondents studied suggested this as a plausible direction. Many of the older people we studied sensed some type of change and felt it to be different from that of illness. The labeling of the subjective experience, however, varied, with some respondents reporting only a vague sense of feeling different, whereas others said that they were going to die soon. Comments such as these suggest that more thorough and sensitive phenomenologic reports would be a useful avenue for research in the terminal phase of life.

A SECOND EXPLORATION

In a second exploration, the focus was on emotional life when death is approaching. For this exploration, respondents from the longitudinal study of the process of becoming institutionalized were used (Tobin & Lieberman, 1976). There were 172 respondents, 100 of whom were interviewed for 12 to 16 hours in 4 to 6 sessions while on waiting lists to enter homes for aged people (85 actually entered the homes), 35 of whom were in a matched community sample, 37 of whom were in a sample of persons who were residents of the homes for 1 to 3 years. Of the 172, 40 died within 12 months. These 40 were paired with 40 who survived an average of 3 years beyond the last interview session. Matching was based on a hierarchical sequence of comparison criteria: living arrangement, sex, age, birthplace, marital status, and educational level.

Although measures of cognitive functioning were included to provide a basis for comparison with findings from the earlier study on psychological factors associated with impending death, the emphasis was on indices of emotional life. The measures tapped five affective realms: emotional states (anxiety, mood tone, and so forth), orientation to emotional life, health and body orientation, self-image, and time perception.

Differences occurred in three of the five realms: cognitive functioning, orientation of emotional life, and self-image. Generally, those nearer death manifested poorer cognitive functioning; were less affectively complex and less introspective; portrayed themselves as less aggressive and more docile, dependent, and intimacy-oriented than their paired counterparts; and used less evidence from their current life to validate their self-image but relied less on distortion for validation. In some areas, for example, in anxiety and mood tone, whether measured by self-report or projective data, and in self-reports or projective indices of health and body image, anticipated associations with impending death were not found. These findings substantiated the results of the previous exploration in which impending death was found to be associated with cognitive decline. Most important was the finding regarding affects; not affect states per se, but rather, orientation to emotional life. Those closer to death are apparently not more depressed, as is frequently reported in clinical papers, but they do avoid introspection. The magnitude and consistency of differences on measures of orientation to emotional life suggest that this finding is not an artifact, and that those approaching death are unwilling, or possibly unable, to look inward because at some level of consciousness they recognize their impending death. It is as if they avoid introspection because of the fear of what they might discover. Although the nature of this monitoring process is unclear, the pattern of findings does indeed suggest a reduction in introspection without necessarily a modification in type or intensity of affect per se. Despite the almost universal focus of the psychological literature on the association of proximity to death with anxiety and withdrawal from others, our data, including impressions of the interviewers, did not reveal this association. Rather, there is a slight but measurable shift in the content of self-concept from assertiveness in interpersonal interactions toward dependency and affiliation.

To be specific, all direct statements related to death that respondents made in the interviews were collated for both groups, and the responses for each person were typed on a card without identifying information. The raw data, then, consisted of 80 paragraphs comprising all statements each respondent had made about death. Two scales that could be reliably rated were developed to discriminate individual differences; a 3-point scale rating degree of preoccupation with one's own death and a 4-point scale of fear of death. Inspection of the distribution for these scales showed low preoccupation and low fear for approximately 40% of the death-near group, suggesting either that the sensitivity of these scales was poor or that the phenomenon tapped by these measures applied only to a subsample of those near death. Further analysis was required to determine the significance of the large number of death-near individuals who did not respond as anticipated on these two scales. Perhaps the low degree of introspection previously noted as characteristic of those close to death was an important influence. Many of these individuals may have been unable to discuss their thoughts about death and dying directly. This possibility led us to develop measures less amenable to the respondent's conscious control.

Stories told to interviewers when presented with a set of institutional Thematic Apperceptive Test (TAT) cards developed by Lieberman and Martin Lakin (1963). Four types of symbols were analyzed; first, direct references to death and dying such as struggling to save one's life; second, issues of rebirth; third, inscrutable events or mysterious trips; and fourth, death figures or the specter of death, such as a figure with hands folded or face covered. Then the 80 respondents were rated for the presence or absence of one or more of the death symbols for each TAT response. The results of this blind analysis indicated that death symbols were rated as present for 34 of the 40 death-near respondents and for only 9 of the 40 death-far controls. Thus, although spontaneous comments did not reveal extensive preoccupations and fears, projective data did reveal that symbols of death occur among those closer to death. To what extent these symbols intrude into consciousness cannot be determined with any specificity.

A THIRD EXPLORATION

In a third exploration, 41 death-near respondents were compared to 41 matched death-far respondents from among community residents who were participating in a longitudinal study. The findings replicated those from the earlier explorations. Added, however, were queries on how they envisioned their death. The two groups differed significantly in how they envisioned their deaths. Those near death showed a much higher proportion of "happy-magical" responses and "concern about suffering" responses than the death-far group. Death-near and death-far groups were about equally divided in the response categories of "natural process," "denial," and "finalism." The death-far group held an almost exclusive claim on the categories of "traditional religiosity" and "mystery." Of interest is that the death-near group was responsible for more than three of four (77%) of the happy-magical responses, which reflects a sense of personal urgency and almost desperate conviction that something happy, pleasurable, and good is waiting for them after death. Although not revealed by these data, it is my speculation that these were the more religious respondents, whose vision of the afterlife was reunion with now deceased beloved persons.

IMPLICATIONS OF THE THREE EXPLORATIONS

Declines in ego functioning were found among individuals nearer to death in all three explorations. The first exploration revealed that cognitive decrements were idiosyncratic; that is, absolute levels were not predictive, rather decrements were found only when a respondent's late trials were compared to earlier ones. In the second exploration, those nearer death manifested more cognitive impairment than their matched pairs who were farther from death. In the last exploration, respondents near death showed more psychiatric symptoms. This cumulative evidence supports an association between decline in ego functioning and impending death.

Deterioration in ego functioning with impending death can be explained as either the behavioral manifestations of central nervous system disorganization or as a reaction to disturbing affects caused by inner awareness of changes prodromal to death. Probably both explanations are accurate. Evidence for a reactive process is found in the lessened propensity to introspection in those closer to death and greater passivity when portraying the self in interaction with others. Both kinds of evidence suggest some active process in which painful underlying or latent meanings and affects are screened from consciousness. The success of this process is suggested by the inconsistent evidence for differences in emotional states between those nearer and those farther from death. In the first two explorations, differences were not found in emotional states, whereas in the third exploration there was a modest association between depression and impending death but not between anxiety and impending death. There was also an increased prevalence of preoccupations with death and fears of death among death-near respondents in the second exploration. Because these preoccupations were neither intense nor ubiquitous, it appears that many if not most elderly people approaching death are able to contain the experience and thereby limit conscious pain.

What is the nature of the underlying experience of approaching death? The most consistent finding was that death-near respondents introduced symbols reflecting death when telling stories to TAT cards. What are the likely mechanisms of such symbols? As shown in the first study, acute illness crises from which respondents recovered did not produce such symbols. Neither did those who recovered from acute illnesses show the same pattern of decline as those who died soon thereafter. It seems equally unlikely that the signaling process was set off by self-detected changes related to decrements of aging such as social and personal losses, physical incapacities, and the many onslaughts undermining self-image. Most if not all respondents had suffered multiple losses and physical decrements associated with advanced age. Environmental settings generate such death symbols in those close to death. If environment influenced production of symbols, more institutionalized respondents should have shown death symbols, inasmuch as the old age home itself is sometimes perceived as symbolic of death; that is, as a "death house."

The kinds of symbols and losses introduced into projective responses suggest that a variety of meanings are attributed to an inner, possibly diffuse and ambiguous experience. For some, the meanings of the internal changes prodromal to death are narrowly focused on separation or bodily decay, while for others the meanings are not as specific, encompassing a sense of nonexistence itself. Despite the diversity of symbols employed to superimpose meaning on inner changes, the nature of the underlying psychological experience is probably the potential dissolution of the self. The presence of these covert meanings suggests the usefulness of an explanatory model that includes signal anxiety. A subconscious experience of prodromal disorganization or disintegrative somatic changes is detected and experienced as a threat to the self, with subsequent signal anxiety. In response to the signal, the detected changes are symbolized, and attempts are made to defend again the anxiety. Although depression may be associated with such symbolization, manifest anxiety is not. Only through further study will it be possible to determine whether this absence of manifest anxiety is specific to very old people, who apparently are more accepting of their own finitude than are younger people. On the other hand, elderly people may be more likely than younger people to become cognitively disorganized in the absence of manifest anxiety because of a less efficient central nervous system. The burden of defending against internal threat may overwhelm an already weakened ego.

The lack of substantial evidence for manifest anxiety in the phase of terminal drop is not surprising if we assume that death is acceptable when it is expected. With life's journey completed, elderly persons who consider themselves old are likely to be accepting of death and also not to respond with fear to inner signals of impending death. For those who have not yet completed their journey, impending death may indeed be cause of concern and manifest anxiety.

WHEN IN UNSTABLE SITUATIONS

Differences in emotional life, therefore, were compared between those who were undergoing the terminal drop phase in the unstable situation of being institutionalized to those in the community and those who had been living in institutions for 1 to 3 years. Twenty-two pairs were waiting to enter homes for aged persons or had recently entered such homes (unstable environmental circumstance). Eighteen pairs had lived in the homes from 3 to 5 years or were living in the community (stable environmental circumstance). The matched pairs, now divided into two groups, were compared to determine whether psychological processes associated with nearness to death differed depending on whether the respondent was in a transitional situation.

The death-near respondents in an unstable circumstance showed more preoccupation and fear than the death-far respondents. No differences were found, however, in preoccupation and fear between death-near and death-far respondents in stable circumstances. Approximately 40% of all death-near respondents had shown preoccupation and fear. When the sample of pairs was divided between those in stable and unstable environmental circumstances, preoccupation and fear were characteristic mainly of those in unstable circumstances.

Mr. Robin, a respondent in the death-near group who was in the unstable circumstance of waiting to enter a home for aged people introduced a variety of death symbols when telling stories to TAT cards. One example is his response to a roommate scene showing two elderly persons sitting across from each other on their beds carrying on a conversation:

Those two men are having a conversation. This fellow (left) is trying to con-
vert him (right). the old man on the right says, "I'm trying to change your
opinion." Then he goes on to say, "You say you're going to live longer than
Winston Churchill, but you're not." By the way, did you know I'm still
waiting for the Messiah? The Christian Messiah that is, has come, but we
Jews have been waiting for the real Messiah for 5,000 years. I prophesy his
coming."

Mr. Robin shared these kinds of death symbols and themes with death-
near respondents independent of whether they were in the process of being
relocated. The direct inquiry into his thoughts and feelings about death,
however, revealed preoccupations and fears characteristic primarily of those
in the process of being relocated; that is, in the unstable situation. Asked to
complete the sentence *"Death is. . . ,"* he responded:

"I'll go to sleep (said bitterly). I ain't so strong; weakest part is not being
well. Death is nothing, just going to sleep. One hour is just another hour
gone. Time means nothing. Everyone tries to plan, but it is impossible. No
future. I don't think about things."

This response was scored high for preoccupation. Later in the interview
he revealed his fears by associating his death with separation:

"I'm better than many people. I prepare myself always. I even have the
stone next to my wife. I told the children that if I possibly . . . the best thing
is just to go. Each day goes by. Death is like a shot. Time is gone, I plan
ahead. Next year I'd like to go to Europe, but I don't know if I can go. The
future is the best thing if I have a companion. The future is to get a com-
panion, go out together and not to lose one's mind."

Symbols of death, therefore, were evident among those near
death independent of situation. Whether the experience signaled by
approaching death is contained, however, depends on the external situation. Environmental change constitutes a severe transition for
elderly persons. Previous patterns of relationships, meanings of significant others, and the self-image are challenged and tested by dis-
ruption of the environment. Individuals in a state of transition may
have been more distressed and reactive over impending death but not
because their approaching death was of greater concern. Rather, they
were being forced to make new adaptations and face anew previously
solved problems. If death were the essential threat, rather than adaptation to a stressful situation, more signs of avoidance, denial, or other
psychological mechanisms would be expected in response to impending death.

The findings regarding the psychology of terminal decline
when old are congruent with the acceptance of death, of nonbeing.
Fears when very old, if there is no unfinished business, are less of
nonbeing and more of the process of dying. Then as death approaches

toward the end of the life span, the previous level of integrality decays, which becomes reflected in diminished cognitive capacities. Concurrently, at a less than conscious level, the decay becomes symbolized, only to be experienced more consciously if in a disequilibrium that makes new adaptive demands. By returning to a homeostatic equilibrium, the experience of the decay of integrality can again be contained and self-preserved. The establishment once again of equilibrium is of particular importance for depressed elderly persons, a topic that will be included in the next section.

Assisting Suicide

Assisted suicide has become a hot topic. Dr. Kervorkian, who brags about how many people he has assisted in committing suicide, may be assisting people who feel depressed. Lifting the depression could, however, ameliorate feelings of depression and thereby the wish to do away with oneself. An illustration:

Her Right to Die

 Mrs. Bains, a 75-year-old dehydrated and malnourished woman, was transferred to the general hospital from a psychiatric hospital following an attempt to starve herself to death. The discussion at the multidisciplinary geriatric staff conference focused on the rights of patients to terminate their lives if they no longer wished to live. There was a consensus that Mrs. Bains was undergoing an existential crisis and now felt hopeless and forlorn but was not clinically depressed. The kind of hopelessness perceived to be evidenced by Mrs. Bains is apparently associated with suicide. Although the tone of the discussion suggested agreement that she had a right to do away with her life, counseling was recommended to reestablish a reason for living. Because she had been a writer of children's books, one approach suggested was to encourage her to write, to compose, for example, her autobiography.

When Mrs. Bains was brought into the conference to be interviewed, it was my impression that her stated wish to commit suicide did not ring true. To be sure, a few weeks earlier she began to starve herself, and had not a neighbor come by to say hello, she would have been successful. Yet something had changed, and now it appeared that she was not suicidal. What had changed was that a male attendant befriended her and reestablished for her a lifelong pattern of being admired by men for her cleverness and wit. Her comments on her past revealed that her intellectual father had admired his precocious daughter, his only child, and also that her husband was so in love with her that he agreed that having children would only detract from their love. It was rather evident that she did not want a child to compete for her

husband's love, and that without children, she could reenact being the only and special child with her husband. After her husband's death she was able to maintain this interpersonal dynamic by taking a young artist into her house. When he left, the crises began that led to her decision to do away with herself.

Unfortunately, Mrs. Bains would soon be discharged from the hospital without the male aide. Counseling her to return to writing did not appear necessary. Unless admired by a man, her writing apparently by itself had little meaning. For her, feeling admired by a man was a precondition for the gratification she obtained from writing children's literature, apparently playing out the little girl in herself. Necessary was placement in a noninstitutional setting in which she could maintain her lifelong sense of self. A social worker was able to identify an adult home that had a male administrator who was certain to be enchanted by Mrs. Bains.

Only through an understanding of Mrs. Bains persistent way of relating to others and the psychodynamics reflected in these relationships was it possible to appreciate the shift from her wish for death to her wish for life. Whereas I believe, as many do, that we should allow self-determination in deciding to end one's life, we must be cautious in interpreting patients' wishes. For the patient who requests "Do Not Resuscitate," the decision to let the patient die, passive euthanasia, may sometimes be made rather easily. But for Mrs. Bains and for other patients who are fully lucid, it is our challenge to attempt to reestablish authentic autonomy, a preservation of the self, although out patients may resist our efforts to do so.

When, however, a person is kept alive with no quality of life left, the physician may face a difficult decision, as occurs when a patient is kept alive by a gastric feeding tube. Withdrawal of the tube then becomes active euthanasia.

Comatose for Five Months

Miss Coons, at 86, lay comatose in the hospital for 5 months. Because of the persistence of her coma, her sister, age 83, implored her sister's physician and lawyer to remove her gastric feeding tube and finally to let her sister die a natural death. Her sister said, "She always told me that she did not want to be a living vegetable." A judge agreed. Nursing staff, however, feared that other patients would perceive them as also letting them die, and when the gastric tube was removed, they began to feed and bathe Miss Coons. Also, other patients began to provide attention to Miss Coons. Apparently, the attention, the skin contact she lacked for several months, helped to revive her as she slowly came out of her coma. She opened her eyes and seemed to recognize her sister. But did her sister and doctor and the judge make the correct decision? I believe so. Miss Coons was comatose for 4 months with

irreversible brain damage. Her only living relative, her 83-year-old sister had to make the decision for her. Unfortunately, Miss Coons did not have a living will and also had not given her sister durable power of attorney. The hospital administration followed their lawyers' advice not to remove the tube even if demanded by the sister. The sister could change her mind after Miss Coon's death and sue the hospital.

Regarding letting people die, Goldfarb (1983) has written in an edited book entitled *The Right to Die*:

If our beliefs that a person be allowed to die should he request it (however extensive our review) or that we can let him die (after adequate review of the details) are based upon giving him greater freedom to live and enjoy life as an individual, they would seem acceptable. However, there appears at present to be a glamorization of dying and of being dead which is part of a movement toward enjoining people to savor dying and to welcome death. Dying, we are told, must be dealt with like any other loss, which we first deny, than deal with by stages of anger, bargaining, and finally acceptance. It is acceptance of death, then as early as possible that we should learn? Or should we learn to treasure life so much that the passage through its later stages is fully lived when we see death near? (p. 18)

CHAPTER 7

Aging Successfully

Margaret *Gatz and Steven Zarit* (1999) have identified the criteria currently used for assessing successful aging, their "keys to mental health in old age." The four criteria are: deriving pleasure from activities, mastery in dealing with the issues of life, achieving a congruence between one's aspirations and achievement, and sustaining an optimistic outlook. Note that the criterion of congruence is similar to Erik Erikson's (1950) acceptance of one's life as it has been lived. In turn, the four criteria form a set that is similar to the set that we (Neugarten, Havighurst, & Tobin, 1961) developed almost 4 decades ago when we asked whether there was a need for different criteria of successful aging for the old and the young. Our measure, the Life Satisfaction Rating (LSR) was comprised of the following five components: zest versus apathy (component A), resolution and fortitude (B), congruence between desired and achieved life goals (C), positive self-concept (D), and mood tone (E). These components or criteria obviously parallel the criteria or keys to mental health identified by Gatz and Zarit.

Influencing life satisfaction is the preservation of the self. Without preservation of the self and the maintenance of integrality, life satisfaction when very old cannot be achieved. On the other hand, the self can be preserved and integrality maintained but with lower life satisfaction, particularly when the age-associated assaults of physical illness and death of loved ones are devastating. Also, some people have lifelong low self-esteem or chronic depression that limits their ability to have high life satisfaction in late life. Most very old individuals, however, preserve the self, maintain integrality, and have at least moderate life satisfaction.

Identifying criteria for successful aging dates back to ancient times and possibly even to the dawn of humankind. Cicero, as noted in chapter 2, made wisdom the essential criterion of successful aging when discussing how the wise man accepts death at an old age with equanimity. By this criterion of wisdom, most older old persons are aging successfully because it is normative to accept death while fearing the process of dying. Whereas magnified fear of the process of dying and being preoccupied with further deterioration, pain, and confusion should be incorporated into any definition of unsuccessful aging, fears and preoccupations, as discussed previously, are not normative; rather they are characteristic of very old people in situational crises and with unfinished business.

Most recently some additional kinds of criteria have been promulgated, such as productive aging and physically healthy aging. These criteria, however, may be inadequate for advanced old age. Productive aging may be relevant to the postretirement young-old years, but only for those who seek to be productive. Most very old people do not pursue what we would consider to be productive activities. They pursue what is meaningful to them and feel themselves to be meaningful and worthy people. In turn, whereas all wish to be physically healthy and to retain full vitality until death at a ripe old age, this is not the reality. Successful aging necessitates neither productivity nor full vitality. They may help in achieving successful aging, as does the preservation of the self, including the adaptive mechanisms used for preservation, but productivity and full vitality are not criteria in themselves.

Objective and Subjective Well-Being

A distinction must be made between objective well-being and subjective well-being. Objective well-being refers to readily observable conditions such as health and financial resources, whereas subjective or psychological well-being refers to inner, less observable feelings of morale, happiness, satisfaction, and so forth. The two kinds of well-being are related because the objective conditions of health and socioeconomic status influence subjective feelings of well-being. Yet the association is far from perfect. Expectations must be considered.

Simply put, the wealthy need more than the poor to feel satisfied. Those, on the other hand, who have limited resources but fewer expectations can make do with less, and even though they have minimal resources can feel satisfied. Because the oldest old people were reared with fewer expectations and later experienced the Great Depression and World War II, they are likely to feel that their finances are adequate if they can meet their basic daily needs and have a few discretionary dollars to give presents to grandchildren and to sequester for a rainy day. They also can feel their health is adequate if not overly dependent on others for care. It is, however, the other group, those who have the greatest expectations and the greatest resources who are the most vocal. In setting the political agenda, they have been called "the greedy geezers." How is it possible to transcend the inroads made on objective well-being, especially from illnesses, and maintain subjective well-being? Listen to Jack Sampson.

So, What Else Is New?

"Did I tell you already that if my name doesn't appear in the obituaries that I have another day? Ain't it grand? I never thought I would live so long. Every day is an added day. My health has deteriorated, especially this last year. A blood vessel in my eye popped, but still I can drive. A small stroke affected by speech, but with the help of a speech therapist, I can talk okay again. My congestive heart failure makes it hard to move around. So, what else is new? If I can stay like this, it will be okay. I hope for a little longer. You can't dwell on what you can't do. What's past is past. You do what you can do. And you enjoy what you can do. Otherwise you give up. It helps to know that the worst days are past, the days when we didn't have enough to eat but made do. And the kids are doing fine, grandchildren too and even great grandchildren. The future? I have no future. I know I'll go first. So I worry about Marilyn. It will be hard for her. We've taken care of each other. When we first came down here, more than 15 years ago, we were healthier, but Marilyn had her colitis and her arthritis, and I had a steel rod in my leg. I was still able to do some work on our apartment and some work for others, too, but I had to give it up as I became unsteadier on my feet. I was still working until almost 80. Now I'm what you would call retired, enjoying the leisure life. It was terribly hard giving up working, but now we take care of each other and do what we can."

Sometimes lower socioeconomic status, reflected in scanty income and little education, and also ill health are transcended in a personally successful aging:

I'm Still Making It

 An interviewer on a project developed to investigate why older people do not avail themselves of a congregate dining program in their senior housing complex was assigned Mrs. Smith, a 77-year-old African-American woman, Mrs. Smith was described as "thin as a reed," "as rickety as an old three-legged stool," and "with a terrible cough that shook her old body." It was readily apparent that she was in ill health and had little money. When asked if she knew about the dining program she said, "I know that I could get a hot lunch." She then answered the query on why she does not go there for lunch, "My business is my business. When I came up north over 50 years ago, I froze every winter. Look outside. It's snowing and my radiator's on. Feel it. Its hot. Since I moved into this building 3 years ago, I don't freeze anymore. Why should I walk to the other building for lunch and freeze. I have every-thing I need right here. My son brings me groceries once a week. I have my Bible and my TV." The interviewer wanted to be helpful and asked whether she would enjoy the company of others and the programs at the dining pro-gram. "That," said a now belligerent Mrs. Smith, "is what I mean when I say my business is my business. I don't want to be around people who don't appreciate what God has given them. He has given me enough, and if I had my way, I would give back Social Security. The Lord giveth and not you or anybody else. I have had my downs and now I'm up. I made it with the Lord's help and I'm still making it. this is a good time for me. Touch the radiator. I appreciate what I got, and what I got is enough for me."

The interviewer at the debriefing session became tearful when discussing how Mrs. Smith refused to let her be helpful. She would not attend the meal program, allow her to drive her to a medical clinic for care of her chronic cough, and was afraid that at any moment Mrs. Smith would tear up her Social Security check. By what criteria should Mrs. Smith's aging be judged? This question was debated by the interviewers and project staff, who reached a consen-sus that the criteria of health and income indicated very low objective well-being, but satisfaction with current life indicated a rather high level of well-being and personal satisfaction with her aging that tran-scended objective standards.

Few positive life expectations can come from the many hard-ships experienced by ordinary people who were reared in the early part of the 1900s. Death was ubiquitous when a child. Common is to hear of death of siblings and also of parents. Not unusual was to lose a mother in childbirth. Marilyn's mother had to marry her father when her mother's sister, who was married to her father, died when giving birth. This was a general practice a century ago. Low expectations that allow feelings of transcendence later take many forms.

They Called Me Grandma

An 88-year-old college-educated professional volunteer, Molly, told the interviewer that she was not expected to live to adulthood. "I was sickly as a child and lost a whole year of school. I remember sitting on the porch watching my classmates walking to school. One called me 'the old grandma' because my mother put a shawl across my shoulders to keep me warm. My mother told me I had a bad heart. I know she didn't expect me to live long. But I did. I went to school and kept going. I sure fooled them and have had a very full and long life."

After detailing the development of our measure of life satisfaction, there will be a discussion of issues related to enhancing life satisfaction, to mental health, and to clinical practice.

Measuring Life Satisfaction

At the individual level, subjective well-being has been assessed in many ways. Now a much used measure in surveys is the Bradburn Affect Balance Scale. On it, higher feelings of well-being are inferred from self-assessments of high positive affects coupled with low negative affects. When, however, we began work in the late 1950s to develop a measure specifically appropriate for older people, only positive feelings were being queried. Indeed, the inadequacy of a unidimensional measure that only focused on positive feelings stimulated our developing a new measure, the LSR.

Our collaborators on the first large scale study of adult life had developed a Morale Index consisting of four questions, of which one was "Do you wish you could see more of your relatives than you do now? Less? Your neighbors? Your friends?" Answers were scored as positive if respondents answered "Things are all right as they are." Our concern was that the Morale Index was a unidimensional measure reflecting for the most part satisfaction with or possibly resignation or conformity to the status quo. The Morale Index seemed, therefore, not to reflect our own concepts of subjective or psychological well-being.

Our concepts were not crystallized when we began the process of developing one or more measures of subjective well-being. We knew, however, that we needed to encompass more than current mood and contentment with the status quo. Our group, which included doctoral students who were in the Adult Development and Aging Program in the Committee on Human Development at the University of Chicago, began by working back and forth from interview data gathered from 177 respondents aged 50 to 90 and a long laundry list of probable components (of something we ultimately called life satisfaction) that would be particularly appropriate for older persons. We considered other labels such as adjustments, morale, and psychological well-being; but adjustment was discarded because it carries the implication that conformity is the most desirable pattern of behavior, existing morale measures stayed too close to current mood, and psychological well-being seemed to us to be an awkward phrase. Also, satisfaction made more sense than something like happiness. Many very old people are not so happy with their present lives because of losses but feel satisfied with how their lives have been lived and what they still can do. Happiness appears more relevant to younger people, who can feel good about their current circumstances, and even find gratification from peak experiences, but at the same time not feel satisfied because of accomplishments yet to be achieved. Life satisfaction, particularly germane to older people, became for us divisible into five components after cutting down the laundry list and combining concepts. The term "life satisfaction," although recognizing it is not altogether adequate, comes close to representing the five components.

Operational definitions of the following components were obtained: zest versus apathy; resolution and fortitude; congruence between desired and achieved goals; positive self-concept; and mood tone. More detailed definitions appear in the scales reproduced below, but in brief, an individual was regarded as being at the positive end of the continuum of psychological well-being to the extent that she or he: (A) takes pleasure from the activities that constitute everyday life; (B) regards life as meaningful and accepts resolutely that which life has been; (C) feels has succeeded in achieving major goals; (D) holds a positive image of self; and (E) maintains happy and optimistic attitudes and mood. Each of these five components was rated on a 5-point scale (with 5 = high); and the ratings were summed to obtain an overall rating, with a possible range from 5 to 25.

In making the LSR, all the interview data on each respondent were utilized. Thus the ratings are based, not on direct self reports of satisfaction (although some questions of this type were included in the interviews), but on the inferences drawn by the raters from all the information available on respondents, including interpersonal relationships and how others reacted toward the respondent.

Four rounds of interviewing were spaced over approximately 2.5 years; in those few cases in which marked changes had occurred in respondents' life situations within that interval of time and where psychological well-being seemed to have changed accordingly, the rating represented the situation at the most recent point in time, at Interview 4.

The Life Satisfaction Rating Scales:

A. *Zest vs. apathy.* Rated here were enthusiasm of responses and a degree of ego involvement in any of various activities, persons, or ideas, whether these are activities that involve the respondent with other people, are "good" or "socially approved" or "status-giving." Thus, the respondent who "just loves to sit home and knit" was rated as high as the respondent who "loves to get out and meet people." Although a low rating was given for listlessness and apathy, physical energy per se was not to be involved in this rating. Low ratings were given for being "bored with most things", for "I have to force myself to do things", and also for meaningless (and unenjoyed) hyperactivity.

B. *Resolution and fortitude.* Rated was the extent to which the person accepts personal responsibility for her or his life, the opposite of feeling resigned, or of merely condoning or passively accepting that which life has brought, the extent to which life is accepted as meaningful and inevitable, and is relatively unafraid of death. This is not to be confused with autonomy or the extent to which the respondent's life has been self-propelled or characterized by initiative. The respondent may not have been a person of high initiative, but yet may accept resolutely and relatively positively that which life has been. The respondent may feel life was a series of hard knocks, but has stood up under them, which would be a high rating. There are two types of low ratings; the highly intropunitive, where the respondent blames herself or himself overly much; and the extrapunitive, where others or the world in general are blamed for whatever failures or disappointments have been experienced.

C. *Congruence between desired and achieved goals.* Here we rate the extent to which the respondent feels she or he has achieved goals in life, whatever those goals might be; feels has succeeded in accomplishing what is personally regarded as important. High ratings go, for instance, to the person who says, "I've managed to keep out of jail" just as to the one who says, "I managed to send all my kids through college." Low ratings go to the respondent who feels he or she has missed most opportunities, or who says, "I've never been suited to my work" or "I always wanted to be a doctor, but never could get there." Low ratings also go to the respondent who wants most to be "loved," but instead feels merely "approved." (Expressions of regret for lack of education are not counted because they are stereotyped responses among all but the group of highest social status.)

D. *Self-concept.*   Rated is the respondent's concept of self—physical as well as psychological and social attributes. High ratings go to the person who is concerned with grooming and appearance; who thinks of self as wise and mellow (and thus is comfortable in giving advice to others); who feels proud of accomplishments; who feels deserves whatever good breaks has had; who feels is important to someone else. Low ratings are given to the respondent who feels "old," weak, sick, incompetent; who feels self a burden to others; who speaks disparagingly of self or of old people.

E. *Mood tone.*   High ratings are for the respondent who expresses happy, optimistic attitudes and mood; who uses spontaneous, positively toned affective terms for people and things; who takes pleasure from life and expresses it. Low ratings for depression, "feel blue and lonely"; for feelings of bitterness; for frequent irritability and anger. (Here we consider not only the respondent's verbalized attitudes in the interview; but made inferences from all we know of his interpersonal relationships, how others react toward the respondent.)

It is apparent that ratings encompass adaptive processes previously discussed. Zest versus apathy (A) is similar to involvement in meaningful activities, no matter how few. Resolution and fortitude (B) contains a sense of control, as well as a determination to persist, especially for those who feel "bloody but unbowed." The adaptive use of reminiscence is also considered because it is an essential aspect in perceiving a congruence between expected and achieved life goals (C).

Yet, the LSR may contain too many aspects. Resolution and fortitude (B) also includes acceptance of death. As discussed in the preceding chapter, people of advanced age who continue to be productive, like still-working visual artists, are unwilling to accept their deaths because they have unfinished business at the end of their life cycles. Their ratings on the LSR would correspondingly be lowered, even though on the components, including other aspects of resolution and fortitude, they would manifest high life satisfaction.

While preservation of the self is not measured directly, the extent of preservation can be inferred from ratings. Higher scores surely reflect the persistence of the self, particularly as reflected in the first three components: the ability to carry out and to enjoy some personally meaningful activities (A), the determination to persist (B), and perceiving oneself as having achieved life goals (C). At the same time that these three components (A, B, and C) may be rated very highly, losses of others and deteriorating physical capacity may diminish an ability to see oneself as healthy and competent (D, self-concept) and cause pessimism and bitterness (E, mood).

Total scores, however, neither tell us the extent of the preservation of the self nor patterns. Two individuals rated in the midrange may indeed be quite different, one person being relatively content with current activities but unable to perceive a congruence between expected and achieved goals, and the other being satisfied with how life has been lived but unhappy with the current circumstances. We shall return to patterns shortly but first more on the LSR.

The ratings depended on scoring by judges who had read all the recorded interview material, but who had not themselves interviewed the respondent. In seeking to establish an outside criterion by which these ratings could be validated, the investigators thought it desirable to have an experienced clinical psychologist interview the respondents and then make his own ratings of life satisfaction. For various practical reasons, it was not until some 18 to 22 months had elapsed after interview 4 that these clinical interviews were begun. By this time, a fifth and sixth wave of interviewing had intervened, and there had been further attrition of the study population due not only to deaths and geographic moves, but also to refusals. Nevertheless, over a 3-month period, 80 respondents were interviewed at length by the clinical psychologist; and it is his ratings (LSR-C1) that constitute a validity check on the LSR. These interviews and ratings were made by the clinician without any prior knowledge of the respondent; that is, without reading any of the earlier interviews and without discussion of the case with other members of the research staff.

The 80 cases were representative of the 177 as regards gender, age, and socioeconomic status. They had, however, a slightly higher average score on the LSR. (The average score for the 177 was 17.8; for the 80 interviewed by the clinician, it was 18.9). In other words, a disproportionate number of drop-outs in the 18- to 24-month interval were persons who were low on life satisfaction.

Using the average of the two judges' ratings for the LSR score, the association between LSR and LSR-C1 for the 80 cases was quite high (a correlation of .64). Of 400 paired judgments, 76% represented exact agreement or agreement within 1 step on the 5-step scale.

Further study was made of several cases for whom there was marked disagreement between the LSR and the LSR-C1. As anticipated, these cases were of two types. First, there were a few who had been rated higher on LSR for which it seemed a reasonable explanation that the clinical psychologist had succeeded in probing beneath the respondent's defenses and had obtained a truer picture of his feelings.

Hidden Feelings

Mrs. Bell, for instance, was a woman whose facade was successful throughout the first four interviews in convincing the judges reading the interviews that she was a person who had achieved all her major goals; that she was resolute, competent, and happy, even in the face of repeated physical illnesses. In the more intensive interview, however, she broke down and wept and said she felt life had been unjust, and that she had been an unlucky person. It was the clinician's interpretation that she had long been depressed, and that the somatic illnesses had been a defense against the depression. She was a woman with a strong moral code and with tremendous pride who went through life feeling that at no time must she reveal her disappointments.

Second, there were a few cases in which the respondent's life situation had changed drastically in the interval between the LSR and the LSR-C1 ratings. The respondent had suffered severe illness or had been widowed, and the crisis had brought on a depression. In a few instances, however, the change had been for the better, as reflected in a higher LSR-C1 rating.

Change for the Better

One man, at the time of Interview 4, had just been widowed. A year earlier he had been retired from his job as a salesman, and he was worried about money as well as being depressed over the death of his wife. When seen by the clinical psychologist, however, he freely discussed the fact that 2 years earlier he had experienced a depression, but that now he was recovered. He had found a new job selling door to door, and he enjoyed what he called his "contacts with the public." He was living in a small apartment near his daughter's family, and he described with enthusiasm his grandchildren and outings he has with them on weekends.

In general, the correlation between LSR and LSR-C1 was interpreted by the investigators as providing a satisfactory degree of validation for the LSR given the various factors already mentioned: the lapse of time between the two ratings and the fact that a number of persons low on life satisfaction had dropped out of the study, thus narrowing the range of LSR scores for the 80 cases (a fact that, in turn, tended to lower the coefficient of correlation); the reality that the LSR was based only on recorded interview data, and the LSR-C1 on face-to-face interaction; and the greater depth of the clinical psychologist's interviews.

It is of some interest in this connection that the correlation between LSR and LSR-C1 was higher for the older members of the sample. (For 30 cases aged 70 and over, $r = .70$; for the 50 cases aged 69 and below, $r = .53$). It may be that the aged individual has less of a tendency to give conforming or "normative" responses in the regular interview situation than does the younger individual and thus provides fewer instances in which the clinical psychologist's depth questions revealed a different level of functioning than shown by replies to the more structured interviews. It might be, on the other hand, that in some manner, of which the investigators were unaware, they devised interview questions and rating scales for life satisfaction that are more appropriate for the very old respondent than for the somewhat younger respondent and that, as a result, different judges were more likely to agree in their evaluations of persons over 70. It is not uncommon for clinicians to remark that a half-hour interview is sufficient to evaluate the adjustment or mental health of an old person; but that it takes considerably more time to make a similar evaluation of a young person.

We also developed a self-administered measure, the Life Satisfaction Index A. Index B was additionally developed to be used in an interview format. Index A and its derivatives consist of 20 or so items that respondents are requested to either agree or disagree with. The items, scattered in administration, reflect each of the five components of the LSR. For example, zest versus apathy is assessed by "Most of the things I do are boring or monotonous." and "The things I do are as interesting as they ever were." Resolution is reflected in "I expect some interesting things to happen in the future." and "I have made plans for things I'll be doing a month or a year from now." Congruence is contained in "As I look back on my life, I feel fairly well satisfied." and "I would not change my past life if I could." Self-esteem is represented by "Compared to other people my age I make a good appearance." and "I feel my age, but it does not bother me." Mood, in turn, is captured by "This is the dreariest time of my life." and "My life could be happier than it is now."

When, however, scores for an older sample are submitted to statistical analysis to determine dimensions of the scale (by factor analysis), only three clear dimensions emerge: positive affects or feelings, negative affects (or feelings), and congruence between expected and achieved goals. Positive and negative affects are included, as noted earlier, in the popular Bradburn Affect Balance Scale, but Life Satisfaction Indices add congruence, a third dimension that is especially salient to the oldest old person. How the three dimensions apply to the oldest old person, and can be independent, is discussed next.

Mr. Sampson, while enjoying some current activities, is very bothered by what he can no longer do. No longer can he apply his trade and no longer can he walk even one block without great pain. At times he contrasts his current physical condition with his prowess earlier in life, but more often he will say "What's past is past." and then talk about his current activities. His choice not to dwell on the past when discussing physical deficits contrasts with his regaling of listeners with stories from his past life. Preoccupied with his vigors in the past in the context of his physical limitations only makes him depressed, whereas reconstructing his early life and making the past vivid reaffirms his concept of self. This distinction in how the past is evoked for adaptation is sometimes missed. The investigators in the 85+ Study were surprised when their respondents did not introduce the past when discussing current activities and interpreted this finding as how avoidance of the past facilitates success in advanced aging. The past, however, is likely to be avoided when telling of what can and cannot be done in the here-and-now. To make the contrast between the here-and-now and back then is dysfunctional and increases dissatisfaction.

From a different perspective, the often admixture of negative and positive affects makes it possible to agree that things are not as interesting as they were, and that few plans are made for the future while also feeling that a good appearance is made, old age is not a bother, and that this is not the dreariest time of life. To return to the LSR for a moment, the total average score (the average, as noted earlier, was 17.8) reflects higher ratings on (A) zest versus apathy, (B) resolution and fortitude, (C) and congruence, and a lower rating (D) on mood. The pattern of overall high positive affects but with depressive mood is not an atypical pattern among oldest old people.

We Would Dance Up a Storm

 Mrs. Miller, an 83-year-old vivacious woman who was widowed 10 years ago, said her life was wonderful. She said, I had the best husband a girl could find. It was like a dream. We loved to dance." Together the Millers danced through life, and in Mr. Miller's last few years they took up square dancing. "Come see my costumes." There they were, all neatly pressed and ready to wear. Now very excited, she began to explain in minute detail where she had worn each of the dozen costumes. She had to be slowed down

and returned to the interview questions if ever the interview was to be completed. She did so reluctantly and in a few minutes was discussing how much she liked to visit with her family and her girl friends. "It seems like the phone is attached to my ear. I have to keep up on everything and everybody. I have to know everything about everybody in my family and in the families of my girl friends." It was now winter so she stays at home too much, but whenever its nice she joins her friends for lunch at the congregate dining program. "It's at Stella's church. Stella is my girl friend I was telling you about, the one who was one of 16 kids. It's a Catholic church. So beautiful you could not believe. I'm Lutheran you know. A good one too. But I like going to Stella's church for lunch and other things we do there." But when asked what she misses most, she became weepy. "I told you. We would dance up a storm. Life's too much the same without Eddie. I make the best of it. What else can I do. I miss him so much I sometimes get a knot in the pit of my stomach when I think about how good it was. I tell him so. You may think its foolish but every night before I go to sleep, I talk to him. His picture is right by my bed. I tell him about my day and how much I miss him." Tears were now rolling down her cheeks. As she wiped them off, she said, "I'm just an old lady who is rambling on. But your life should be so good. Whoops. Its late and I have to get ready to go to my other church, the Catholic church for lunch. Stel is picking me up." Now bubbly again, the interviewer who had a slight cold was summarily dismissed with a peck on the cheek and a word of advice, "You should dance up a storm, you'd feel better."

Mrs. Miller is not atypical in manifesting a mixture of positive and negative affects. Life can be satisfying despite losses as expectations change, but losses nevertheless exact their toll and are experienced as unhappiness. It is not surprising that more unhappiness or depressive symptoms are evidenced among elderly people but not major, or clinical, depression.

Unhappiness, Clinical Depression, and Hopelessness

Distinctions, therefore, must be made between unhappiness and clinical depression and hopelessness. To be unhappy is not necessarily to be either clinically depressed or to feel hopelessness. Clinical depression refers to a set of behaviors that includes more than unhappiness or feeling blue to encompass behaviorial systems such as apathy, an absence of initiative, loss of appetite, and sleeplessness. Mrs. Miller is unhappy in missing Eddie and her past good life, but she is not clinically depressed because she is certainly not apathetic, shows no lack of initiative, has a good appetite, and, although she sleeps in spurts like other older people, she has no difficulty in falling to sleep.

For younger people, loss of sexual interests is also pathognomonic of clinical depression, a criterion that is less relevant for very old people, particularly for those without a partner. For those, however, with a partner, both of whom do not have debilitating illnesses, sexual activity can be retained until the end of the life cycle.

Hopelessness, in turn, is characterized by perceiving life as meaningless; as devoid of any future pleasure and no means of making life meaningful. Persons who are clinically depressed may also feel hopelessness, but people can feel hopelessness without being clinically depressed. Indeed, older persons who say their lives are meaningless and wish to commit suicide must be taken at their words. Adolescents who commit suicide are often not clinically depressed but, rather, seeing no viable future for themselves, take their own lives. Similarly, persons suffering from severe bipolar manic-depression are likely to take their lives as they emerge from their deep clinical depression and know that they are facing a manic phase followed again by clinical depression. Unable to alter the course of their affliction, and now with sufficient energy to act on their hopelessness, which they did not have when deeply depressed, suicide impulses may be acted on. At Drexel Home for the Aged we were mindful of how suicide was most likely to occur for our residents who talked of their hopelessness but were not clinically depressed. Recall Mrs. Bains from the previous chapter who stated she wished to die, but in actuality after admission to the hospital this was no longer so. Only through an understanding of Mrs. Bains' persistent way of relating to others and the psychodynamics reflected in these relationships was it possible to appreciate the shift from her wish for death to her wish for life.

Practice Wisdom

Depression per se has been found quite amenable to treatment independent of age. Specific to aged clients are the writings on treatment of the oldest old persons when in acute crises, particularly Alvin Goldfarb's (1959) inflating beliefs in mastery and Jerome Grunes' (1982) recapturing of early memories. In Goldfarb's augmenting of his elderly patients' feelings of potency and in Grunes' reviving the reconstruction of organized memories of his elderly patients, both psychotherapists are facilitating mythmaking. As discussed earlier, mythmaking is inherent to beliefs in one's greater mastery than is realistic and also to reconstructing the past, wherein significant others become bigger-than-life heros and antiheroes. In these mythmaking processes in psychotherapy with elderly people, as in their spontaneous occurrence among very old people, the reality principle recedes in importance: Grunes refers to a "historical sense of self," that is, "less subtly organized," and Goldfarb to "inflating" a belief in mastery. Less critical, therefore, than strict adherence to reality is that these mechanisms preserve the self.

Shared also by both psychoanalysts is the importance of enhancing self-worth. For Grunes, self-worth is evoked by the therapist while recathecting the past, whereas for Goldfarb, self-worth comes from identification with the powers of the therapist and from beliefs in one's personal powers to transcend limitations. Anger for Goldfarb becomes useful in this process, particularly in "organizing action," which is not unlike one kind of rationale for the benefits of aggressiveness to very old people when confronting life crises.

The approaches of Goldfarb and Grunes are compatible, and, actually, each approach leads to the explicit goal of the other approach. The 87-year-old woman who regains her sense of narcissism by recapturing memories of a father who "loved me best of all" is also reestablishing a belief that those in her current environment recognize her when she wears a pretty dress, and then interpreting, and often misinterpreting, responses to her as admiration, appreciation, and love. In turn, when Goldfarb has discussed how his urging the woman in her 9th decade whose hands are crippled with arthritis to return to knitting, it becomes obvious that he had very purposively selected a meaningful activity from her past that provides her a way of organizing and structuring her memories. Whereas Goldfarb used this case to illustrate how the reestablishment of a rather mundane activity can help move a patient from depression and dependency toward exaggerated feelings of mastery and independence, the interaction also includes a recathexis of the past in which the elderly woman became more vivid to herself.

Thus, the approaches of Goldfarb and Grunes are mutually reinforcing. At the simplest level, both use talking cures (variably referred to as psychotherapy, treatment, or counseling) to provide crisis management, or supportive therapy, for those elderly persons in advanced age who are experiencing psychological stress. Whereas Goldfarb focused on the inability to reestablish beliefs in control of the external environment, Grunes focused on the inability to maintain an organized reconstruction of the past. Inabilities to retain inflated beliefs in control and to organize vivid reconstructions of the past are symptoms of inner psychological stress, particularly among very old people. In supportive therapy with an empathic clinician, the reestablishment of adapted inflated beliefs in mastery reduces the disorganizing psychological stress, permitting a recathexis of past memories in an organized and vivid manner. In turn, the empathic clinician who facilitates a reorganization of recollections, by reducing inner stress, facilitates coping with the external world.

Above all, shared by both therapists is a therapeutic optimism. Whereas some psychodynamically oriented therapists emphasize, as Irving Yalom (1987) "the loss of possibility" and as Robert Nemiroff and Calvin Colarusso (1985)"the race against time," and still others, as Martin Berezin (1987) "ego depletion"; for Grunes and for Goldfarb, narcissistically injured, frail, elderly individuals can be helped to transcend these realities. And, in my perspective, we can do so by encouraging the use of the normative psychological mechanisms that are employed by those now old: Assuring adaptive coping by enhancing a sense of control and mobilizing assertiveness and also by recapturing the past and making it vivid. The past then becomes useful for establishing again the perception of a congruence between expected and achieved life goals.

Particularly salient to the oldest old person is the congruence between expected and achieved life goals. Mrs. Miller, who danced up a storm in her earlier years, is, fortunately, able to perceive this kind of congruence. So, too, were the Sampsons, who achieved more in life than they expected. But sometimes congruence, once achieved, is undermined.

She No Longer Recognizes Me

 Mr. Stanley becomes animated when he attends his senior center, but when alone he has uncontrollable crying spells because he had to place his wife in a nursing home when her Alzheimer's disease became "so bad that she was going to the toilet in bed" (incontinent of feces). He cannot bear to visit her because she no longer recognizes him. Having promised her that he would never place her in a nursing home, he feels that he has abandoned her. The feelings of guilt and shame sometimes get so intense that he even has considered suicide.

Before his wife's illness, when they attended the senior center together, Mr. Stanley was able to perceive a congruence. Now he feels cheated, and no longer can he say that he accomplished more than he had expected. He is not unlike survivors of widowhood who suffer an initial period of disequilibrium because of the thwarting of expectations of a companionate old age. Mourning that follows acute grief after the death of a beloved mate in advanced old age, however, is generally shorter than in the younger years as a new life as a widow becomes established.

Now the paradox may be evident that those with the least expectations who had the most difficult early lives may perceive that they accomplished more than they anticipated. It was these kinds of people for whom Grunes' and Goldfarbs' acute crisis psychotherapies were most helpful in ameliorating depression and confusion when they began their work in homes for aged persons more than 3 decades ago.

RECONSTRUCTIVE PSYCHOTHERAPY

Reconstructive, or insight, psychotherapy with very old people was impeded by Sigmund Freud's admonition that older patients are too rigid to benefit from psychoanalysis. Karl Abraham (1927) disagreed with Freud and reported the successful psychoanalysis of older patients, although older patients were considered to be those above 50 years of age. Reports now abound of psychotherapeutic successes with patients in their seventies, eighties, and even nineties. Among those who have counteracted the resistance to using insight therapies with the very old is Robert Butler (1963), who focused on how the inevitable life review evoked by nearness to death can be used therapeutically to resolve life-long conflicts. Butler's optimism has a counterpart in George Pollock's (1987) perspectives of how early losses can be successfully resolved by very old persons and lead to liberation. The therapeutic process, by assisting in the liberation, can awaken creativity and eventuate in dignity, self-respect, and usefulness. Insight therapies are not precluded because of age. Again, it is the nature of the psychopathology and the age of the psychopathology, not the age of the patient, that must be the first consideration.

Reconstructive psychotherapy can benefit the very old person, but there may be a need for modifications in processes and outcomes. Grunes (1987), for example, argues for the need for a special kind of empathy because of psychological distance and the countertransference issues evoked. Martin Berezin (1987) disagrees with Grunes and cautions that the presence of limited possibilities and narcissistic depletion casts a shadow on the therapeutic encounter. Wayne Myers (1984) believes that if the capacity for insight exists (and a neurotic transference can be developed), psychodynamic therapy proceeds independent of the age of the person.

Thus, there are differences among experienced clinicians in how the process is modified, but there are also differences in expected outcomes. Berezin's view leads to different criteria of successful outcomes for older persons than for younger persons, who have more extended futures. Certainly Pollock's views suggest the same criteria for older and younger persons. Not considered, however, are criteria for successful reconstructive therapy that includes the normative psychological processes inherent in the unique psychology of very old people. Should a goal be to assist in making the past vivid or to overinflate beliefs in mastery? Should these processes, which are goals of Grunes' and Goldfarbs' supportive psychotherapy, also be goals for reconstructive psychotherapy? The functions these processes serve for the preservation of the self of those who are very old would suggest that they should indeed be incorporated as goals.

What Do We Do Differently

Because practice wisdom is so important in informing us about counseling the aging, a systematic investigation was designed with Joseph Gustafson to determine whether clinicians who work with elderly people would affirm aforementioned processes and possibly add additional processes. Our approach was to include a diversity of practitioners, administrators, and therapists but, for convenience, to focus only on social workers (Tobin & Gustafson, 1987). To be sure, everyone has their own approach to working with people. Some practitioners devote all or most of our time to direct treatment, others to case management, and still others to planning and administration. Also, some have a more psychodynamic orientation, some a humanistic, others a cognitive, and still others a behavioral orientation; and some combine orientations into a personal eclecticism. Can we expect that despite these differences there are some commonalities in working with the aged? Possibly, these commonalities reflect shared characteristics of workers who purposively select to work with elderly people. A more likely explanation is that commonalities are a function of shared characteristics of elderly people. That is, shared characteristics among them must in some way influence how to work with them in ways that are different from work with younger people.

Researchers, however, have not yet provided sufficient evidence that the content of treatment is, or should be, different. A review of the literature, as well as personal clinical experience and the clinical experience of others, led to the identification of five dimensions of potential differences: activity, touching, use of reminiscence, perceptions of the worker by the client (transference), and concerns evoked in the worker (countertransference). A study was thus undertaken to assess the validity of these dimensions. It was found that 541 respondents (subscribers to the *Journal of Gerontological Social Work*) tended to agree with the 20 statements characterizing the five dimensions.

Activity of workers, as expected, was perceived to be greater with elderly people, including more coordination of services, more reaching out to difficult families, giving more concrete assistance, and more talking by the worker in sessions. The necessity for greater activity can be explained by the nature of elderly clients, who are more likely to have a multiplicity of problems in which physical deficits, social losses, and psychological decrements interact in a context of lessened social supports and inexperience in mobilizing formal supports. From one perspective, therefore, the problems confronting older clients are more concrete, less amenable to change, and thus necessitate activity beyond the therapeutic encounter itself. Thus, case management has been advocated that encompasses developing a treatment or service plan, delivering services, and monitoring and modifying service delivery as needed. It appears, then, that it is the different needs of elderly clients that dictates the greater activity of workers.

It is possible, however, to wish to do too much. Instructive is a report by child psychoanalysts Raymond Poggi and David Berland (1985) on their experience in a senior citizens' apartment building. To be helpful to residents, Poggi and Berland chose to provide a group experience to women in a residential setting. After the first few sessions, they became aware that they were not perceiving group members as women. When they discussed their attitudes toward participants with each other, they realized that they were desexualizing them, which certainly is unlikely to occur when psychoanalysts work with persons of other ages. They attributed their attitudes primarily to being perceived by the women as "boys" rather than as therapists; and, secondarily, to feeling a need to rescue them through providing assurance and concrete assistance. Fortunately, they corrected their misguided approach and began to perceive the elderly women as the women saw themselves—people with persistent sexual identities despite losses. Indeed, these women, as people of any age, have a need to be perceived as possessing their sexual identities. As they began to understand that being perceived as boys reflected the women's attempt to retain their identities rather than as a purposeful infantilization of them, they were able to allow themselves to be perceived as boys without a threat to their professionalism. Moreover, they concluded that while providing assurance and concrete assistance is important, it could not supplant facilitating the capturing of the persistent and stable self.

Touching reflects an extension of the workers' active approach to the elderly client's needs. Whereas clients may not fully understand other activities of workers, touching is something that is readily understood and experienced. It is experienced as a form of caring for those who need help and assurance when in turmoil. Touching was acknowledged as a form of easily recognized caring, that they touched the elderly clients more, and that support is conveyed better by touching than by words. It is more, however, than a show of caring. The "laying on of hands as a form of symbolic healing" emerged in discussion with one experienced clinician struggling to understand why he, trained in psychoanalysis not to touch, did indeed touch and found it important to do so. Grunes, when teaching the meaningfulness of touching, emphasized how elderly people can feel untouchable because of bodily deterioration that makes them feel unattractive and thus unlovable.

The value of reminiscence to elderly clients is, of course, not new to clinical social workers who have been taught and have learned through experience that helping clients to exploit their ego strengths and coping capacities involves discussing the ways in which successful adaptation has occurred in the past. This, too, is important in elderly clients but more specific to them than for persons of other ages is the use of the past to recapture and reaffirm the current self (agreed on by close to 9 of 10 respondents). There was not much agreement, however, that having a life span makes reminiscence better suited to elderly clients. The usefulness of the past, apparently, is not a function of its length per se, but rather how it can be used and made vivid to maintain a constancy of the self when confronted with a loosening of a sense of identity from age-associated decrements and losses.

Transference refers to projections onto the worker of meanings, wishes, and thoughts that are redirected from other persons. Although it occurs in all relationships, and presumably in exaggerated forms in helping relationships, interventions vary as to the use of transference in treatment. Independent of how, or whether, the transference is used by workers, it is not uncommon for workers to notice that the transference of older clients is somewhat different than among younger clients. Most common is for workers to observe that they are being perceived more as an authority figure. The usual explanation for this projection focuses on how elderly people have been socialized to respect authority figures, especially members of the health professions and particularly physicians (61% agreed). Beyond relating to the worker as an authority figure was the expectation that workers would perceive older people as projecting more omnipotence onto them. Most respondents, however, did not perceive this as a difference (40.5%).

There are probably qualities of transference that were not captured by the survey items. For example, when helping elderly people to recapture themselves through reminiscence, the worker may feel that he or she is experienced by the client as a person from the client's early life in a different way from what occurs with younger people. It was difficult, however, for experienced clinicians to put this qualitative difference into words. This elusive transference, as well as others, certainly needs more in-depth clinical and empirical study.

Regarding countertransference, in much the same way that individual clients evoke projections by workers onto them, client groups with similar problems will evoke common concerns among workers. Substance abuse clients may evoke concerns with self-indulgence and passivity; clients mourning death of a loved one, with concerns of losing others; and clients who have abused children or spouse, with concerns regarding potential to harm others. So too, elderly clients, because they share common situations and problems, can evoke shared concerns among workers. Based on these data, concerns regarding dependency, helplessness, death, and aging of parents are the most common shared themes. In addition, some workers sometimes feel like a child when relating to elderly clients, but this feeling was not at all widespread.

This small percentage of clinicians (about one of eight) who reported sometimes feeling like a child was surprising. I certainly have often felt like an older person's child when relating to an elderly client. Perhaps "feel like a child" suggests an infantalization, which the clinicians did not feel. Recall that the child psychoanalysts Robert Poggi and David Berland felt infantalized when attempting to assist women in high-rise congregate housing. Fears of infantalization may cause a withdrawal from treating elderly individuals:

The Resentment of Infantilization

At 72, Mrs. Victor, who best fit the diagnosis of narcissistic character disorder, was in extreme distress. She wanted to leave her current husband, but felt herself to be "too old-looking to get another man." Yet, she was well

preserved for her age, and the trainee's first impression was of a very attractive woman in her late forties or early fifties. But the trainee perceived this potential client as not amenable to treatment. In the initial diagnostic session, Mrs. Victor had referred to the trainee as "honey," "dearie," "sweetie," and other prosaic terms of endearment that made the trainee feel like a little girl. The trainee resisted the interpretation that her wish not to treat Mrs. Victor was because of feelings of being infantilized, but she continued to see Mrs. Victor under supervision.

Mrs. Victor had never stayed with a man for more than 5 years until she met her current husband 6 years ago. Having been married three times previously, she hesitated in marrying Mr. Victor, but gave in when he insisted, "It was marriage or nothing." His wealth was an added incentive. Then, in the fourth year of the marriage she got her "itch." "The romance, you know, goes after awhile and I got my itch to move on." Nothing had really changed, except Mrs. Victor has a lifelong lacunae that she fills by overly romanticized attachments that subdue the inner emptiness. The feeling of emptiness had returned, but, now perceiving herself as no longer the "beautiful girl I have always been," she feared leaving the marriage. Not unlike many others with a similar diagnosis, Mrs. Victor was a quite bright and accomplished person.

Gradually, through supervision, the trainee became aware of her resentment at being infantilized. Her mother, she realized, used such terms of endearment to control her through infantalizations. The trainees then began to perceive Mrs. Victor as a candidate for the kind of treatment available to patients with narcissistic character disorders and began the treatment of Mrs. Victor in earnest.

Perceiving older persons as untreatable can usually be traced to transference kinds of concerns. This is indeed sad because elderly persons are treatable. Of course, it is not always easy to maintain therapeutic optimism when confronted with an elderly client who has suffered from many losses and is now in acute pain. Yet Jerome Grunes, Alvin Goldfarb, and many others have been able to do so by maintaining a belief in their therapeutic interventions. Too often, for example, clinically depressed elderly people are misperceived as intractable to therapy. Yet, depression is treatable at any age, as are other treatable mental illnesses. It is the age of the disease and not the age of the person that must be considered.

The evocation of concerns provides insight into why some workers may avoid working with elderly clients. We may not all become substance abusers, but we will all have (or have had) parents who will become older, frailer, and more dependent. And, of course, we ourselves will all grow older. Why then do workers choose to work with elderly patients? Why risk experiencing feelings of losing parents through death (and becoming an orphan) and one's own dying?

Obviously there are gratifications in helping elderly clients, and concerns that are evoked also present opportunities to work through these concerns. Still, more must be learned about the many and specific gratifications that can accrue in working with elderly persons. Clearly, part of the gratification should be a function of how the work permits the worker to be active, how caring is communicated by touching, how reminiscence by an older person provides a poignant moment of exchange in which the octogenarian seems to be transformed into a young and vital teenager or young adult, and how the projections onto the worker become so personally meaningful. Also, seeing the stability that most elderly persons exhibit can be quite reassuring for their own aging.

But if those who work with older people provide more concrete assistance because old people are needy, psychotherapists may not wish to treat elderly people because they perceive them as in great need of concrete assistance and not psychotherapy. Apparently our respondents touched old people more because they perceived old people as more needy, especially when accurately perceiving their older clients and patients as feeling unattractive and unloved. Therapists may indeed be intimated by their needs when perceiving the depletion among the old and, as well, the impossibility of filling voids.

Elderly individuals certainly need touching because they feel so untouchable; that is, not only untouched or unloved because of loss of a life-long spouse, but also, not worthy of being touched because of age-associated physical deterioration and perceived disfigurations in appearance. Touching in these circumstances should not be perceived by psychodynamically oriented practitioners as a violation of their therapeutic principles but rather as an aid to the therapeutic encounter, as a way to help the person reestablish a sense of self-worthiness. A most recent and interesting example of the usefulness of touching has been provided by Muzza Eaton, Iola L. Mitchell-Bonair, and Erika Friedmann (1986), who found that gentle touching of elderly institutionalized patients with organic brain syndrome improved their nutritional intake more than verbal encouragement alone.

Thus, older persons may be perceived as needing interventions other than psychotherapy, such as concrete assistance and stroking. Also inhibiting perceiving older persons as amenable to psychotherapy are feelings evoked when elderly persons reminiscence. To gerontologic social workers reminiscence is perceived as useful in reaffirming the self. To those, however, who fear their own aging, reminiscence may be perceived as living in the past and, moreover, a sign that life is too short, and that possibilities are too limited when you are old.

Lastly, the typical countertransference issues were evident, although, as noted earlier, not to the degree expected among our respondents who work with elderly people. Particularly interesting was that only 65% of the respondents agreed, "I am aware of fears of my own death." Such fears are more likely to be found among younger people (whereas old people are more concerned, generally, with disability and how they will die) and thus are most likely to be ubiquitous among our respondents. Also, apparently, the probability of having fears of becoming dependent and helpless when working with the elderly turns off psychotherapists. Adding to the turning off are issues associated with care for the therapists' own parents that are, of course, inseparable from lifelong relations with parents. Given the responses of those who work with elderly clients, a fear of the evocation of countertransference issues is a likely reason why therapist do not choose to work with elderly people.

In turn, given the kinds of reasons for why respondents work differently with elderly clients, it may very well be that the important question I must address is: Why should anyone wish to work with elderly people? Although this question shall be left for others to address, it certainly appears that the respondents did enjoy working with elderly people and found their work to be meaningful. Possibly, the responses to the questions on reminiscence capture one aspect of the reason for working with the elderly. Not only do practitioners obtain pleasure from the voyeuristic listening to the reconstructions of the past but, also, to the transformation of the client when reminiscing in becoming increasingly vivid to self, which may provide a kind of pleasure from treatment that is unique to working with elderly clients. Indeed, this perspective is quite congruent with the unique psychology of the very old, in which the blending of the past and the present for self-definition, as well as making the past vivid to reaffirm the self, are apparently normative occurrences. In turn, assertiveness and beliefs in mastery afford to workers a sense of intellectual discovery and, also, provide ways of working with elderly clients that can provide special rewards.

PART FOUR

When Care Is Needed

First to be considered is care at home, then care in hospitals and nursing homes, and lastly when care is needed for a victim of Alzheimer's disease.

Home care is of significantly greater frequency than nursing home care. As many as three times as many elderly persons are being cared for at home as are cared for in long-term care facilities; that is, whereas 5% of persons 65 and over reside in long-term care facilities at any one time, about 15% of elderly persons who have the same incapacities remain at home to be cared for by their families (Weissert, 1985). The 5% is, however, a deceptive statistic because living beyond 65 is associated with nearly a one in two chance of spending part of one's old age in a nursing home. Still, caregiving by children for their elderly parents has become so commonplace that it is the main preoccupation of couples at retirement. Yet, spouses are caregivers before adult children. Women who invariably marry older men typically care for their husbands and then are cared for by their children after becoming widowed. To be clarified in chapter 8 is how processes that facilitate adaptation of elderly care receivers are particularly irksome to caregivers. Also considered are feelings of caregivers, including anger, that are associated with difficulties in maintaining control of the caregiving situation.

Regarding hospitalization, the primary focus is on iatrogensis, the inadvertent adverse effects from treatment. Also discussed in chapter 9 is the process of becoming institutionalized when old and the predictors of adaptation, specifically control through magical mastery and aggressiveness as contrasted to lethal passivity. Control and aggressiveness, although related, have also been found to be independent predictors of vulnerability to the stress of relocation. (Becoming institutionalized has been reported in the Tobin and Lieberman book Last Home for the Aged: Critical Implications of Institutionalization and predictors of vulnerability in the Lieberman and Tobin book The Experience of Old Age: Stress, Coping and Survival.) Issues in institutional care are also reviewed.

Deselfing Alzheimer's disease forms the third, and last, chapter of this set. Diagnosis, treatment, and the loss of self in Alzheimer's disease are discussed in chapter 10.

CHAPTER 8

Family Care at Home

*T*he *Sampsons take care* of each other. Both have difficulties in the activities of daily living from limited mobility, but only Jack is sufficiently impaired to approximate residents in nursing homes:

We Take Care of Each Other

Marilyn Sampson said, "We used to fight like cats and dogs, mostly over money when the kids were small. Now we take care of each other. Without him I don't know what I would do. He drives, only in the daytime when he can see. We go to the early bird to eat pretty early. It's still light when we come back home. I gave up driving a long time ago. He shops, and sometimes I go with him. I can't be on my feet too long. Jack can't either, but he leans on the cart and gets what we need. We buy enough for a few days and then package what we don't have for dinner and put it into the freezer. What else? Every morning I take out his 20 pills and carefully arrange them. Some he takes when he gets up, some after breakfast, some in the afternoon, some after dinner, and some when he goes to bed. If I didn't do it, he would forget about taking all his pills. He is not forgetful, just doesn't want to take medication. He's still a tough guy and taking pills bothers him. Not me. I'm an old fogy. The pills are the easy part. When he came back from the hospital after his prostate surgery, it was hard. I couldn't hold him up to help him take a shower. We had an aide come in, Mary. She was a big lady. Jack loved her, but to me, she was too bossy. She would stay a few minutes longer and feel like we owed her something, like she had a right to tell us what to do. She gossiped about other people. So I was afraid to tell her anything. She would ask questions, you know, of a private nature, and I would tell her nothing. But we needed her, and she did her job. Thank God!"

Jack added, "Marilyn takes good care of me now. She knows when I take the little pills and the big pills, the blue ones and the white ones. After my prostate surgery, she and Mary, this real big aide, made sure I could get back on my feet, on my legs that aren't good anymore. I can't even walk a block. If the elevator stopped working, I couldn't even make it to the second floor, to our apartment. Since you saw us, it's not only my legs. I have a bad valve in my heart, and when I exert myself, I go into what's called heart failure. I can't catch my breath. Just the other day I moved a table for Marilyn. It was only a few feet, but it was too much. I had to sit down to catch my breath."

In caring for each other, they relate to each other from moment-to-moment, in interpersonal contact that reaffirms their identities. Recall the movie *On Golden Pond*. When Norman (played by Henry Fonda), the retired professor who is one day away from his 80th birthday, becomes disoriented in the woods behind his summer house, he panics and runs around in circles but finally arrives at the house. Breathless and with obviously frightening heart palpitations, he sits beside his wife (Katherine Hepburn) on the couch, and as he catches his breath, he turns toward her and tenderly says in a voice strained with a mixture of anxiety and relief, "When I look into your face, I can be *myself* again." This moment in the movie dramatically and poignantly captures how families help us to be ourselves. Indeed, for the very old, the greater the embeddedness in family life, the more the possibility of preserving the self. Unfortunately, however, the psychological mechanisms used by very old persons to preserve their senses of self, as noted earlier, may be troublesome to family members.

A family consultation session will be detailed followed by using the session to illustrate how psychological processes useful for preserving the self of a man in his nineties were sources of annoyance and concern for his offspring, who themselves were in their young-old years. Next is a discussion of the kinds of typical feelings of family caregivers that are particularly relevant in work with families, including rage from inadequacy in providing care, fears from risk taking, frustrations associated with providers, and gratifications. The chapter continues with a section on providing emotional support to the older care receiver, and ends with the question: Who is the client?

An Illustration of Family Dynamics

I was asked by Jane, the granddaughter of a couple in their nineties, to meet with her, her father Joe, her mother Beth, and her father's sister Aunt Sue to consult on the caregiving arrangements for her grandparents. Jane said that her father Joe was becoming quite anxious about the caregiving arrangements. His sister, her Aunt Sue, was the primary caregiver to his parents, who had decided to remain for the winter in their summer home so that Aunt Sue, who was living in the home, could provide care to them. Nothing dramatic had occurred, but Joe feared that his sister may become burned out.

My meeting with Jane, Father Joe, Mother Beth, and Aunt Sue began with Father Joe encouraging Aunt Sue to voice her complaints about her father. His request of Aunt Sue, said in a rather quiet voice but with an unmistakenly sarcastic tone, was something like, "Tell Dr. Tobin all those things that bother you about Dad, the kinds of things you always tell me about." He then added in an aside to me that was loud enough for all to hear, "Sue said that she did not want to attend this family meeting because she gets so angry, and that's not good for her."

So Aunt Sue began her litany of complaints, "Our father expects me to do everything for him, and he doesn't appreciate anything I do. He never appreciated anything mother did for him, and now he doesn't appreciate what I do for him. And he yells at me. At times he even thinks that I'm trying to hurt him. It's hard to take."

As if embarrassed by her anger, Aunt Sue stopped and lowered her head. Father Joe, however, encouraged her to continue, "What about his overdoing?" So Aunt Sue continued. One day, she related, he tried to carry some firewood into the house, which he could not do, and this activity frightened her. When she tried to discuss with him this kind of harmful behavior, he discussed how capably he built up a large business, that he still had all his faculties, that he wished to do things for himself, and that it was none of her business. Moreover, she felt that his constant allusions to, and embellished stories about, his great success as a businessman were purposely used to irk her because she had married a man who tried to emulate her father but was unsuccessful in business. Eventually he took to drink and they were divorced.

Mother Beth redirected the focus toward Joe's recent anxiety. Joe, however, could not verbalize why he had become anxious. Daughter Jane, then said that it might be because he was considering slowing down now that he was close to 65. "No," said Joe "I have been slowing down, and the business is in good shape." "How," asked Beth, "do you feel now that dad does not come into the office everyday?" This was the first autumn that his father had not come into the office for at least 1 hour each day. "Good and bad," said Joe "because I like seeing Dad up and about, but in the last few years he hasn't really understood the direction of the company. And frankly, he thinks he does, but I don't have the heart to tell him anything different. It is especially difficult when he acts suspicious, like I'm not telling him the truth." Beth then commented, "I have sensed that you have been somewhat relieved that the old man isn't there to tell you how he built up the business and ignore all that you have done to keep it going." Joe responded, "After 40 years, you learn to accept that."

The conversation stopped, and everyone turned to me. I asked "What about Grandma?" All agreed that Grandpa would not have been successful had not Grandma been there to encourage and support his ventures. She was his sounding board, and all chuckled when reminiscing about how her sense of business was probably better than Grandpa's.

Then, rather suddenly, the precipitant for the session was brought out. Every year Grandpa goes into the hospital for an annual checkup. During the week he is away, Grandma uses the time away from her spouse of over 70 years to visit one of her three daughters. This year, however, she said that she was too frail and did not want to bother her daughters or to be among vigorous noisy grandchildren. Instead she was thinking of going into the hospital herself for a complete checkup. This thought of Grandma's frightened Aunt Sue, as well as father Joe, because their mother has always insulated them from their father. Also, they were aware and frightened of her increasing frailty.

Joe, who was now fidgeting, suddenly sprang up and said that he needed to go to the bathroom and to get a cup of coffee. It was now 1 hour into a session that lasted for more than 2 hours. A break seemed sensible. When we all returned to our chairs, Joe was sweating and his face was ashen. What was wrong? After a few minutes of silence, Beth said something to the effect "So that's what it's all about Joe. You are still Mama's little boy and the thought of Mama not being there to help you with Dad is the problem."

In a low and strained voice, Joe began by denying that this was the problem. But then his daughter Jane said very directly that the purpose of this session was to obtain guidance, and that indeed it was the change in his mother that was bothering him, that he should share his feelings with us. With an apparent sigh of relief, he began to talk about his mother. Whenever he decided on a new direction for the business, he first went to his mother, as did his father. If she agreed his decision was a wise or sensible one, then she gently convinced her husband that he should accept his son's judgment. What often happened, however, was that his father took the decision as his own without giving any credit to his son. For Joe, it was only his mother who truly understood his importance. Without her, there would be no one who understood how much of a man he had become, and that he no longer walked in the shadow of his father.

It was a sad moment for Joe but also one in which support could be given to him. His wife, sister, and daughter assured him in no uncertain terms that they were aware of what he had contributed. After reviewing some of the important decisions he had made, Mother Beth lightened the air by saying "Maybe now you can slow down, and we can go on some long vacations. We have to spend the money you made some way." Turning to Aunt Sue, Mother Beth asked if their going away would be a hardship because they would not be available if there were a crisis. Now very thoughtfully Aunt Sue replied, "I'm always scared something will happen. I can't enjoy myself. You go away."

There was never a second session. I left it to Jane to contact me if the family wished to continue or if Joe, by himself, wished to be seen in counseling. About 2 months later, Jane told me that the situation remained stable with Aunt Sue continuing to complain angrily and vociferously, but enjoying being the "special and best child."

The lengthy single session with this family certainly revealed the kinds of complaints found among caregivers in response to behaviors that preserve the self. It also revealed the persistence of family psychodynamics and, fortunately, how lifelong dysfunctional psychodynamics can be made manifest and begun to be worked through. Joe was able to use this session to begin to free himself from preoccupations that have been very troublesome for him.

Complaints About Functional Behaviors

Aunt Sue, as well as Father Joe, indeed complained about adaptive behaviors that are helpful to Grandpa, which are encompassed under the unique psychology of very old people: a nasty aggressiveness, magical mastery, and repetitive vivid reminiscence. And they also complained that Grandpa is still himself.

AGGRESSIVENESS

Grandpa was always feisty. His determination led him to build an enormously successful business and to make him a millionaire several times over. But he was not known to be a particularly distrustful or suspicious person. Yet now Joe is concerned that his father "acts suspicious, like I'm not telling the truth." Aunt Sue not only concurs but augments this impression, "At times he even thinks I'm going to hurt him." The concerns are about Grandpa's functional paranoia, distrust, and suspicion, which is unaccompanied by anything as serious as delusions of persecution. Still, the attacks on them by their father are hard to take.

As a member of a support group for family caregivers said of her impaired father, "What I do for him is never enough and, you can bet, he always tells me so." Another said, "He keeps telling me what I do that is wrong." And still another, "I don't mind if she (her mother) doesn't trust anybody else. But I take care of her. And I do the best I can." It may be best for the homebound mother who lives with this caregiving daughter to externalize her anger toward her plight, but it certainly is not best for the daughter onto whom the rage is displaced, especially when the beleaguered daughter is devoting many hours to caring for her mother and taking much time away from her husband and children.

MAGICAL MASTERY

Magical mastery, also evident in Grandpa's behavior, is a cause of concern. As portrayed by Aunt Sue, he tries to participate in some of the physical activities that assure him of his manliness such as carrying firewood into the house. Joe, on the other hand, is disturbed by his father's belief that he understands the company as it now is. Fortunately, Joe is sufficiently sensitive to his father's needs that he does not confront him with the unreality of his beneficial illusions. Most caregivers have concerns about magical mastery, particularly when the elderly family member is doing something that may be harmful. "She can't see anymore to cook but there she is turning on the stove. She will catch on fire. She wears this inflammable night gown to cook her breakfast." Or "He doesn't know how dangerous he is to himself." Often have I heard, "She doesn't know that she can't take care of herself anymore."

REPETITIVE REMINISCENCE

Hurtful to Aunt Sue is her father's incessant talking about how he built his business. These reminiscences, which are a source of great self-esteem to her father, are disturbing to Aunt Sue, particularly because of how she interprets them. In the telling of his great successes, her father is perceived as putting her down because of her marriage to an unsuccessful businessman. The content of the discussion during the consultation session, however, suggests that Grandpa was not the least bit interested in Aunt Sue's long forgotten divorce but, rather, interested in recalling his business success when now he is no longer the prominent businessman he once had been.

Other caregivers also complain about repetitive reminiscence, "I'm going to bring someone in to tell his stories to. At least three times a day he tells me about growing up in the old country." Or, "Whenever we have a conversation, we never finish it because she starts to tell stories about the good old days." "How often," said the distraught daughter "must I hear the same old stories of how my dad struggled to feed us in the Depression. Sure, he is trying to say that my helping him now is only paying him back for what he did for us. When I try to tell him I would do for him anyway, and that he should read the paper like he used to so we have something to talk about, 2 minutes later he is back talking about how we starved but made it."

PERSISTENT FAMILY DYNAMICS

As a listener at the family session I was very impressed with how Grandpa has been able to be himself through his midnineties. He, apparently, is as arrogant as ever and as unwilling as ever to give credit to anybody, including his wife, who is seen by her children as the real wise one in the family. It is the persistence of Grandpa's identity that makes Aunt Sue most uncomfortable because it is a constant reminder of her failure in finding a suitable mate; for her, a mate acceptable to her father. Grandpa, in being himself, is also a reminder to his son Joe that he should not feel so successful because he took over a thriving business built by his father. Fortunately, at 65, Joe is beginning to reject this internalized evaluation of his father. Thus the session not only revealed the kinds of complaints found among caregivers about psychological mechanisms useful for preservation of the self, but also the persistence of family psychodynamics.

Caregiving family members often complain about how parents say things that trigger lifelong sensitive issues such as "Papa really knows what to say that hurts me!" Or "Mama always compares me to my sister who was always favored!" Each person in their old-old years, in trying to be themselves, will attempt to play out their lifelong relationships with their children. But it certainly is difficult for caregivers when characteristic ways of interacting trigger underlying resentments and conflicts. Because of the persistence of these psychodynamics in the relationship, it is erroneous to consider a role reversal in which the parent who was once the caregiver is now the care receiver. Family interaction is always characterized by interdependence, a complex mixture of dependence and independence among members. Of course, there are differences. Caring for an infant contains the anticipation of a rewarding future of growth and development, whereas caring for a debilitated parent contains a downward course followed by death. And older people are likely to provide more monetary assistance to adult children than their children provide to them. It is, however, the persistence of psychodynamics that is most characteristic of caring relationships among very old people, and it is this very persistence, albeit a disturbance to caregivers, that helps in the preservation of the self.

Gerontological social worker Elaine Brody illustrates this persistence when telling of the daughter who was giving her incontinent mother a sponge bath. Mother, in a prone position looked up at her disheveled daughter and said "I always liked you in red." Mother, with her chatter about clothes and appearances, redefined the moment to maintain a persistent relationship. The daughter, who has a sister whom the mother has always thought was prettier, winces, bites her tongue, and tries to continue to be gentle.

Feelings of Family Caregivers

The more that feelings of family caregivers are understood, the more it becomes possible to help them to continue to contribute to the emotional well-being, as well as to the preservation of self, of their impaired member. For example, the complaints about behaviors that are beneficial to care receivers are often only the tip of the iceberg. Below the surface, and sometimes just below, may be rage; a rage that is likely to be evoked by feelings toward the family member for whom care is being provided for causing feelings of inadequacy. Some other feelings of caregiving family members of which workers must be aware are the fears when risks are taken, the guilt of taking time away from other members of the family, the frustrations in relating to providers, and also the gratifications. Feelings are indeed many, complex, and usually quite ambivalent.

AN UNDERLYING RAGE

Feelings of inadequacy when giving care are generated by a desire, often unconscious but rather unavoidable, to make the recipient of care healthy again. Aunt Sue was able to express some of her feelings of inadequacy when she communicated that she could not vacation away from her parents because she carries around this feeling of having to be with them when an inevitable crisis occurs. Her feeling is less of guilt regarding what she is not doing for her parents and more of inadequacy, of not being able to do anything that will keep them healthy. For Aunt Sue, these feelings are fused with her feelings of being angry, possibly enraged, for not being sufficiently appreciated for the dedication to caring and for having her defenses penetrated with a consequent resurrecting of painful inner experiences left over from her earlier years.

FEARS FROM RISK TAKING

Aunt Sue was not providing the kind of care that causes great fears in risk taking. Barbara Hasselkuss' (1988) in-depth interviews with caregivers identified this fear as a major theme:

> A fear of change, or anything which might cause a change, was usually present. "Now he's got a sore on the other foot, so now I'm worried about that one." Activities were governed by their perceived safety ("We planned to stay longer [vacation], but the glucose count started to go up, and we just felt uncomfortable—we'd had so many frightening things happen—so we came home"). Some care procedures were perceived as risky ("We used a condom catheter when he first came home; you were always afraid of getting that too tight"). Risk associated with leaving the care receiver home alone was sometimes handled by putting the care receiver to bed during the caregiver's absence. "Oh, I wouldn't leave him in the wheelchair, he gets into things. He loves to smoke and I don't trust him, he'd burn up, so he's better off in bed." (p. 688)

DESERTING OTHERS

Beyond risk taking, it is very common for caregiving middle-aged children to feel guilty about taking time away from others. Deserting others was found by my then doctoral student Mary Smith to be a dominant theme in counseling in Ronald Toseland's project, which focused on comparing the effectiveness in reducing caregiver's strain by professionals and by peers in support groups and in individual counseling. Smith, then a doctoral student, was one of the professional counselors, and she also supervised and monitored professionals and peers who provided individual counseling to the middle-aged female caregivers.

Smith observed that many who are caring for elderly parents felt they were neglecting their spouse, that they lost their privacy and at times their intimacy with their husband, and that their marriage was under a great deal of stress. Some used much energy to shelter their husband from feeling any burden or responsibility for the care of the frail elderly parent. One woman said, "My husband is a wonderful, patient man, I don't want to burden him with any responsibilities regarding the care of our parent." Another commented, "I don't like to complain to my husband. It just gets him angry. He doesn't understand why I can't get others to help with Mom." Few women felt that their husbands understood them, nor that they would actually help them. Most were fearful that their husbands would just get more angry, become more sullen or withdrawn, or insist on nursing home placement if they were asked to assume more caregiving responsibilities. It was the impression of counselors that those marriages presently very stormy were likely to have been shaky before caregiving. Whereas, to be sure, caregiving puts an added stress on relationships, mutually supportive relationships tend to survive these stresses better than insecure, unhappy relationships. During counseling, concerns about marital relationships were discussed to alleviate conflict.

Parent-child issues were present with some of the caregivers but were not as prevalent as marital problems. Caregivers felt that their parent-child problems were present because of the stages their children were going through. Yet, these adult daughters felt they could, and did, mobilize their children into sharing some of the daily chores regarding care of their grandparents. There was a sense of control felt by the women over their children, which was not present with their spouses.

Relationships between siblings was also a major topic of discussion, which encompassed siblings of the caregiver, as well as siblings of the care receiver. The primary caregiver often felt stuck in her role and had difficulty thinking how she could effectively mobilize others into the role of caregiving. Letting her siblings know how she felt and what kinds of help she would appreciate was something that was worked on regularly during the counseling sessions. Statements such as the following were made by the clients. "I know I chose this role. It is my problem now." "I don't want to appear that I can't handle Mom." "I don't want to sound like a cry baby." "My brother has his own problems. What good would it do to burden him with more problems?" "They live so far away. Why tell them what it's really like for me? They can't do anything, anyway." These and similar statements were made regularly by the caregivers. Help was given to the clients in sharing some of their burden and feelings with other family members, as was provided to Aunt Sue.

FRUSTRATIONS RELATED TO PROVIDERS

A recurrent theme in counseling is frustrations related to providers. The most frequent complaint was to find and keep qualified, competent, and reliable home-health aides. Fear of rejection by aides was a major problem that caregivers often verbalized. Daughters often felt at the mercy of these employees and felt powerless to do anything to change the situation. Assistance was, however, provided in counseling sessions, as caregivers learned how to relate to aides in different ways, how to make better use of them, how to make their jobs a little more interesting, and how to reward the aides with appropriate praise and encouragement. Other concerns were associated with a lack of information regarding existing services, as well as a lack of knowledge of how to access them.

A theme of tensions with professionals, rather than aides as Smith reported, has been identified by Barbara Hasselkuss (1988). One of Hasselkuss' caregivers commented, "The occupational therapist wanted to come early and watch me, what I did and everything, and it made me so nervous. So I asked the occupational therapist not to come anymore." (p. 688). At times caregivers commented that health professionals made remarks that undermined caregiver's efforts. A caregiver reported that the nurse chided her for feeding the care receiver greasy potato pancakes that could "close an artery and clog it, that he wasn't getting enough blood to the brain."

It is quite understandable why Mary Smith found that caregivers often do not feel in control and need to exert too much control. At any moment the situation can become out of control from changes in the elderly care receiver's status, from relations with family members, and from tensions with health providers (Smith, Smith, & Toseland, 1991). Sometimes caregivers respond by exerting too much control, particularly when unacceptable feelings of rage are provoked by care receivers' behaviors. As described by Mary Smith (personal communication):

Sometime children who are caregivers are unaware that their anger relates to how the care receiver makes them feel inadequate. As an outside observer, it is certainly understandable that a caregiver would feel toward a parent for whom they are providing care that the parent has placed him or her in an intolerable position. The frail elderly care receiver has become the source for feelings of inadequacy, as well as for raising issues that relate back to childhood that have been repressed for a lifetime. A common way to deal with some of these less conscious feelings is to focus the anger on specific behaviors. The caregiving child becomes angry at, for example, suspicious or paranoid behavior that all too often makes caregiving extremely difficult. The paradox is, of course, that the projection of blame for disability by the elderly family caregiver onto others is very functional. Once again, when internal deterioration occurs it is best to blame others rather than oneself.

GRATIFICATIONS

Aunt Sue, of course, does not only have negative feelings. She also has feelings that she is a good child and, moreover, a better child than her sibling Joe, who has not, as she has, assumed the responsibilities for caring for their parents. Fortunately, usually the gratifications from caregiving outweigh the felt burdens. The gratifications that families receive from caring for an impaired member regardless of age make it easier for caregivers to express those negative feelings that they may have bottled up. The opportunity to verbalize negative feelings in a support group is particularly helpful. Although the negative feelings toward care receivers can be dangerous to the holder, most caregivers can, when made conscious of them, deal with them. Indeed, for most caregivers it comes as a relief that others have similar feelings and are not overwhelmed by them. In one group of family caregivers, when a daughter who was providing care to her mother mentioned her frustration and anger, another member of the group who was providing home care to her father blurted out, "I get so angry with him that there are times when I just want to kill him!" She was, fortunately, ready to deal with these feelings of great frustration and anger. In listening to others, it became apparent to her that she was not alone in having these feelings and, more importantly, that she was doing an excellent job of giving care while maintaining control over her feelings. She learned that just being there, the day-to-day face-to-face contact, was of the most importance. Also she learned, as she must, what it is possible to do and what it is impossible to do.

BEING A MORAL PERSON

As observed by Mary Smith in counseling, "These women frequently reaffirmed the morality of their decision to be caregivers, believing they were superior to others who relinquished responsibility when they placed their parents in nursing homes." Feelings of being a moral person, of fulfilling family obligations that transcend conflicts in relationships, accounts for the great extent of family caregiving. Indeed, the ties that bind families together are no greater in evidence than when care is needed by elderly members. As noted earlier, although about 5% of all elderly people are in nursing homes at any one time, possibly as many as three times this percentage of them whose physical and mental status is comparable to those in nursing homes are being cared for in their own homes. About one-half apparently can leave their homes but need care, protection, and surveillance to do so, whereas the other one-half may be homebound, with half of the homebound being bedridden.

Providing Emotional Support

It is thus obvious that care at home rather than in a congregate setting enhances the retention of self. To be explored briefly is the emotional security from families before home care is warranted. My studies with Regina Kulys (Kulys & Tobin, 1980) replicated what others have found; less than 10% of persons 65 and over report being concerned about the future. Because, obviously, age-associated losses are going to occur, it has been easy to interpret the lack of future concern among the more than 90% as reflecting denial, an unwillingness to face the future. Found, however, was that those who are not worried are not only those least likely to use denial, but are also the least anxious and depressed and, moreover, have the greatest amount of familial supports. Because of event uncertainty and the uncertainty of timing of events ("anything can happen at anytime"), to worry about what will happen is actually to be preoccupied; and it is the presence and availability of family that reduces preoccupations and permits elderly persons to use present interaction for preservation of the self.

To further explore the role of family in the process of self-preservation, the person designated by respondents as their "responsible other" was also interviewed. To identify responsible others, respondents were asked: "If you were admitted to the hospital and had to name someone who would be responsible for you and your affairs, whom would you choose?" As others have found, there is a principle of substitution so that the first person named, if available, was a spouse; if unavailable, a child was named; and if neither a spouse nor a child was available, other family members were named, usually a sibling. Only when spouses, children, and other family members were unavailable, were friends named.

For the 50 dyads composed of parents and children, feelings of security among parents were found by another doctoral student, Mary Schlesinger (Schlesinger, Tobin, & Kulys, 1981), to be related to their ability to say that responsible children would take their wishes into account if decisions needed to be made for future care. Paradoxically, greater amounts of interaction between parent and child were associated with lessened feelings of security which, however, becomes quite understandable because increased interaction occurs when adverse events cause both lessened security and greater need for attention by children.

KNOWLEDGE OF SERVICES

Most associated with feelings of security of parents was the extent of personal care services of which responsible children had knowledge. Apparently, knowledge of concrete services by children provides the necessary reassurance that meaningful concern will be given, a kind of concern that reassures parents that they will, for example, be able to use community services to stay at home. This reassurance suggests once again that what is most meaningful to the elderly person is that the maintenance and retention of self will persist. Albeit conflicts occur in the parent-child relationship, when formal services are known by the child and this knowledge communicated to the parent, feelings of security of parents are enhanced.

CHILDREN DESCRIBED CLEARER

Each parent and responsible child was asked to describe him or herself and also to describe the other person as they think the other person would describe him or herself. The parent was better able to describe the child as the child described self than was the child able to describe the parent as the parent described self. One interpretation of this finding is that it is very important for parents to have a clear picture of children that are likely to be responsible for their future care. Yet, also evident in the data was the portrayal by parents of negative aspects of self that children seem to feel would not be used in parents' self-descriptions. The acceptance of previously unacceptable motives and self-perceptions is common among elderly people. As discussed earlier, if the central task in advanced old age is to be oneself, then previously unacceptable thoughts and feelings become open to consciousness if they serve to preserve the core self.

SPOUSES AND CHILDREN AS CAREGIVERS

Concerns of spouses may be quite different than the concerns of children. Spouses tend to feel less ambivalent about providing care than do children and say: "He (or she) would take care of me if I needed care." Husbands, however, experience less strain because, apparently, they focus more on instrumental assistance than emotional support, which is certainly easier to provide to a frail and failing spouse who may also have Alzheimer's disease. Yet the sense of capacity experienced by husbands and wives does not ameliorate the strain from the instrumental tasks of providing assistance that may indeed be a taxing burden on spouses who themselves may be in their eighties and even nineties. Also, the emotional strain must certainly be enormous for spouses who are witnessing the deterioration of a life-long mate. An obvious concern, therefore, is with relief from the incessant burdens of caregiving, as well as how to obtain supportive services. Also, the caregiving spouse cannot help but ask: "What will happen next?" Most painful is the thought of having to place a mate in a nursing home. Even when others, such as the family physician, say "It's time," the spouse may become quite agitated and upset. It is likely that the wife who is providing care will have feelings such as, "He would never let this happen to me."

The concerns of children include those of caregiving spouses, but because of the absence of the reciprocity of marital relationships, concerns may be rather different. Often, for example, it is the very daughter who has felt most unloved who assumes the burden of caregiving as a means of gaining a feeling of being loved. For this child, caring for a parent often becomes a vehicle of discharging hostility toward siblings, as when the caregiving daughter verbalized to her sister something like, "I care more for Mother than you do." Regardless of whether the caregiver feels herself to be an unloved or a loved daughter, it is often the unstated, or less conscious emotions, that cause difficulty. One such preconscious feeling is generated when the adult child is giving care to a widowed parent, and the thought of losing a second parent (and becoming an orphan) can be very frightening. The cared-for parent represents the patina between the child and his or her Maker. Although not verbalized, preoccupations with one's own death are evoked. Concerns and preoccupations with dying are indeed concerns of caregivers in their middle years.

Who Is the Client?

Working with these families challenges us to determine who is the client. Hopefully, as noted earlier, we do not trade off the good of our elderly clients for the good of their caregivers. But it is never an easy task, especially when the emotional pain associated with caregiving to a deteriorating elderly family member is too much to bear. Because it is too easy to identify with the burden on adult children who are closer in age to the therapist, it is imperative that the therapeutic alliance be primarily with the older person. Jerome Grunes (1987) has recommended that the first interview be only with the elderly person and afterward with family members included. Martin Berezin (1987), however, advocates beginning the therapeutic process by interviewing the older person and family members together because of the more comprehensive portrait of family dynamics that can be obtained. Yet, Rodney Coe (1987), after reviewing the literature on medical encounters between physicians and older people in which family members participated, concluded that collusion between physicians and family members is the norm and diminishes communication with, as well as a sensitivity to, the older patient. One reason for the collusion is the desire of the physician and other health professionals for the patient to comply with the therapeutic regimen. Compliance that leads to passivity and then adverse, and possibly even lethal, consequences will be considered in the next chapter.

CHAPTER 9

In Hospitals and Nursing Homes

The Sampsons have been in the hospital but as of now have not needed nursing home care. They are, however, not unfamiliar with hospitals, discharge planning, and nursing homes; the three topics that are covered here.

Hospital Iatrogenesis

The causes for psychological distress that will be focused on here are classified as iatrogenic. Iatrogenesis refers, in a narrow sense, to deleterious effects induced inadvertently by a physician in the treatment of a patient. The awareness that iatrogenic illness can result from treatment is reflected in the Hippocratic tradition, in which physicians are directed to do no harm, at least to favor good in the balance of good over harm in treatment. Because physicians are not alone in inadvertently doing harm, a broadened definition is used here to encompass effects by health care personnel, in addition to physicians, and also by hospital policies and procedures.

They Gave Me An Infection

At 72 Jack Sampson was hit by a car that shattered his left leg. "I went to get a quart of milk and the Sunday paper on a Saturday night. As I opened the door to get back into the car, he hit me. I was told that the impact lifted me over the hood of my car. I had to feel sorry for the kid who hit me. He was 16, an honor student who only recently got his license. He was driving slowly, but somebody told him to never go over the double yellow line and

he didn't. Instead he banged into me. Wow he really banged me up. They put a steel rod in my leg, and I've never been the same. I feel every change in the weather."

"The first thing I remember in the hospital is seeing a cross on the wall. Where the hell am I? If I was Catholic, I would have guessed sooner that I was in a Catholic hospital. Then I saw my family all around the bed. I was scared. I guess I realized that I was in the hospital, but at first I didn't know why. I felt no pain. They gave me morphine. Slowly it came back to me, what happened. The surgery was good, excellent. My surgeon was a real pro. I recovered fast and was waiting to go home when I get an infection, a urinary infection, an infection of my bladder. So the surgeon saves my life, and they don't take care of the catheter. They overlooked me, to put it politely. My surgeon was mad and a nun, an administrator, apologized to me for what I think they call a sin of omission."

SUSCEPTIBILITY OF THE AGED

Patients of all ages are susceptible to hospital iatrogenesis, but elderly patients are particularly susceptible because of less physiological homeostatic reserve and comorbidity, their multiplicity of illnesses. The presence of many illnesses makes it common for elderly people to be treated with many medications when hospitalized. When one or more physician specialists may prescribe appropriate medications for the conditions being treated, the accumulation and interaction of drugs can indeed cause adverse consequences. A geriatrician, from a medication review, can, however, usually reduce the number of drugs and also substitute drugs that interact with other noninteracting drugs and thereby reduce complications.

Hospital iatrogensis became of interest to me early in my career during my clinical training at Drexel Home for the Aged. Residents of the home who were transferred temporarily to the hospital, even with careful following by the home's medical director, were likely to be returned confused and depressed, and sometimes with needless medication to improve psychological status. Discussions at staff meetings often suggested that residents' confusion or depression was induced by hospital practices. It was not uncommon, for example, for the medical director to comment on how a drug given in too high a dose to one of our hospitalized elderly residents was likely to be responsible for his or her medical complication, a complication that included or led to confusion or depression, or sometimes both. Or the psychiatrist would comment that once again night hospital personnel misinterpreted cyclical sleep patterns and gave medication to induce sleep; but while it helped the patient to sleep, it also caused drowsiness and lethargy throughout the day. Then a member of the nursing department or social services department would tell about the resident who returned from the hospital quite depressed because of how floor personnel acted. Our hospitalized residents frequently reacted strongly to being chided for minor infractions of hospital rules, such as turning the television set on too loud, which was necessary because of impaired hearing. Calling the elegant Mrs. Weiss by her first name, which was taboo in the Drexel Home for the Aged except for her closest of friends, obviously worsened the situation.

A rare exception to considering the topic of iatrogenesis in geriatric medicine texts is the chapter, Iatrogenesis, in *Essentials of Clinical Geriatrics, Second Edition* (Kane, Ouslander, & Abrass, 1989). The chapter begins with a discussion of the narrowing of the therapeutic window with age as a consequence of the decreasing responsivity to therapy and the increasing susceptibility to toxic effects. Although they note that the "therapeutic window is perhaps more easily recognized in the pharmacological treatment of the elderly" (p. 332), they add such common iatrogenic problems as bed rest, enforced dependency, transfer trauma, and overzealous labeling of dementia and incontinence. Labeling is of particular relevancy for psychological effects and is a function of expectations of elderly patients that can indeed be harmful to them.

ATTRIBUTION TO EXISTING MEDICAL CONDITIONS

Despite the many possible causes for iatrogenic psychological effects, investigators have invariably attributed greater complication rates among elderly patients to their initial medical condition. Knight Steele and his associates (Steele, Gertman, Crescenzi, & Anderson, 1981) reported that the increase in complications with age was largely a result of the number of drugs given for medical conditions at admission. Although they looked for psychiatric disturbances from other iatrogenic causes, the search was thwarted because there was inadequate documentation in medical records. Obviously, however, there is an awareness among practitioners that there are many iatrogenic causes for confusion and depression in hospitalizations.

CONFUSION AND DEPRESSION

The causes of confusion and depression, for convenience, can be divided into preadmission and postadmission causes; and, in turn, between physiologic and psychosocial causes. Preadmission physiologic causes include medical status, medications, and nutritional status; and psychosocial causes include the lack of social supports and disruptive meanings of hospitalization. Postadmission physiologic causes include diagnostic tests and procedures, treatments, medications, nutrition, sleep deprivation, immobilization; and psychosocial causes include social dislocation, encompassing depersonalization by staff, physical and emotional isolation, and labeling. Social dislocation to a hospital, however, is more than living in a foreign environment. Beyond the geography and routines being different, the removing of personal belongings augments depersonalization. Then, the wearing of a hospital gown like all other patients and residing in a sterile hospital room can only compound depersonalization. Furthermore, preadmission and postadmission causes may interact when, for example, admission in poor medical status necessitates additional medications while in the hospital, or when a lack of social supports causes a greater preadmission fear of nursing home placement leading to anxiety, agitation, and sleep deprivation after admission.

The most obvious expectations that induce iatrogenicis are anticipations of Alzheimer's disease. Illustrative is a case in which Alzheimer's disease was wrongly diagnosed:

Be a Good Patient

In common with other elderly hospitalized patients, when my Aunt Frieda was hospitalized in California, family members urged her to be a good patient. To Frieda being a good patient was not only to "do what the doctors order" but also not to bother any of the staff with requests or complaints. Initially she was only anxious, but then she also became apathetic and withdrawn. The charge nurse noted this change and suggested to one of the house staff physicians, a first-year resident in internal medicine, to call in a psychiatrist. When my cousin told me a psychiatric consultant had been requested, I immediately called the charge nurse, who told me that my aunt was obviously confused and may have Alzheimer's disease. I responded that it was unlikely that she had Alzheimer's disease because 3 days before, when she was admitted to the hospital, she was oriented to time and place. I then suggested that my aunt had pseudodementia (a false dementia when depressed) because in her apathetic state she was unconcerned about where she was and the time of day or month. I also discussed my fear that a psychiatric resident unfamiliar with the causes for disorientation among elderly hospitalized patients would be too quick to suggest medication that could interact with her other medications. Since her brief admission to the hospital the number of drugs in her polypharmacy had risen at an alarming rate as she began to be seen by a variety of specialists for her diverse ailments.

Also, a sedative would only increase her passivity. I then suggested waiting on the consultation until I could talk to my aunt.

My phone call to her revealed not only her apathy but also her anger, which she was trying valiantly to hide in her determination to be a good patient. She was, however, enraged at her daughter, my cousin, for what she perceived as attempts to control her, at her physician for not being more definitive in his diagnosis and treatment, and at the nurses for making her follow their routines. After I told her that she must speak up and not permit the anger to be bottled up within her, she began to reveal her suppressed anger. Deflecting her anger toward me, she bitterly said, "What do you expect me to do!" She felt impotent, unable to cope with her dreadful situation. I responded that it was her life, and that if she wanted something, it was up to her to speak out. The conversation then abruptly ended when she said, in a voice that was barely audible, that she was too tired to talk.

The following afternoon my cousin called and vilified me for making her mother angry. No longer was mother a good patient! After my cousin's 20 minute tirade, I interjected a question on her mother's behavior. She was now getting out of bed and certainly more oriented in place and time. The conversation ended with my cousin acknowledging these improvements but still bitter regarding my interference.

In this instance, an elderly person was successfully mobilized. As frequently occurs, however, it is not always to the betterment of relations with others. My cousin still recalls how upsetting it was to her when her mother started to be an ornery patient. As discussed in the previous chapter, behaviors that are best for elderly patients may indeed be discomforting to family members. But Frieda is also a classic illustration of how expectations lead to interpreting of behaviors as signs of dementia among elderly hospitalized patients. Her inability to locate herself in time and place was quick to be assessed as Alzheimer's disease when it was actually a result of her depression and thus a pseudodementia. Paradoxically, the charge nurse, who had revealed to me that she was trained in geriatric nursing, believed that she was not only acting correctly but acting more professionally than nurses untrained in geriatric nursing because she was aware that older patients may be suffering from Alzheimer's disease. Calling in a psychiatrist appeared to her to be the best of professional practice. Yet, if the psychiatrist was not sufficiently educated to Alzheimer's disease and additionally chose to intervene vigorously by using potent psychotropic drugs, not only could the drugs lead to iatrogenic effects, but so too could diagnostic procedures employed to rule out all other causes for a presumptive diagnosis of Alzheimer's disease.

Also, unfortunately, not too uncommon is to interpret the confusion in "sundowning" as Alzheimer's disease. Sundowning refers to the rather prevalent confusion in hospitalized patients as evening approaches. The combination of a foreign environment and drowsiness from bedfastness and soporific medication is likely to cause a transient confusion as daylight fades. Although sundowning occurs independent of age, it is more likely to be interpreted as Alzheimer's disease among elderly patients. Again, a quick history can reveal that the confusion is not part of the insidious progressive symptomatology characteristic of Alzheimer's disease. Rather, the patient is suffering from an acute episode that contradicts the diagnosis of Alzheimer's disease.

The foreignness of the environment per se can be a cause for confusion. As a member of a geriatric consultation team at a major teaching hospital, I became familiar with innumerable patients whose confusion was caused by the newness of environment.

If She Were To Wet Her Panties

Mrs. Andrews was found to be wandering in the hall at 2 a.m. and was unsure of where she was. She was extremely agitated but with a few reassuring words became calm. She did not want to return to her room but rather wanted to call her daughter to take her home immediately. With more assurance, she regained her composure, as well as orientation and returned to her bed. In the morning, her daughter confided to the nurse that her mother had gotten up to urinate, but because she did not know the location of toilet, wet herself. An extremely fastidious woman, Mrs. Andrews then became extremely upset with consequent confusion and agitation.

Fortunately for Mrs. Andrews the night nurse recognized the acute quality of the confusion and did not overrespond. The recognition by her that nocturnal urination is common among elderly patients and can, in turn, lead to wetting oneself in a foreign environment was evidenced in a later comment, "Mrs. A. reminds me of my mother. If she were to wet her panties like that, she would even be in worse shape. Whenever she gets anxious, she can't think or doesn't think right. She would think she had Alzheimer's disease." These comments certainly capture the disorganizing force of a foreign environment, as well as the greater disorganization of behavior by anxiety among older persons than among younger persons. An essential cause for Mrs. Andrew's anxiety was her feelings of loss of control. For her, fastidiousness is a way of mastering the world. Wetting herself made her feel that control was lost and not to be regained and, if the night nurse was correct, that now she was suffering from Alzheimer's disease. Fortunately, a perceptive nurse responded calmly and helped Mrs. Andrews to regain her sense of control. Had another nurse with a different response been on the floor, Mrs. Andrew's confusion and agitation may have persisted and led to needless medication with possibly further iatrogenic effects.

DEPRESSION

My Aunt Frieda illustrates the role of depression in fulfilling the expectation that elderly patients who are confused are suffering from dementia. Yet, because Frieda's depression was not expressed in a dramatic form, but rather in apathy and suppressed anger, hospital personnel did not respond to the depression. They are, however, likely to have the erroneous belief that elderly patients suffer more from clinical depression than persons of other ages. But epidemiologic studies have clearly revealed that they have no greater incidence of clinical depression (Blazer, Hughes, & George, 1987; Gurland, Deen, Cross, & Golden, 1980). As with the expectation of Alzheimer's disease, expectations of depression can lead to treatment that can cause iatrogenic effects. To expect that elderly patients will be clinically depressed because of a multiplicity of losses can cause a disregard for obvious reasons for depressions that may be handled without the kinds of interventions that can cause iatrogenic effects.

For example, a rather frequent phenomenon in hospitals that causes overmedication is when the elderly patient is told that "It's time to enter a nursing home." Typical is the case of the elderly female patient who was given medication for her depression and when the depression lifted, success was attributed to the drug:

You Will Not Be Going Home

When Mrs. Carson a widowed lady of 82 with no family, was told shortly after being admitted to the hospital that it was not possible for her to return home, she became depressed, for which she was medicated. Because of unresponsiveness to queries used to assess her mental status, an immediate diagnosis of dementia was made. Fortunately, however, a geriatric nurse surmised that the deterioration was really a pseudodementia, and not a true dementia, because shortly before she became depressed she was perfectly lucid. The nurse, moreover, appreciated the cause for Mrs. Carson's depression was the realization that she would not return home. Yet, the geriatric nurse felt that it was necessary to medicate Mrs. Carson and communicated her feelings to the attending physician.

As Mrs. Carson wrestled with her problem that she had no alternative but to enter a long-term care facility, she began to consider the necessity of a nursing home that would sustain her, that would help her survive. Eventually she decided that the county home, to which a friend had gone, would be suitable for her. With this resolution the depression lifted.

As accomplished by elderly people who adapt best to institutionalization, Mrs. Carson transformed the situation so that the decision to enter a nursing home became her own and, also, the nursing home she chose became an ideal environment for her. She then began to talk about the gains that would accrue from entering the county nursing home. She would make friends and participate in activities. The loss of independence in relinquishing her apartment receded into the background, and she appropriately focused on the impending event.

There was no need to medicate Mrs. Carson. Her medication did not alleviate the depression but, rather, her working through the decision that "It's time . . ." was the cause for its alleviation. What could have helped Mrs. Carson was assistance in transforming the dreaded reality of nursing home placement into an acceptable solution through the use of magical coping. Without this assistance, Mrs. Carson was able to transform the situation to her liking, but she may be one of the few patients able to do so. Others are less fortunate in being unable to transform the situation without professional assistance.

OTHER EXPECTATIONS

Another kind of harmful expectation relates to accepting verbalizations reflecting accommodations to impairments as the absence of impairments. If, for example, very old patients are asked if they have sensory problems, hearing or visual losses, or back pains, they are likely to report no problems. But accommodation to impairments does not mean that problems are not present nor that these problems cannot be treated. Ninety year olds are less likely than 80 year olds to complain of problems, and 80 year olds less likely then 70 year olds. If mobile and lucid, and the self is preserved, complaints are likely to be fewer. Yet accommodation to treatable deficits must be understood, and, whenever possible, deficits remediated. These kinds of omission can also be considered as a kind of iatrogenesis.

A more flagrant kind of iatrogenesis is evident when it is expected that a percentage of elderly patients will suffer from a condition associated with a disease; for example, that among debilitated bedridden patients, pressure sores will occur. To accept any percentage as unavoidable, however, is to dismiss the possibility of preventing pressure sores that may be preventable. The acceptance of debilitating problems among very old patients applies also to psychological status.

I'm Too Old

 The new young medical social worker remarked that people in their seventies are usually depressed. She illustrated her comments with a visibly depressed woman, Mrs. Burke, who had been admitted to the hospital for chronic obs' uctive pulmonary disease. Mrs. Burke, the social worker said, was preoc upied with whether she would be bedridden and would have to go to a nursing home. Although weepy and only able to communicate in a strained, sad voice, Mrs. Burke could be heard to say, "It's come. I can't care for myself. I'm too old." The worker did not recognize that it was her fears of being immobile and possible nursing home placement that evoked the current feelings of becoming old and not her chronologic age. Yet, if Mrs. Burke recovered sufficiently to care for herself at home, a possibly premature transition to becoming "old" may have been reversed. Because treatment was not followed through after discharge, her disposition and later affect status is unknown.

Mrs. Burke, like others, when under the duress of hospitalization, can undergo the transition to becoming old and often, besides being preoccupied with immobility and nursing home placement, become preoccupied with how death will occur. And, like others, when hospitalized patients become melancholic, they are likely to be unable to use the beneficial psychological mechanisms of aggressiveness and blending the present and the past, as well as making the past vivid, to reaffirm the sense of a persistent identity.

Iatrogenic psychological effects are nurtured daily in the hospital. In the *New York Times* on March 23, 1986, there was a review of Theodore Geisel's new book, *You're Only Old Once*. Commenting on his new Dr. Seuss book for adults he said, "I still climb Mount Everest just as often as I used to. I play polo as often as I used to. But to walk down to the hardware store I found a little more difficult. I have a feeling if I stay out of hospitals I may live forever." Geisel then revealed how hospital personnel can indeed be harmful. When being wheeled into the hospital room on a gurney for an eye operation, the attendant pulled out one of Dr. Seuss's books and asked him to autograph it. Geisel commented, "He probably thought it would be the last one I ever gave. It was very flattering, but I wanted to sock him."

Discharge Planning

Costly hospital stays have been reduced by discharging patients as soon as possible. Given iatrogenic effects, this is fine. But now that patients are being discharged "quicker and sicker," more attention must be directed toward discharge planning. This attention has not occurred.

Were We Mad

"When I went in to take care of my diverticulitis," Marilyn Sampson said bitterly, "the other doctor, Dr. Lessor, what a shmo, came by to discharge me. My doctor, my internist, was away at a meeting, so his partner came. He, the other guy, just popped in, told me I was going home and started to tell me, really Jack, what I should do at home. I told Jack to write it all down but before he could get a pencil and a pad the guy was gone. I called Nellie, my doctor's nurse, the next morning for instructions and to tell her how mad I was. Our doctor, Dr. Stein, called when he returned. He takes the time."

Dr. Lessor is not unlike many physicians who spend too little time talking to their elderly patients and also talk to family members rather than directly to older patients. When anxious and with sensory losses, instructions may not register. Talking to family members and not to the patients themselves reduces their role in decision-making for their care, which in turn decreases their sense of control.

IT'S TIME

The Sampsons have fortunately been able to return home after their hospital stays rather than be relocated to a rehabilitation facility or a nursing home. As discussed earlier, sometimes health professionals tell family members that "Its time. Its time to consider a nursing home." before the family wishes to or is prepared to relinquish care. A recommendation to relinquish care to a nursing home must be approached cautiously by health professionals. Families, in turn, must understand that the final decision is theirs, and that the recommendation is only advice and not an order to be followed. Those who give advice, albeit with the best of intentions, may know too little about the family and base their recommendations more on what they would do than on what the family would prefer to do or is capable of doing. Sound hospital care is inseparable from discharge planning, which must begin as soon as possible. Without considerations of after-hospital placement and care, treatment can be misguided:

Shock Him

I was asked by the chief of the in-patient psychiatry unit to consult on a depressed patient in his late seventies who had suffered a psychotic depressive episode 30 years before when he was in his forties. The episode had been

resolved with electric shock therapy. Although I was unaware of my task when I accepted the assignment, I was expected to convince Mr. Lawrence to again accept shock treatments. On the day I was to consult on Mr. Lawrence I was told that he had become even more depressed and now was mute.

After the psychiatric resident presented Mr. Lawrence's history, a marginal person who had minimal attachments to others, we briefly discussed the precipitating events that had led to his current hospitalization on a locked psychiatric unit. Mr. Lawrence had been living alone and because of the inclement weather had not shopped for food and had become increasingly malnourished and dehydrated. A neighbor called the police when she realized she had not seen Mr. Lawrence recently and feared that he had died in his apartment. On entering his apartment, it was apparent that Mr. Lawrence was incoherent. She called the police, who took him to the emergency room where a short conversation between Mr. Lawrence and the psychiatric resident on call led to a psychiatric rather than to an acute medical unit.

When Mr. Lawrence was wheeled into the conference room, I noted that despite a face that was fixed in a depressive demeanor, he raised his eyes slightly to look around the room and for a moment fixed on two young female psychiatric residents who were attending the staff conference. He was wheeled about 2 feet away from me, and I pulled up my chair, gently touched him on his wrist and said something to the effect "It's nice being the center of attention of attractive young ladies." Although it seemed like 5 minutes, he slowly opened his eyes and slightly turned his head to look at me. We then began our conversation. He was aware that he had not been eating properly, and that each day he had told himself he must go out to buy food. He apparently blacked out and awoke very frightened in a cold sweat and disoriented. He was reluctant to discuss the depressive episode 30 years ago, but it was apparent that he feared that once again he would receive shock treatments.

Rather abruptly, his psychiatrist asked if he could talk to the patient, and he too pulled up a chair very close to Mr. Lawrence and asked "Would you be willing to sign the consent form so that we can give you shock treatment?" Immediately Mr. Lawrence's face returned to a taut depressed expression, and he became mute, refusing to continue the conversation. Further questioning did not elicit any answers.

After Mr. Lawrence was wheeled out of the room, the chief of service asked me how we could convince Mr. Lawrence to accept shock treatment. His psychiatrist, however, asked whether I thought shock was necessary. I sidestepped this question because the chief of service was determined to do so, and I responded that I was more concerned with what will happen to Mr. Lawrence after his discharge. A lively discussion then ensued with the social worker who had been thinking about placement. It appeared both to her, and to me, too, that discharge to an adult home where he would feel secure would be sensible, if not ideal, for Mr. Lawrence. All he wished at this time in his life was to be warm in winter and not to be hungry. Even a minimal amount of attention to those basic needs would indeed elicit a very favorable response from Mr. Lawrence.

A focus on discharge placement, rather than on his acceptance of electric shock therapy, would, I believe, have enormously benefitted Mr. Lawrence. Attempts to communicate with him about his aftercare would, that is, probably have elicited some verbal comments, lifting his mutism; and talking to him about placement could have obviated the necessity for shock treatments, a procedure with obvious iatrogenic consequences for Mr. Lawrence, who shudders when he recalls his shock treatments decades earlier.

QUICKER AND SICKER

Nowadays with patients being discharged quicker and sicker, there is, however, too little opportunity to work through placement in a facility. The harassed discharge planner must, for example, tell families that they have almost no time at all to locate a nursing home. As they scramble to find an empty bed, under enormous strain if the elderly patient is on Medicaid (a "non-self-payer") or unable to feed him or herself ("a feeder"), workers are unable to adequately assist residents-to-be for the impending relocations. When, with great relief, a nursing home is found that they can justify as appropriate, relocation occurs swiftly and with increasing frequency, with no warning to the patient.

The Process of Becoming Institutionalized

Morton Lieberman and I have reported on our studies of relocation to institutions in two books (Lieberman & Tobin, 1983; Tobin & Lieberman, 1976). In all, we followed over 600 elderly persons from before to after relocation and included control groups who were not being relocated. Here I shall first discuss our findings on the process of becoming institutionalized, including the preadmission redefinition of self, the postadmission first month syndrome, and then the reestablishment of self. Next, findings on the prediction of vulnerability to institutionalization will be covered.

REDEFINING OF ONESELF BEFORE ADMISSION

As noted previously, the message that "It's time to go to a nursing home" evokes a painful and distressing change in self-concept. The resident-to-be has become what has been feared. That is, before placement is considered, the best nursing homes are perceived as assuring survival when no other alternatives are available. The underlying feeling, however, is often that going to a nursing home is to be abandoned to a "death house". Then, when "It's time," the metamorphosis occurs to becoming the kind of person that has been dreaded. Residents-to-be who successfully deal with the inner experience of being abandoned while awaiting admission to nursing homes focus on anticipations of physical care, security, and activities and also use magical mastery, transforming the nursing home into an environment that is closer to the ideal and convincing themselves that the relocation is of their own choosing.

THE FIRST MONTH SYNDROME

Shortly after admission, there is an inevitable adverse response to the relocation. Entering and living in a the foreign environment of a nursing home is associated with what Jerome Grunes has labeled "the first month syndrome." Unless psychotic, the newly admitted resident will manifest behavioral changes. Some become quite disorganized, others become extremely depressed, and still others become both disorganized and depressed.

AFTER THE FIRST MONTH

After the first month syndrome, most residents of nursing homes of good psychosocial quality are able to reestablish their conception of self. Indeed, our data suggested great stability in the self from before to 2 months after admission because by 2 months after admission, portraits of the self approximated portraits before admission. Adverse changes to 2 months after admission in the *Last Home for the Aged* study were limited to more hopelessness (less optimism about the future but not more clinical depression nor less life satisfaction); an increase in bodily preoccupation and a perception of less capacity for self care, suggesting the adoption of the role of patient among other old sick people; and a lessening of feelings of affiliation with others, reflecting, apparently, an experience not unlike sibling rivalry with other residents.

Concurrently, there was an amelioration of the feelings of being abandoned by family. Indeed, the tendency was toward mythicizing of living children, particularly in reminiscent data, which is an exaggerated expression of the age-associated process of mythicizing significant figures from the past. Although a child may still be alive and a frequent visitor, the increased psychological distance created by institutionalization and the need to preserve the self in the face of institutional demands may cause an exaggeration in the mythicizing of this adult child. The exaggerated response is likely to be reinforced by the institutional environment, where the coin of the realm is famous offspring who are attentive and caring, and where family attention provides leverages for personal prestige and, also, for more attentive staff caring.

THE LATENT LEVEL

Although entering and living in the best of nursing homes was not associated with changes that would support belief in the "destructiveness of institutions," the shift at the more latent less conscious level was not, however, as modest as the manifest changes in psychological status. The earliest memories revealed a significant shift from abandonment toward the introduction of themes of mutilation and death. This shift in recollections sometimes occurred when the same incident was reported at both times:

She Had Hair Like Braids

 Before admission Mrs. Wagner offered the following earliest memory: "I remember my mother. She had hair like braids, open and falling upon her shoulder. She was sitting up in her bed and near her on her table was a bottle of honey and I remember asking her for honey. That's all I remember— nothing before and nothing behind. I still can see her sitting in bed. I must have been 2 years, 2 or 3. Closer to 2, I guess. But that's a picture I have." After admission she recalled: "I remember my mother's death. I remember at least one moment of it. She had honey on her bed and I wanted some of that honey. I didn't really understand that she was dying. I was almost 3 years old. That's all I remember. I can see her face clearly even now. She had two braids hanging down. This picture is all I remember of her."

The contrast between the two memories suggests that a breakthrough of repression had occurred in which previously withheld, archaic material was now being expressed. It would appear that in the first report, the pain of mother's death is defended against, but it breaks through in the second telling of the same incident. In the reconstruction of the same incident at both times, there is a central theme of oral deprivation (i. e., wanting but not getting the honey), as well as the personally meaningful symbolism of mother's braids.

More often, however, the increase in loss when becoming institutionalized was associated with a shift in incidents, as in the following example of the repeat earliest memory.

From Swimming to Coffins

When on the waiting list, Mrs. Rosen said, "I liked to go swimming and mother wouldn't let me. Once I stood on the pier and fell in. I remember how they took me out and took me to my mother. That's all I remember. I wasn't sick." And after admission: "Didn't have coffins in the old country like they do here. My father died. I remember my sister was still a breast baby. . . . It was a cold day. My mother said don't go. But he was a stubborn man, and so he got pneumonia and died."

Contrasts with thematic changes in the control groups suggest that one-third would not have shifted to these themes of more narcissistic loss had they not entered the homes. The shift is, apparently, specifically related to entering and living in the homes, and to living in a total institutional environment with sick elderly people in a home that is to be the last one. With such a significant shift, from abandonment to increased vulnerability, it was indeed surprising that so little change was observed in psychological status. Most likely the ability to successfully contain, to defend against, the latent meanings is a function of entering the best of contemporary long-term care facilities. Yet even these facilities exact their toll, as reflected in the latent meaning of institutional life itself, in the adoption of the patient role, in a lessening of futurity, and in portraying oneself as less willing to be close to others.

BY THE END OF 1 YEAR

By the end of 1 year postadmission, more than one half of the sample had either died or had extremely deteriorated. Those able to be interviewed again showed only a lessening of affiliation in relation to others and a lessening of body preoccupation. All other measures did not show a change. This pattern of stability with only focal changes in affiliation and body preoccupation among the intact survivors masks the global outcomes: 41 of the 85 elderly people who were relocated had died or had become extremely deteriorated. To what extent these 41 would have shown these outcomes had they not entered and lived in the nursing homes is impossible to know.

PREDICTORS OF VULNERABILITY TO THE STRESS
OF INSTITUTIONALIZATION

Assessments of the possible psychological predictors of morbidity and mortality were made while on waiting lists preceding admission. Measures were sorted out into nine dimensions that have either been explicitly discussed as, or inferred to be, predictors of outcome to stress: functional capacities, affects, hope, the self-system, personality traits, reminiscence, coping with the impending event, interpersonal relations, and accumulated stress. The two outcome groups (the intact survivors and the nonintact) were then contrasted on these measures, and simultaneously, the corresponding two outcome groups were contrasted for the two control samples. Thus, any measure that differentiated, or predicted, for the sample that underwent the stress of institutionalization and also predicted for the sample not undergoing this stress could not be a predictor of vulnerability to the stress of institutionalization but, rather, would be a characteristic associated with survival. Stated another way, if a measure only predicted for the sample undergoing stress could the attribute being measured be considered a sensitizer to the stress of institutionalization and not associated with survival per se.

Measures in several dimensions were associated with survival: function capacities, affects, hope, self-system, coping, and interpersonal relations. But only one dimension was a sensitizer to the stress of institutionalization: Passivity was associated with morbidity and mortality among those entering the homes but not with morbidity and mortality for those in stable environments.

A dimension that was not relevant for control samples was coping with the impending event of institutionalization. When residents on the waiting list were assessed, however, for how they were mastering the impending event of institutionalization, it was found that those who transformed the situation so as to make the move totally voluntary and also to perceive the relocation environment as ideal were those most likely to survive intact through 1 year following admission. This kind of magical coping (as well as aggressiveness and hopefulness) was found to enhance adaptation in three additional relocation situations, which are described in the Lieberman and Tobin 1983 book *The Experience of Old Age*.

THE QUALITY OF ENVIRONMENTS

Not unexpectedly, the quality of the psychosocial environment also predicted outcomes. This was most clear in our fourth study, the *en masse* relocation of 427 state mental hospital patients to 142 nursing and boarding homes. The relocated group of 427 had a death rate 1 year after relocation of 18%, and the carefully matched control group of 100 who were not relocated had a death rate in the same interval of only 6%. Those who remained alive following the relocation were likely to have entered facilities of good psychosocial quality.

To be specific, the beneficial psychosocial qualities were, first, warmth expressed in interpersonal relations between residents and staff and, also, between residents; second, activities and other forms of stimulation that are perceived and interacted with; third, tolerance for deviancies such as aggression, drinking, wandering, complaining, and incontinence; and forth, and lastly, individuation defined as the extent to which residents are perceived and treated as individuals in being allowed and encouraged to express individuality. It is a pattern of qualities that reflect the acceptance of aggressiveness, magical coping, mythmaking in reminiscence, and certainly the preservation of self.

CONTROL IN NURSING HOME ADAPTATION

Among the personal characteristics fostered by the survival-enhancing environments is a sense of control, a construct that has been introduced throughout this volume, for example, in the previous chapter when discussing autonomy and self-determination. The most impressive studies of control in nursing home adaptation have been carried out by Judith Rodin and Ellen Langer (1977). Experimental group participants were encouraged to make decisions for themselves. Langer wrote in her 1987 book *Mindfullness*:

> Those in the experimental group were emphatically encouraged to make more decision for themselves. We tried to come up with decisions that mattered and at the same time would not disturb the staff. For example, these residents were asked to choose where to receive visitors: inside the home or outdoors, in their rooms, in the dining room, in the lounge, and so on. They were also told that a movie would be shown the next week on Thursday and Friday and that they should decide whether they wanted to see it and, if so, when. In addition to choices of this sort, residents in the experimental group were each given a house-plant to care for. They were to choose when and how much to water the

plants, whether to put them in the window or to shield them from too much sun, and so forth. (p. 82)

Effects were dramatic. Three weeks after the experiment ended, residents in the experimental group participated more in activities, were happier, and were more alert. Eighteen months later, 30% of the residents in the comparison group had died but only 15% in the experimental group. Not unexpectedly, the relationship that was found between control and survival for nursing home residents mirrors our finding of how aggression and magical coping are associated with intact survivorship for those entering homes: Clearly, what is lethal for the very old is passivity and the lack of a sense of control, of autonomy, and of mastery.

Thus, residents-to-be must not, if at all possible, be permitted to be passive and without control. In discharge, planning when in the process of relocation to a nursing home, residents-to-be must be encouraged to participate in decision-making on their own behalf and even if unrealistic, to believe they are in control.

At admission, staff must determine how best to structure the new resident's institutional life to enhance control. At Drexel Home for the Aged an initial treatment plan was developed based on the resident's characteristic way of coping and how the self is preserved. Over the years, we became rather creative. One example was providing the newly admitted paranoid resident with a roommate who was a "paranee", someone whose sense of self includes being critical of others. In turn, whenever a resident could be placed with a roommate who needed to nurture a more dependent partner, the marriage was made. We were not, however, always successful. Jerome Hammerman, a director of the Home, liked to tell the story of a new resident, a gentle and soft-spoken man, who timidly asked if he could talk to him for a few minutes. "Mr. Hammerman," he said, "you know you might have a nice home here, but how can you give an old man like me a man to live with. I only lived with a woman, my wife, for over 60 years."

Assuring successful passage through the phase of the 1st month syndrome can often be difficult. Adverse effects must be acknowledged. Indeed my test of an inadequate (or, if you will, lying) administrator is to ask how residents adjust initially. If the response is "They do fine," I become suspicious. Confusion and depression is to be expected initially, but by the end of 1 month or so, with assistance from staff, the resident can be expected to reestablish a sense of self-sameness, albeit with underlying feelings of being a patient among the old, sick people and being closer to death. Still, these underlying feelings can be readily contained by a sense of control, as is the case in nursing homes with high quality psychosocial environments. Some ways to promote these kinds of institutional environments will be covered next.

The Facilitory Environment

Some of the basic principles for developing nursing home environments that facilitate adaptation have been provided by Jacqueline Edelson and Walter Lyons in the introduction to their excellent book *Institutional Care of the Mentally Impaired Elderly* (1985). They begin by admonishing the reader not to confuse mental disease with treatable "excess disability." Expectations, for example, can too easily cause staff to discourage use of residual capacities of residents of their facilities who have organic brain damage. Many years ago, Elaine Brody and her associates (Brody, Kleban, Lawton, & Silverman, 1971) found that excess disabilities could be reduced or eliminated in an institutional setting among the more aggressive residents:

> The fact remains that certain personality characteristics described with the "aggression factor" were strongly predictive of the treatment potential of these individuals. . . . Aggressive, stubborn, nonconforming individuals elicit negative reactions from others and therefore tend to be regarded as maladjusted; difficult, and inflexible. They may be viewed as unpleasant, undisciplined children in the conscious and unconscious attitudes of the staff. They may be all these things, but our data suggest very clearly that within this aggressive behavior is a force for self improvement. . . . It may be these "fighters" who become management problems rather than yield to a structured environment. They, rather than the "adjusted" people improved when direction and means of implementation were given to help them to retrieve functions that had been important in previous years. (p. 139)

Unless the more passive elderly individuals become aggressive, even the best of therapeutic intentions and interventions may fail. Note that the factor of "aggressiveness" that was associated with therapeutic success was not simple mobilization, or nonpassivity, but rather a kind of determined nastiness that usually alienates others. Indeed, it is precisely this kind of aggressiveness that we found insulates the very old from the deleterious effects of stress.

Edelson and Lyons (1985) wrote that care must be provided "that is rehabilitative whenever possible, prosthetic whenever necessary, and at all times humane, identity-preserving, and ego-supporting" (p. xix). Identity-preserving is the same as preservation of the self and, of interest, is that in their next chapter, Edelson and Lyons explain how promoting mastery is the essence of ego-supporting efforts using Goldfarb's formulation of inflating beliefs in mastery.

Next Edelson and Lyons, from their many years of experience at the Baycrest Geriatric Center in Toronto, note that "institutional arrangements that support direct care staff in establishing a supportive relationship with impaired residents focuses attention on how interdisciplinary teams work" (p. xxi). Thus individual mental health practitioners, separately or as members of teams, can best be used to structure ongoing supportive relationships between staff and individual residents.

Finally, they state: "As changes are made to meet the needs of the mentally impaired elderly, there will be resistance to change" (p. xxii). The obvious challenge to professionals is to facilitate change, but a paradox is that facilities must be assisted in changing so that they become settings where identities are not changed. Fortunately, mental health professionals are precisely those professionals who know only too well how hard it is to reduce resistance to change but, also, at the same time, know how to reduce the resistance.

An institutional orientation to enhancing residents' functioning must penetrate interactions between residents and staff at all levels. Such penetrations occur through staff's understanding of residents' behavior, but there are many barriers that must be overcome if there is to be accurate appraisals of behaviors, particularly of demented residents. Staff, like family, find it difficult to understand how seemingly pathologic processes are actually functional. Aggressiveness, nastiness, and even paranoid behaviors can, as has been shown, facilitate for adaptation to stress. Staff must learn to understand, tolerate, and even nurture verbally abusive aggressive and paranoid behaviors directed at them by residents. Obviously this is a difficult task, a task too difficult for some staff. It is also a task that is not assumed by staff in many facilities where even the most minor of deviations from ideal compliance and gratefulness are not tolerated.

TOLERATING DEVIANCY

An illustration of intolerance of the nonideal resident was provided by a graduate social work student who selected to write about, for an assignment in a course on psychopathology, a 67-year-old woman who resided in a nursing home. The student, in his fifties, a minister whose newly self-appointed ministry was to work with, and for, elderly people, prepared an excellent case report.

"A Histrionic"

 Mrs. Green, who was in the nursing home recovering from a stroke, was always self-centered and impulsive. She had, for example, abandoned two children, one with each of two husbands that she left. A third husband had died within the past 2 years. The student voiced his concern that Mrs. Green was labeled by the professional staff as "a histrionic who is always manipulating and demanding." His concern was that staff members were vilifying this lady rather than providing her with the care and attention she needed for her recovery. When I asked the student to describe Mrs. Green as a person, he became flustered and responded that she is self-centered, but then added that "That is no reason to treat her so badly." "So, "I asked "is the judgment of the staff wrong?" He was unwilling to accept, at this time, that there was agreement in the diagnosis and continued to focus on her bad treatment. After returning to Mrs. Green in the next three class sessions, it became apparent that the diagnosis was correct, and that Mrs. Green was neither an admirable woman nor particularly likeable. Moreover, he began to realize that the task of the staff, and especially his task because he was now Mrs. Green's caseworker, was to help her in being who she is. It was not love she needed, and indeed he could not love her, but he could help her to retain her persistent self-centered identity. As he became more open in discussing his feelings with his supervisor, it became apparent to him that although she, too, disliked Mrs. Green, she was able to accept Mrs.Green for the person she is and, also, to assist staff to do the same.

In this instance, some staff were sufficiently professional and mature to accept Mrs. Green's distasteful behavior. It would have been more difficult if Mrs. Green was verbally abusive rather than self-aggrandizing and demanding of attention. Similarly, staff must learn that magical thinking of residents can also be functional for adaptation and survival.

UNDERSTANDING MEANINGS OF BEHAVIOR

Yet entry-level staff cannot begin to understand the meanings of these seemingly pathologic behaviors unless senior professionals do. Professionals however, can too easily interpret facilitatory processes as psychopathologic if they use models developed for younger persons. We are taught that "good coping necessitates realistic appraisals" of one's capacities, and that abusive behavior toward others reflects "bad object relations." Although such generalizations may generally be correct, they may be completely wrong when applied to very old persons, particularly when they are under duress.

Staff must learn that bizarre behaviors often have meanings related to the striving for preservation of self. Once this principle is understood it becomes increasingly possible to see continuity between bizarre behavior and premorbid personality traits. In turn, as the bizarre behaviors become intelligible, staff can tolerate, or even encourage, seemingly aberrant behaviors that help the patient be him or herself.

A poignant example occurred at Drexel Home for the Aged when a social work trainee wished to change the fondling behavior of Mrs. Lewis, a quite confused female resident.

Why the Fondling?

A confused resident, Mrs. Lewis, was fondling the breasts and genitalia of other women, which was particularly offensive to staff members. Psychiatrist Grunes had explained to select staff members that Mrs. Lewis' fondling was a reflection of the relationship with her deceased husband. Her daughter had related how her parents were such a loving couple that they always held hands and were constantly touching and gently petting each other. Mrs. Lewis was actually rather terrified of men and thus sought out women to replace her lost and needed tactile contact. Grunes' approach was to let her form a tactile relationship with a self-centered woman who appreciated Mrs. Lewis' attention and to confine the fondling, as much as possible, to secluded areas in the facility. Had the fondling behavior been extinguished, it was believed, Mrs. Lewis' deterioration would have rapidly accelerated.

Interventions must not be targeted on behaviors that preserve the self, but, rather, behaviors that diminish the self must be targeted for change. For reinforcement to be effective, procedures must be incorporated into the service plan and be part of everyday routines. Implementation must be by staff who, whether as members of nursing, occupational therapy, or social service departments, assure the creation of a sustaining environment for each resident. It is not easy to be objective. They have, as Rose Dobrof (1983) has noted, good reasons for feeling angry, helpless and demoralized, frustrated, and even betrayed. Feelings of anger toward residents are reflected in comments such as "How can he say these things to me? After all I have done for him?" Anger toward the family may be justified in a comment such as "Don't they even care about that old man? He probably just sits there like that because they never visit him." Thoughts about the other staff members and supervisors include "They leave all the dirty work for me. Nobody ever shows any appreciation around here." Feelings of helplessness and demoralization are reflected in "It doesn't seem to matter what we do, they never get any better." Should not the aide feel frustrated when saying "I must have explained that to her six times already." The terrible feeling of betrayal is captured by the comment." After everything I have done for her, she doesn't even know who I am." There is obviously no easy way to reduce these painful feelings. Necessary, however, is to provide a sense of efficacy to the hands-on staff.

FAMILY VISITING TO MENTALLY IMPAIRED RESIDENTS

The best of homes always encourage family visiting. With many homes, however, as the residential population becomes more impaired mentally, there is a tendency for lessened visiting of family members. Attempts to maintain visiting patterns through family groups, such as family members of new residents, keep families involved in the home. Yet, as Florence Safford (1980) found, members of families of more confused residents participate in these groups but do not necessarily visit either the floor of their resident family members or the resident. In withdrawing from interaction with deteriorating residents, some family members simply deny that their visiting has lessened, while others become terribly upset with themselves and their inability to tolerate the deterioration, and still others vociferously blame the home for causing the deterioration. Common to families is displacing the anger toward themselves and toward the resident onto the home.

The extreme pain in passively watching the deterioration of a loved one is quite evident. As noted earlier, families welcomed relief from their psychological pain through being encouraged not to visit. Occasionally, of course, family members should not be encouraged to visit if it is too upsetting to them or to the resident. Surely, however, a general discouragement of family visiting can provide great relief to families but certainly is dysfunctional for residents in reducing the maintenance of their identities and diminishing the perception of their uniqueness by staff. Thus, a task is to develop an approach to families that encourages their presence on residents' floors and, also, encourages face-to-face contact with even the most intractably confused family member.

VISITING AND HELPFUL TO MOURNING

Another kind of observation is important to developing a structural approach. That is, those family members who continued to visit a slowly deteriorating resident until the time of death are less likely to have a protracted mourning process following the death of the resident. These family members, however, are not without feelings of inadequacy and rage during stages of deterioration. Thus, the approach must allow for displaced rage that we know can be beneficial for family members. It is better than rage turned inward causing heightened depression and certainly better than rage expressed toward the resident.

Fostering Family Involvement

Family members can indeed be annoying and disruptive to care but their visiting is the *sine qua non* of good institutional care. Elsewhere I (Tobin, 1995) have discussed five interventions designed to foster family involvement in institutional care: Reducing apprehension and anxiety of family members; face-to-face visiting that enhances the sense of self of residents, particularly of Alzheimer's disease victims; sharing by family members in the caring for residents; facilitating cooperation and interdependence between family members and nursing assistants; and furthering an identification with the facility as a caring community. A variety of interventions are appropriate for meeting these objectives, including family counseling, family support groups, educational programs for family members, and fundamental changes regarding institutional staff and policy.

REDUCING FAMILY APPREHENSION

Perhaps the easiest and quickest way to reduce apprehension by family members is for administrators to say to them: "We give the best of care here, so you don't have to visit so much." Although their apprehension may be reduced if such simple-minded advice is followed, it will surely also result in harm to the institutionalized elderly relative. Unfortunately, this kind of advice is given too often, as the following example reveals.

A Good Business

I was asked to discuss my work on institutionalization at the annual meeting of a state proprietary nursing home association. My talk, and the discussion thereafter, seemed to reflect an acceptance by the administrators of the need for family involvement. But then at lunch a cheerful man dressed in an expensive, well-tailored suit who owned several rural nursing homes said, "Let me tell you about families. I've been in the undertaker business all my life, and what they want is for me to take over. You get them all upset if you involve them too much. I tell them I treat every resident like one of my own family, and I tell my people to tell them that we are doing God's work and to let us do His work."

By not visiting, families avoid perceiving that their elder is "just another resident" whose uniqueness is easily overlooked by staff who are more oriented toward organizational efficiency than individualized care. Not visiting also permits family members to avoid witnessing the physical and mental deterioration of their loved one. These benefits to family members do not offset the potential harm to the elderly resident, who is left without meaningful family interaction.

What are institutions for these elderly patients doing to resolve this apparent dilemma? Rhonda Montgomery (1982, 1983) systematically examined staff-family relationships and nursing home policies. She reported subtle but noticeable differences in how policies create expectations of families. Some homes have no expectations of families, considering them outsiders, "visitors"; others view families as "servants" who should be available to assist in providing care to residents and when they do not do so, as neglectful; and still others perceive families as "clients" with whom the staff should spend time.

When families are viewed as clients, programs are developed to incorporate them into the life of the home, thereby reducing their apprehension. This process usually begins before admission by encouraging familiarity with the home through written materials and visiting and sometimes by having family members meet in groups. As evidenced by the following example, the content of such groups can become quite threatening to the home's staff and administration.

A Family Upset

A new resident family members group was developed at Drexel Home for the Aged, led by the newly hired director of social services. After a meeting of one of these groups, the director sought me out for my advice in my role as a consulting clinical psychologist to the home. A recently admitted resident had told her son that her roommate chided her for leaving her watch on

the bureau because it was likely to be stolen. Thievery became the topic of discussion at the family members group, and the more the director mini-mized the problem, the more angry the group became. One daughter even threatened to take her father out of the home. How to be honest about thiev-ery and other problems without upsetting new family members became the content of the consultation.

After admission, families can continue to meet together in, for example, family support groups, family councils, programs that train families how to communicate to their residents who have dementia, and group counseling sessions. Individual formal and informal coun-seling of family members is also essential for maintaining involve-ment, assuring comfort, and alleviating apprehension.

We must not, however, overlook the fact that the more family members visit and become a part of the home, the more likely it is that their caregiving burden will continue. Effective programs to reduce apprehension require viewing each family individually, particularly with respect to the family member's perceived burden. Each family, for example, brings its own unique, well-established, and persistent style of family interaction to the nursing home visit. Particularly destructive can be visits by a middle-aged daughter who has a long-term symbiotic relationship with her institutionalized mother. It is not uncommon for such a daughter to have been the primary caregiver at home before admission, having taken on this role to obtain the love from her mother that she feels has been denied her. At Drexel Home for the Aged, for example, we often had to discourage these daughters from visiting because of their sometimes not so hidden abusive verbal behavior toward their mothers.

Family visitors must be assured that their visits to resident rel-atives in the home make a difference. Otherwise, like my friend Joan in the following example, they may have doubts.

Making a Difference

 Joan visited her mother at Drexel Home for the Aged almost every day, watching her mother's slow, progressive deterioration from Alzheimer's dis-ease. Whenever I socialized with Joan, she would tell me about her mother's worsening condition and how hard it was for her to visit. She questioned whether the visits were doing any good. I stopped by one day to see her mother and chatted with a lovely nursing assistant. The assistant verified that Joan's mother sometimes did not recognize her during a visit; but a few hours after the visit, the mother was "bursting" to tell the nursing assistant that her daughter had been to see her.

Mothers may not recognize their daughters or may think their daughters are their mothers, but it is not unusual for mothers to later tell staff persons that their daughters visited them. Family members must be told so and assured that visits are important to confused, as well as nonconfused, residents.

Florence Safford (1980) found, as we did at Drexel Home for the Aged, that the amount of time spent with a resident whose cognitive functioning is deteriorating may lessen, but total time spent in the home remains about the same, with family members using the time to visit other residents. Visits to residents without family are particularly helpful.

Given the extent of senile dementia among nursing home residents, educating family members to communicate with residents becomes important for successful visits, Irene Burnside (1981), a nurse with experience in long-term care settings, has discussed "bedside" helper techniques in communicating with residents who have senile dementia. These techniques include reinforcing reality, using touch, supporting denial if it is therapeutic, and helping to express feelings. As the first step, it is critical that staff are educated to these techniques so that they, in turn, can educate families.

FAMILY SHARING IN CARING

Nursing homes can go beyond reducing family apprehensions and assisting good visits by developing ways that family members share in care with staff. However, role expectations need to be made clear. The task of encouraging others to visit the elderly resident, for example, was perceived in one study (Schwartz & Vogel, 1990) by families to be their unique responsibility. Staff, on the other hand, perceived this as a task that they shared with families. This kind of discrepancy can and should be easily corrected by discussions with families.

More important, family members should be included in initial and follow-up treatment planning and then be active in delivery of care. It is most crucial for family members to provide biographic information to be used for individualizing care. Mary Pietrukowicz and Mitzi Johnson (1991), for example, used such information to develop short vignettes of residents for nursing assistants, which increased the assistants' individualizing of residents. Biographic data are also useful to professional staff so that they can understand the meanings of behavior, particularly bizarre behaviors that have meanings related to the striving for preservation of self. Sound biographic information makes it possible to see the continuity between bizarre postmorbid and premorbid personality traits and behaviors. When bizarre behavior becomes intelligible, family and staff can tolerate, or even encourage, seemingly aberrant behavior that helps the resident be herself or himself.

Families can also be very helpful in either advising or assisting staff regarding their elder's activities of daily living. Bathing may be particularly stressful for residents, especially those who are paranoid or have dementia and particularly dementia victims who are paranoid. Family members can advise on bathing habits, on preferences for baths or showers, on time of day their relatives usually bathed, and on other routines. In addition, if welcomed and encouraged, they can be present at baths for soothing or actual assistance.

But family members must make their own decisions regarding how to participate in the sharing of care. Some may not wish to be involved; others desire too much involvement. The right balance can only occur through discussions and participation. On dementia units, involvement often takes the form of participating in activities.

FACILITATING FAMILY STAFF INTERACTION

A first step in facilitating interaction between family members and nursing home staff is to promote a mutual understanding and respect for the life experiences and social (especially family) context of both groups. In view of the fact that nursing assistants are the primary caregivers in nursing homes, the present discussion focuses on this particular group of staff. It is impossible to develop a "home" unless underpaid and often unappreciated nursing assistants are themselves individualized and are not only insulated from disrespect and verbal abuse by families, but become praised by families for their care to relatives. Families must learn how to relate to nursing assistants so that the latter feel rewarded and replenished rather than victimized and exhausted, feelings they already know all too well. Because they are usually underpaid and overworked, it is common to have a 100% turnover in nursing assistants each year. Even in better nursing homes, it seems that only half of the nursing assistants remain as employees for many years, while the other half turns over about twice each year. Those nursing assistants who do remain for many years must be relied on not only for beneficial care to residents but also to indoctrinate newly hired nursing assistants. It is important for family members to appreciate that nursing assistants, regardless of their tenure in the facility, are likely to live near or below poverty level and have personal problems related to limited economic resources (Tellis-Nayak & Tellis-Nayak, 1989). Given their personal lives and their onerous work as nursing assistants, they have good reasons for feeling demoralized, helpless, and angry. These kinds of negative feelings at work, together with frustrations at home in their personal lives, can lead to abusive behaviors toward residents. Indeed, maltreatment of residents by nursing assistants is apparently quite widespread (Pillemer & Moore, 1989).

Encouraging and exacerbating such abuse are vituperous, direct criticisms by family members of nursing assistants for dereliction in care of their relatives. Unfortunately, nursing assistants are often discouraged from talking to family members and may even be castigated for spending too much time on emotional work with residents. Given that residents come in sicker and more confused, the pressures are to complete work efficiently and quickly even when confronted by abuse from confused residents and racial slurs that are ubiquitous in those homes in which the assistants are Black or Hispanic women and the residents are White.

Family members who are unaware of these circumstances are likely to excoriate assistants when the root problem is actually the bureaucratic organization of contemporary facilities. To counteract the propensity to respond to "bureaucratic demands by narrowly focusing on 'crud' work," nursing assistants must be allowed and encouraged to do emotional work with residents, and they also must be insulated from unwarranted criticisms by family members.

SPLITTING THE INSTITUTIONAL TRANSFERENCE

Abuse by and toward nursing assistants can also be reduced by prevention programs and by creating a rewarding workplace milieu. One approach we took at Drexel Home for the Aged was to insinuate a staff person between families and nursing assistants to reduce unwittingly critical comments and sometimes quite abrasive outbursts directed toward nursing assistants. Guiding our approach was the awareness of how families develop an institutional relationship, or transference, that includes both positive and negative projections. In this sense, the nursing home is perceived by family members as both the life-sustaining, all-giving other and the life-impeding other. Families consider the latter to be the cause of present as well as subsequent deterioration in their elderly relative.

To make this institutional transference useful for the resident, we deliberately encouraged a "split transference," whereby a unit worker became the all-giving, all-loving other, and administrative personnel became the life-impeding others. Hiring unit workers was indeed a careful process in which persons were sought who were genuinely altruistic and giving individuals. This was to ensure that family members would feel more comfortable and confident in discussing concrete needs of the resident with the unit workers than with the nursing assistants.

An example of how this split-transference benefitted all those concerned is revealed by one situation. A family became extremely upset when their elderly relative's tattered but cherished sweater mysteriously disappeared. Although the sweater was very likely misplaced by the confused resident or accidently lost in the laundry process, the family insisted that it was stolen by a nursing assistant. The all-loving unit worker assured the family that "every possible means was being taken to recover the sweater." The family's sense of personal inadequacy and guilt thus was partially alleviated through projection onto the unit worker of feelings and actions of unconditional caring and loving for the family member in the home. This transference also permitted the family to relate to the nursing assistant without an angry outburst.

As noted earlier, one price to be paid for encouraging family involvement in nursing home care is the family's awareness that their relative is only one of many sick and deteriorating elderly people for whom the home is providing care. To offset this family disillusionment, the unit worker's purpose was to enhance fantasies of the home's special concern and caring. The worker thus became perceived as different from all other workers in the home because of her or his special interest in the family member.

Many families explained the worker's special interest, concern, and care by thoughts such as "Mama, after all, is a special person," even when mama was actually only a shell of her former self and not very lucid. These kinds of thoughts echoed the concurrent rationalization by daughters and sons that "I am a special person because of all I have done for Mama." In turn, as the unit workers became perceived as an extension of self, they became more like a family member who is believed to provide attention and caring out of unconditional love and certainly not because it is paid employment. Indeed, for some family members, although the unit worker became the perfect child while the daughter saw herself as the imperfect one, there was nevertheless a sense of satisfaction that the elderly relative's needs were being met with tender loving care.

Underlying rage from anger toward oneself for abandoning the elderly relative and toward the relative for provoking feelings of inadequacy, shame, and guilt were displaced onto the home and may have even diminished. However, these feelings were not completely extinguished. The unit workers assisted in containing the rage through actions and also through explanations regarding how good the home truly was. Yet can the displaced rage ever subside completely, having been generated by anger toward oneself for abandoning the elderly relative and toward the elder for evoking feeling of inadequacy, shame, and guilt? The rage was purposefully redirected away from the all-loving and all-caring unit worker and toward an authority figure: the charge nurse, the chief of social service, the associate director, or the executive director, who became the bad other causing all their woes.

The main point to be made is that rage must be deflected from nursing assistants and toward authority figures. One kind of covert feeling regarding these authority figures is that "If they only cared enough, they would make her well again." Such projections often took the form of irrational tirades, particularly when a symbiotic relationship existed between daughter and mother. If the professional judgment is that interaction between daughter and mother is helpful for the maintenance of the mother's sense of self-identity, then such verbal abuse of staff becomes more tolerable. The staff can learn to understand and to appreciate that the irrational abuse is an expression of the daughter's internal state, expression of her own fear of personal dissolution when observing deterioration in her mother. This is not an easy task. It can only be accomplished by staff who are supported and nourished by administration so that they can withstand personal abuse.

AFTER THE RESIDENT'S DEATH

All the efforts noted previously enhance the family's identification with the facility while the elderly relative is still alive. Although often overlooked, it is also important to assist families in maintaining connectedness with the home after the resident's death. A resolution of the mourning process can be facilitated, for example, by becoming a volunteer. At Drexel Home for the Aged we encouraged families to become members of the Friends of Drexel Home, which raised funds for special programs. Volunteers are often individuals who choose to volunteer in a long-term care home because of their past relationships with deceased parents or a dead husband or a wife. By giving to the home and to residents in the home, they can retain emotional connectedness with family members who are no longer alive. Especially for those volunteers who institutionalized a now dead parent or spouse, residual feelings of having abandoned their family member to a facility can become lessened. Often at Drexel Home for the Aged we asked volunteers to visit a resident who had no family visitors, to give the volunteer a special feeling of being like a family member to an isolated, abandoned resident.

Yet, it must be noted that nursing homes will not be successful in meeting the needs of residents and their families unless reimbursement formulas for care provide more resources for creating a home. Currently almost all costs are for medical care, for the hospital component, and for essential hotel functions. Without the necessary dollars for the psychosocial aspects of care, which include ensuring family involvement, nursing homes must struggle valiantly to counteract the medicalizing impetus. To do so they must develop in-house family policies that counteract prevailing reimbursement formulas; policies that can lead to less profit for proprietary facilities and the need for substantial subventions for not-for-profit facilities and policies that will humanize their care and enhance the well-being of staff, residents, and families.

CHAPTER 10

The Deselfing Alzheimer's Disease

The Sampsons are familiar with Alzheimer's disease from the many of its victims among their acquaintances. Marilyn Sampson discusses one of her experiences:

She Didn't Want to Shut Him Up

"We always saw the Roses at the Family Buffet, but they can't go there any-more because Art is too confused. Now we see them only at the Country Kitchen. They have a nice early bird special. They serve you and use real tablecloths, not plastic. The last time we saw them there, Art looked better than he has in years. He lost a little weight and looked trim and fit. Before he got Alzheimer's, he was a big talker, not obnoxious, more that he just liked to talk about what was happening, his kids, and how it was when he was grow-ing up. Bea, that's his wife, a real sweetie, took me aside and told me that she was having a difficult time. She told me that Art was becoming difficult to understand. Before he was confused and said things over and over. Now he is still confused. Doesn't always know the time of day or where he is. But now he often doesn't make sense. Bea said that's okay at home. She can usu-ally get his meaning and figure out what he wants. But it bothers other peo-ple, and she gets embarrassed, and he gets flustered. So she decided that she would have to stop his talking or she could never go anyplace with him. And she can't leave him alone at home. She didn't want to shut him up. She just didn't have any other choice. If Art stays the same, Bea said that it will be okay. It's been 3 years now and she doesn't want to put him away. He knows who she is, and he is her companion. It's better than living alone. She has been told it will only get worse. There's no cure. And there will come a day when she will have to consider a nursing home. She knows a great deal about the disease from the Alzheimer's Association. She thinks the time will come when he can't remember who she is. "It may be next week or in 5 years."

215

The Disease

The unknown etiology of Alzheimer's disease necessitates making a provisional diagnosis by ruling out other possible causes for senile dementia. Senile, of course, refers to its onset late in life, and dementia to regressing from previous sound mental functioning. Originally, Alzheimer's disease referred to presenile dementia, to a dementia occurring before later life, as well as to a familial disease that is hereditary. Alois Alzheimer, a German neurologist, identified the disease in 1907 when he reported a perplexing case of a 51-year-old woman whose intellectual functioning progressively deteriorated. When death occurred 4 years later she was bedridden and incontinent. An autopsy of her brain revealed "tangles" and "yellow plaques," which have persisted as indicators of the neuropathology in the disease that bears Alzheimer's name. Until the 1970s Alzheimer's disease referred to familial, hereditary presenile dementia, whereas late-life dementia was referred to as senile dementia or chronic brain syndrome or organic brain syndrome. Organic was used to specify a physical cause rather than a functional, or nonphysical, cause as would occur in psychosis. As senile dementia became more prevalent, scientists began focusing attention on the disease and neuroanatomists and pathologists discovered that the microscopic changes at post-mortem were the same in senile dementia as they are in Alzheimer's presenile dementia.

Although the postmortem pathologic changes in the brain were the same, there was an initial resistance to grouping them together because it was unusual to have a family history of the disease in senile dementias of unknown etiology. Senile dementia was becoming rather common in the 1960s and 1970s as people lived longer, and most experts attributed the cause of the disease to deteriorative brain changes associated with aging, a normative degenerative process associated with living a long life. When, however, Congress was debating establishing the National Institute on Aging (NIA) as a new research institute of the National Institutes on Health, less monies would be allocated to NIA if senile dementia was "normal." Robert Butler, the first Director of NIA, argued convincingly that senile dementia was a disease and not a normal process, thus warranting the targeting of funds and research efforts toward finding a cure for the disease. The disease was named Senile Dementia of the Alzheimer's Type (SDAT), but even though there have been vigorous research efforts to determine its cause, as of this date the etiology of SDAT remains elusive.

EARLY AND LIFE DEMENTIA

A consequence of grouping early and late life dementias under the rubric of Alzheimer's disease is that families of late-life victims of senile dementia fear the disease is familial. Unfortunately, a reporter for the New York Times wrote a garbled story several years ago in which it could readily be inferred that SDAT is hereditary.

My Kids Won't Have Kids

 I was asked by the President of a newly formed chapter of the Association for Alzheimer's and Related Disorders to give a general talk on Alzheimer's diseases. Essentially I discussed the content of this chapter, emphasizing early and then later in my talk that late-life dementias are unlikely to be hereditary. A woman who appeared to be in her early sixties was sitting in the first row taking copious notes. Sitting next to her was a man who was an obvious Alzheimer's victim from how he looked around this way and that way ignoring my comments. Although he appeared to be several years older than the woman, closer to 80 than 60, I assumed he was her husband. I noticed this couple not only because of how furiously she wrote down everything I said, but also because she occasionally shook her head in disagreement as if to scold me.

After the lecture she rushed up to me with the older man in tow and said that I must be wrong. It was clear to her from the article in the New York Times that Alzheimer's disease was hereditary. After she read the article she gathered her son and daughter, both in their thirties and married without children, for a family meeting. Both were beginning sparkling careers and had decided to delay having children until their thirties. After, however, their father developed Alzheimer's disease and had to give up his medical practice, and after she read the New York Times article, she felt it best to alert her children to their dismal future. When I asked her when her doctor husband developed the disease, she answered 4 years ago when he was 73. When I asked her if anyone in the family had ever suffered from dementia, she said that her family was free of the disease, but all her husband's family had perished in concentration camps. All I could say was that 73 may be a young age to develop senile dementia, but it certainly happens and suggested that she consider it to be nonfamilial so that she could enjoy grandchildren and her kids their children. Now almost tearful but clearly perplexed, she said that it's such a dreadful disease that maybe her kids should wait a while longer, until a genetic test can resolve the problem. The conversation ended with her last comment, "I pray that they develop the test before the time-clock for pregnancy runs out on my daughter and daughter-in-law."

Twin studies, however, have revealed that among identical twins in advanced old age, one may become a victim of SDAT and the other not a victim, which suggests a nonfamilial etiology. Yet, as with some other ailments, it may be necessary to have a genetic disposition for Alzheimer's disease to be manifested in later life. A genetic marker, as noted by the doctor's wife, will provide a better understanding of familial etiology. Unfortunately, in common with so many medical discoveries, there is a down side to the recent identification of the genetic marker. The person who belongs to a family that has a history of dementia must decide whether to have the test that can determine whether the gene is being carried for this dreaded disease. One of my dearest friends faces this dilemma. A cousin of his, a medical researcher who chose to focus on Alzheimer's disease because of the familial history, has completed a genetic study of my friend, as well as most members of the family. As of this writing, my friend has chosen not to be told whether he carries the gene for the disease.

The prevalence of SDAT is controversial. The estimate by Philip Katzman (Katzman, 1987; Katzman & Kowas, 1994) of one of three chances of having the disease when 90 years of age and over is decidedly different from the rates reported by Dennis Evans and his colleagues (Evans, et al, 1989) from a study in a working-class neighborhood in Boston. They concluded that the prevalence for SDAT for people 65 to 74 was 3%; for those aged 75 to 84, it was 19%; and for those 85 and over, the rate for Alzheimer's disease was an astounding 47%. Experts who side with Katzman's estimate fault the Boston study for generalizing from a sample too restricted to working class people and to a neighborhood where a high rate of drinking causes dementias from alcoholism. Without postmortem studies of the brain, estimates of the prevalence of Alzheimer's disease at this time can only be just that; only estimates. As will become apparent, ruling out other causes for senile dementia is not always possible.

Diagnosis

Alzheimer's disease is an insidious disease that progresses slowly and inexorably from islets of confusion to total confusion in a few years to more than a decade. Insidious refers to having a treacherous, gradual, and cumulative effect. Dementia in its essential meaning of deterioration from former cognitive functioning entails the diminishing of such intellectual abilities as short-term memory, judgment, and language without a loss of consciousness. Personality changes can be expected. The elegant woman may ignore her disheveled appearance; the outgoing man may become withdrawn and silent.

As an insidious disease, the *sine qua non* of diagnosis is the slow progression of confusion. In normative aging, losses in short-term memory cause modest forgetfulness but do not expand to disorientation when in familiar settings or to erratic judgment. A history of intellectual functioning can quickly rule out Alzheimer's disease. If confusion is acute, its suddenness rules out Alzheimer's disease. Recall my Aunt Frieda who was misdiagnosed because she was perfectly lucid the day she was admitted to the hospital, 1 week before she was labeled with Alzheimer's disease. Her mental status at admission and 1 week before admission should have been recorded in her medical records.

The eagerness to diagnose Alzheimer's disease, from the best of intentions, can cause a provisional diagnosis to be communicated to patients and families with devastating consequences. There are many treatable medical conditions that can cause slowly developing intellectual dysfunction including malnutrition, drug intoxication from a single drug or the interaction of medications in the pocket book polypharmacy of many older people including Jack Sampson, thyroid imbalance, vitamin B-12 deficiency, fecal impaction, and a mild heart attack. If diagnosed correctly and when the condition is treated, the confusion will be ameliorated.

ASSESSING CONFUSION

Confusion per se is assessed for orientation to time, place, and person by a mental status exam that requires patients to state the day, month, and year; the place where they are now; and who they are. Patients who are very anxious, especially if they fear a diagnosis of Alzheimer's disease, and in a foreign setting like a doctor's office may respond incorrectly to queries on time and place. Disorientation to the person occurs late in the disease. To rule out anxiety, some neurologists ask the patient for a valued personal possession such as a wallet or house keys before beginning their examination. Then, even when answers to queries on time and place are incorrect, if the patient asks the neurologist to return the wallet or house keys on leaving the office, a diagnosis of a pathologic process is not made. If, however, the valued personal possession is not requested by the patient, and Alzheimer's disease is suspected, examination for treatable medical conditions should follow.

NON-CURABLE MEDICAL CONDITIONS

Slowly developing confusional states, however, can be caused by medical conditions that may not be curable, specifically by tumors and by cerebral mini-strokes. Arteriosclerosis per se does not cause dementia but is associated with mini-strokes that may account for as much as one third of senile dementias with unknown etiologies. The latest rule of thumb is that more than two thirds of nursing home residents, whose average age approximates 85, have senile dementia, and one third of these residents' senile dementias are due to mini-strokes. Cerebral vascular strokes that are more damaging than a series of mini-strokes can be diagnosed from both their suddenness and their accompanying impairments such as slurred speech and motor dysfunction. Mini-strokes usually must wait for their diagnosis at autopsy.

PSYCHOLOGICAL CAUSES FOR DEMENTIA

Psychological causes for confusional states can be grouped into anxiety, depression, and effects from relocation, including their interactions. The elderly patient examined in the doctor's office to confirm a presumptive diagnosis of Alzheimer's disease becomes beset with anxiety and cannot give current answers to the doctor's queries on orientation to time and place. Aunt Frieda becomes depressed in the hospital when not knowing if the prognosis for her medical condition will necessitate transferring to a nursing home rather than returning to her apartment. Elderly persons relocating to nursing homes become confused in a foreign environment, displaying a 1st-month syndrome characterized by disorientation, anxiety and depression, and sometimes frank psychosis.

Anxiety at any age can fractionate behavior. My students know only too well how anxiety affects their performance on tests. A little anxiety in a very old person who has the modest impairments in short-term memory associated with age, like being unable to recall in the morning where their eyeglasses were placed the night before, can quickly deteriorate into massive confusion when experiencing anxiety.

Depression causes a pseudodementia, a false dementia. A depressed person who is apathetic may have the capacity to be oriented to time, place, and person but be too withdrawn to respond to queries about their orientation. My Aunt Frieda was so depressed in the hospital that she could not carry on a conversation. She would only mumble her words, which was interpreted as incoherence by nursing personnel.

Relocation is disorienting regardless of age. Young, healthy Peace Corp volunteers experience culture shock, becoming disoriented in a foreign culture where they cannot communicate with those around them, sometimes suffering acute psychotic breakdowns. Relocation effects are not only evident in hospitalization and when entering nursing homes but also when elderly persons, as well as when younger people, change their community residences:

Is There a Place in the Home For My Mother?

When I entered my office there was an urgent message on my answering machine to call Mel Lesser, a former student and now a child psychoanalyst. I phoned Mel, communicated with his answering machine, and after his therapeutic session with a patient, he called me back. He began with a question, "How can I get my mother into Drexel Home? I want her to have the best of care as soon as possible. She's confused and upset, and it looks like Alzheimer's disease." I slowed him down and asked what had happened. Slowly, and very clinically, he began. "My mother is 83. When my father died last March, 10 months ago, I knew something was pathologic because the mourning process for my father was completed too abruptly. We decided to move her to a nice apartment the week before last to be near my sister who could check on her every day. This morning my sister stopped by on the way to work just to make sure everything was all right, but my mother was weepy and hard to understand. My sister immediately called me, and I then called my mother to make a provisional diagnosis. I want Dr. Grunes to see her to confirm the diagnosis of Alzheimer's disease, but I thought that at the same time I would make sure that she has a place in the best nursing home in the area. I would also like Jerry Grunes' phone number.

"Mel", I said, "before you act hastily let's consider some possibilities to explain her behavior. It is not uncommon for people your mother's age to have a brief mourning period. People in their eighties are not unfamiliar with death, and when it occurs on time late in life, can accept death. Remember that your younger patients are often coping with off-time, premature death. If also your mother cared for your father during his terminal days, she was doing her appropriate anticipatory grief work." Mel interrupted, "He died suddenly but, yes, he had a bad heart, and they would talk about what my mother would do after his death. They both expected my father to die first."

I shifted gears and said, "Let's now look at possible causes for her current confusion. Relocation is especially hard on people. It's like culture shock when younger people become disoriented in a foreign setting. Maybe she looked for something, and it was out of place, like her dentures or her wedding ring. Tell me what kind of person your mother is."

He began, "She is fastidious. You know the type. The living room couch and chairs always had plastic covers. Everything must be perfect before she can leave her apartment. She must look just right and everything must be in place." I let him continue for a few minutes longer and then interrupted. "Let me give you a not too rare scenario for your sister to check out. Your mother, as older people do, gets out of her bed at night to urinate, but being in a new apartment, she turned the wrong way to the bathroom. Then she realized that she did not know where she was and wetted herself. Being fastidious, wetting herself caused more anxiety, increasing her confusion."

Two days later Mel called to tell me that I was partially correct. His mother did have difficulty locating the bathroom at night but had not wet herself. Whereas his sister was reluctant to discuss this kind of personal issue with their mother, his sister told Mel that their mother was relieved to discuss her fear of incontinence. Their mother said something like, "I worry about having to wear those old people's diapers that they are always advertising on TV." So what had happened? Mel's mother felt that she would never adjust to her new apartment. Everything was in the wrong place. She did not want to tell her children that it was a mistake to move, so each day she tried harder to be comfortable in her new home. As she put each thing in its proper place, she began to feel better about the move. But she kept misplacing her house keys and, therefore, could not leave the apartment. In her old home she would set her house keys on a wooden nail in the kitchen, but now there was no wooden nail, and so she would try different places for her keys. For the whole day before Mel's sister came to look in on her, she had been looking for her keys without finding them and becoming increasingly upset, angry at herself, and confused. She was thus in a rather confused state when Mel's sister called him to report their mother's condition.

Mel's sister took off work the next day to calm their mother down and to help her organize her apartment so it would be less confusing to her. A set place was established for her keys, and her bed was placed in a position in relationship to the bathroom so as to approximate the layout in her previous, long-time apartment.

The extent of Mel's mother's confusion, and also what I interpreted to be a fear of leaving her apartment to be in an unfamiliar neighborhood, suggested to me that she may have been in an early stage of Alzheimer's disease. When, about 2 years later, I met Mel at a meeting, he told me that his mother did well for a while but then became increasingly confused. They moved mother into his sister's home when she said that she was tired of working and that caring for their mother at her home was an appropriate, new full-time job and certainly better than a nursing home for their mother.

A controversy exists regarding whether the extent of Alzheimer's disease is associated with lower socioeconomic status. It is my belief that no such association exists. The reason that more intellectual persons are assumed to be less afflicted with this disease is because habitual ways of thinking and adapting persist during initial stages of disorientation when there are incursions on immediate memory. The former professor of literature may not be able to remember what he ate for breakfast but can still recite all of Shakespeare's sonnets. It is my impression, therefore, that the diagnosis of Alzheimer's disease is made later in the course of the disease for more intellectual persons. On the other hand, the blue collar worker who has not been particularly interested in intellectual pursuits may not only exhibit gross deterioration earlier but may not be as devastated by the diagnosis as those who derive stimulation from their intellect. Deriving gratification and identity from the simpler pleasures seems to facilitate adaptation when care is provided by spouses and other family members who relate to victims of the disease in essentially the same ways they have always related to them.

The elderly person should be included in the process of making the diagnosis. Practioners Victoria Bumagin and Dorothy Hirn (1990) have included the elderly person who is assumed to have Alzheimer's disease in the evaluation process and, if amenable, in arranging the evaluation appointment with the physician or geriatric assessment center. These kinds of efforts to involve the potential victim in the diagnostic process enhances a sense of control that can contain anxiety and depression.

A provisional diagnosis of Alzheimer's disease is made when there is a ruling out of possible other causes for an insidious process of losses in immediate memory and of capacities for the activities of daily living, as well as probable changes in personality. This provisional diagnosis begins the first stage of caring when every effort must be made to preserve the former self and to enhance the victim's sense of control. As the deselfing process continues, there is a lengthy middle stage that includes loss of remote, past memories and psychosis, a loss of contact with reality. In the final stage, the victim is in a vegetative phase, completely out of contact and possibly lying quietly in a fetal position.

After Diagnosis

Most crucial in preservation of the self after diagnosis is to assure beneficial caregiving. Hopefully, the family will be calmly apprised that the earliest phase can persist for a lengthy, indefinite time. In turn, the family must also communicate to the family member with the disease that they will provide whatever is necessary to retain integrality.

Advisable is to encourage family members to join and participate in the Association for Alzheimer's Disease and Related Disorders. Whenever a family member has joined the Association following my recommendation, the feedback has been very positive. One daughter reported on how important it was for her to share her concerns with others "in the same boat." She added, "I got some ideas of what to expect next. I don't like it, but it makes sense to know." Not only can caregivers' sense of isolation and loneliness be reduced, but also families can be empowered through advocacy as their family member experiences further deterioration.

Just as victims of the disease should be encouraged to be involved and feel some control in the diagnostic process, so too should victims be encouraged to be involved and feel in control of their everyday and future lives. If, for example, not completed by now, a living will and durable power of attorney should be prepared (Brechling & Schneider, 1993). Concurrently, meaningful activities must be maintained, and the environment made as simplified and manageable as possible. These adaptive coping processes are of the more rational type that are used when very old. The less rational facilitory adaptive mechanisms, especially aggressiveness and functional paranoia that reduce vulnerability by deflecting blame for impairments away from oneself, can be challenges for family members in the same way these mechanisms are challenges for those families caring for members without Alzheimer's disease. Tolerating these behaviors necessitates an understanding of their function and also maturity. Unfortunately, even with the best of care, deselfing will inevitably continue.

The Loss of Self

The struggle to retain the self as the disease continues its course is observed not only by family members but also by practitioners. Donna Cohen and Carl Eisdorfer (1986) titled their book on family caring for Alzheimer's disease patients *The Loss of Self*. They begin their book with quotes from the diary of James Thomas, an Alzheimer's disease victim: "Help me to be strong and free until my self no longer exists" and "Most people expect to die some day, but who ever expected to lose their self first."

The dissolution of the self is catastrophic for the person who is aware of the dissolution in herself or himself. Apparently, a similar process occurs in the early stage of schizophrenia, when the victim of this disease becomes aware that inner mental processes are becoming destructured. Indeed, the early paranoid ideation in schizophrenia may be a way of coping with this awareness in the same way that similar ideation may be a way of coping with the early awareness of Alzheimer's disease. Other parallels are that both diseases have no known cause or cure, and both are insidious because both diseases follow a course of slow and progressive deterioration. Cause for concern exists when the older person exhibits unusual changes in mental abilities that persist and become progressively worse, disrupting life routines and accompanied by unfamiliar or bizarre changes in emotional expression.

Walter Lyons (1982), a caseworker and administrator in the Bay Crest Home for the Aged in Toronto, reported on his frustrating experiences caring for his wife, who was afflicted with Alzheimer's disease. Because of his background, he understood not only some of the principles in providing care, but also his wife's internal feelings. He wrote the following as if these words were hers: "You only know me from the outside, through my 'abnormal' behavior. Will you see me inside, struggling to maintain my assaulted personhood? Will you mistake my struggle to retain some dignity, some feeling of self, for organic disease rather than its consequences?" After noting his wife's struggle to retain "some feelings of self," Lyons continued to describe her thoughts:

> For me, this is a life and death struggle from which I can collapse into crushing defeat and withdrawal, or I can be aroused to a fever pitch of agitation and frustration expressed in pacing, in tearing at my clothing, repetitive movements or sounds. You may think I am "completely out of it," but if you watch me closely I may startle you with my awareness of, for example, the danger of walking down steps or the presence of a person, or I may be searching for a person or an activity which I usually do around this time of day. My attempts to indicate to you that I am missing something may not make sense, and you may write off my behavior as the meaningless actions of a person who lacks memory and does not know what time it is, or where he is. Yet, inside, in my own perception of things, I am reaching for something very real, and trying in my own way to find it or get you to help me.
>
> You may fail to help me do what I can do, by not taking the time and trouble to discover this. It is much simpler to do things for me, because that way is quicker and surer and more efficient. But, do you realize that this may make me more confused, frustrated, sometimes resistive and resentful. Sure, I am cognitively impaired, but that means you have to use your ingenuity and your patience to help me to clue into what you want me to do and try to understand what I want to do.

Then I face the opposite kind of problem, in which, because of my inability, you may think I lack motivation, and therefore you try to pull or push me into doing things in the belief that somehow, if I am not pushed into them and I am not engaged, you are colluding in making me more helpless.

But it is not only your misperceptions of me which add to my problems. It is also what you are feeling deep inside of you, because I know you are terrified by my losses. You are well-meaning, good intentioned, normally kind and considerate. But inside, you cannot help but feel not just pity, but some revulsion; not just empathy, but also some rejection.

When I am incontinent, I do not like it. I can still experience shame and embarrassment. But I am helpless to protect myself against it, especially when you are not tuned into my signals when I want to go. I am also helpless to protect myself against your annoyance and disgust. Do you know how dependent I am upon you to protect my dignity which is so often assaulted?

I know that you really cannot cut down all the barriers that isolate me. But you can look for those things which reduce my frustration, which help smooth the way in the face of what confounds me, if you take the time and make the effort to help me bridge, at least partially, the cognitive gap which separates me from our reality. I am not gone. I am here.

Do you really know how terribly alone I am, closed in and cutoff from so many people and so many things around me? How I try, and why I cry? For God's sake, help me in my terrible isolation. That is my cry and my pain at its most raw and elemental level. (pp. 3–6)

A more poignant description of what it is to be a victim of Alzheimer's disease has not been written. Most essential to Lyons was providing assistance to his wife in being the same person, helping her to do the same things she has always done. Yet not all family caregivers are as aware as Lyons that seemingly bizarre and aimless activities are purposeful. For example, regarding the common and annoying wandering behavior, some wander to release tension by using a lifelong pattern of coping with stress such as taking a brisk walk or a long stroll, others searching for security ("Where is my mother?"), and still others are carrying out a work role. Men who wander may be going to their jobs; women to the grocery store or their kitchens.

How can families be assisted to help the Alzheimer's disease victim retain a sense of self? Just as Lyons learned that his wife was struggling to be herself, family members must learn that bizarre behaviors often have meanings related to the striving for preservation of self. Once this principle is understood by family members, it becomes increasingly possible for them to understand the continuity between current bizarre behaviors and premorbid personality traits. In turn as the bizarre behaviors become intelligible, they can tolerate, or even encourage, aberrant behaviors that help the patient still be himself or herself. Recall the woman who had to touch the breasts of another resident in Drexel Home for the Aged to be herself.

When seeking to understand the meanings of behaviors, caregivers must penetrate exaggerated and inappropriate expressions of emotions, a lack of personal hygiene, and unintelligible communication. Because unintelligible communication often masks residual cognitive abilities that make it possible to understand simple conversations, when there are tactless discussions of childlike behaviors in front of people with Alzheimer's disease, they can naturally become enraged. Beyond disturbing childlike behaviors, caregivers are disturbed by changes in personality and bizarre behaviors. The father who has always been fastidious in his appearance may scatter all his clothes on the floor while searching for a favorite tie. When Mother talks to her long-dead mother as if she is alive and in the room, it is certainly abnormal, but it is also a seeking for security and an expression of her lifelong identity.

Mother or Father may not be the "same person," but she or he is still a person and in many ways is the same person. The extent to which the Alzheimer's disease victim feels like the same person he or she has always been, no matter how bizarre the behavior, must be accepted as the person's reality. The distortions that are so very painful to family members as they watch a loved one lose contact with the here and now may indeed serve the patient's purpose of retaining a sense of self while providing assurance as the disease follows in its inexorable course.

AN INAPPROPRIATE RESPONSE

An example of an inappropriate response to a family member who was a victim of the disease occurred when a husband tied his wife to a chair while he cooked the meals. When she refused to talk to him after he began to restrain her, the husband and home care worker became alarmed because their relationship had immediately deteriorated. To the worker and the husband, however, restraints made sense because his wife had previously not allowed him to prepare food in *her* kitchen. He did not object to adopting the role and responsibilities of "housewife," but he did object to her incessant interference. He only tied her down after he had frequently and painstakingly explained why she should not interfere. She would "shadow" him by standing at his elbow whenever he was in the kitchen, and her interference turned the kitchen into a complete mess. Now he felt that she was being unduly angry at him for taking a necessary step. I suggested to the worker that the husband allow his wife to have the use of the kitchen, that he use a space for meal preparation that she did not ordinarily use, and to call me if he believed that the restraints continued to be needed. The worker has not called back, hopefully because his wife was not tied down, and that although the kitchen was more messy, the wife talked to her husband, and life was calmer.

INABILITY TO DIFFERENTIATE THOUGHTS AND ACTIONS

Too often, overwhelmed spouses and children of Alzheimer's disease victims interpret behaviors as motivated by vindictiveness as occurred in the previous case. At other times, behavior is interpreted as lying, the purposeful telling of untruths. Being bewildered by strange behaviors when caregiving can indeed lead to perceiving the care receiver as doing spiteful things, which, unfortunately, can be a projection of one's own frustrations and angry feelings. When a daughter asks her confused mother who has disheveled hair to comb her hair, and her mother answers that she just did, the mother is not "lying." Rather it is because of her inability to differentiate between thoughts and actions. Her transient thought of hair combing becomes the belief that she did so. Steven Zarit and his associates (Zarit, Orr, & Zarit, 1985) provide many examples in addition to "lying" that are caused by not understanding the effects of memory loss. Repetitive questions are misinterpreted as a wish to be annoying or attract attention and thus, "He should control himself." This behavior more likely reflects an inability to remember asking the question or the loss of appropriate skills to gain attention. Or the family may say that the Alzheimer's disease-patient is denying memory loss when the patient cannot remember. Too often explanations for behaviors that are plausible to families are not at all accurate. Above all, most beneficial to both the patient and the family, and having a calming effect on both, is acceptance.

Self-help groups have been found to be helpful. Whereas previously it was thought that families become increasingly unable to withstand the mental deterioration, Zarit, Orr, and Zarit have also reported that family caregivers in support groups report less experience of burden over time, although the physical burden may be appreciably greater, as described by Nancy Mace and Peter Rabins (1981) in their book *The 36-Hour Day*. This counterintuitive finding apparently relates to how the most trying times are when the victim and the family first become aware of the disease and, also, the subsequent phase when the deselfing process causes a marked deterioration from the premorbid state. The shift that later occurs from a moderate or extreme nonresemblence of self to a total nonresemblence is easier to accept probably because family members have already begun to successfully mourn the loss of the identity of the person.

Still, living with and caring for a family member with Alzheimer's disease has a profound effect on mental health. Richard Schulz and his associates (Schulz, O'Brien, Bookwala, and Fleissner, 1995) reviewed the 40 studies since 1989 of the effects on people caring for family members with dementia. Virtually all studies reported elevated levels of depression, and many reported heightened physical morbidity. The extent of psychological morbidity among family caregivers was associated with increased problem behaviors of care receivers with Alzheimer's disease, less income, poorer self-ratings of health, more perceived stress, and less life satisfaction. Physical morbidity was associated with problem behaviors and cognitive impairment and with caregiver depression, anxiety, and perceived lack of social supports. Although there are measurable effects on health, most effects were primarily psychological.

Mary Mittleman and her colleagues (Mittleman et al., 1995) have reported that a comprehensive support program reduced depression among spouses caring for a wife or husband with Alzheimer's disease. In this support program caregiving spouses in a treatment group not only participated in an Alzheimer's disease caregiver support group in which they were taught how to reduce stress and manage care to reduce the frequency and intensity of troublesome behaviors, but also received individual and family counseling and were provided with informal consultation when requested by the caregiver or other family members. Conflicts with family members were apparently sufficiently resolved to increase satisfaction and thereby enhance the perception of family cohesion without increasing interaction with or assistance from significant others.

The Mittleman et al. study also revealed that after placement of a family member in a nursing home, care burden and depression may continue among spouses and other relatives who previously provided care at home because of (a) feelings of guilt related to abandoning the family member, (b) the time required to travel and visit their relative, and (c) concerns that adequate care and supervision are not being provided in the facilities. Deborah Monahan (1995), who developed support groups and workshops to alleviate burden levels after nursing home placement, reported that support group attendance was significantly associated with lower burden levels.

Specific disorganized behaviors have been ameliorated by behavioral, educational, and supportive interventions, as well as by environmental designs and medications. Jiska Cohen-Mansfield (1996) has reviewed efforts to reduce aggressive behaviors, pacing and wandering, and verbally disruptive behaviors. In turn, Linda Teri (1995) has reported on the Seattle Protocol that uses a combination of behavioral management and caregiver education to reduce depression and agitation. After caregivers are taught how to identify individual behavior problems as well as the antecedents and consequences of each behavior, they "are guided through a systematic approach to change" (p. 299). Reducing depression and agitation make it possible to maximize residual cognitive functioning. Teri wrote, "Strategies are developed for identifying and confronting behavioral disturbances that are associated with the targeted behaviors, interfere with engaging in planned pleasant activities or otherwise cause conflict between patient, caregiver, and others" (p. 299).

The loss of resemblance of self is accelerated when long-term memory begins to fade, when memories of the past become dim and are difficult to recapture. A student who was working in a medical daycare program would take daily walks with an elderly gentleman who could lucidly discuss this terrible problem:

Losing the Past

 The student was told by a victim of this disease, "This Alzheimer's disease is hard on me and especially on my wife. We have been holding our own, comforting each other with the past. Now I am losing my past, and I will no longer be me. And I will not be able to share our history together, our wonderful life together."

MANAGEMENT TECHNIQUES

Alzheimer's victims cared for at home or in long-term settings can be assisted in many concrete ways. Irene Burnside (1981), a nurse with years of experience in nursing homes, in synthesizing techniques for managing patients with cognitive impairments divided these techniques into three categories: techniques for the helper, specifically for memory development, and for manipulation of the environment. Her "bedside" helper techniques include reinforcing reality, using touch, supporting denial if it is therapeutic, and helping clients to express feelings. Reducing duress is particularly important. Situations that provoke agitation, including most new situations, must be recognized. Obviously, when the victim of the disease cannot communicate the source of the agitation, disorganized and aberrant behavior is likely to escalate. Education in communication is indeed very helpful. Can, in turn, family members and staff in nursing homes become more comfortable and more competent, and feel more efficacious in working with patients with dementia? Certainly our observations at Drexel Home for the Aged were that it is possible to enhance staff's functioning and feelings but only by support and reassurance of the more professional staff. The more staff are expected to put out, the more nourishment staff must be provided.

Regarding Burnside's ideas for retention of memory, she has provided a list that is appropriate for any setting. For example, she suggests providing sufficient cues to aid memory and orientation (e.g., props to indicate change of seasons), consistent cues that encourage recognition instead of recall, and multiple cues; avoiding pressure to perform; being sure to communicate what is expected to be remembered; and being sure that familiar objects that reaffirm the continuity of the sense of self are on display.

Environmental manipulations are rather obvious such as using a night light and bright colors and decorations. In nursing homes it is sensible to color-code doors, keep the same staff working with individuals, provide a safe environment that is not too boring but not over stimulating, provide a nonthreatening environment, provide clocks and calendars, and make special efforts to provide a milieu that reduce sundowner's syndrome.

When family and other familiar persons are present to affirm the persistence of the self and use the several kinds of management techniques, there may be a maximization of residual cognitive capacities, which at times can be startling.

Winston Churchill in the Late a.m.

 Sir Martin Roth, Winston Churchill's eminent internist who lectured throughout the world on geriatrics, always included a discussion of his patient Sir Winston Churchill. It went something like this: "My patient Sir

Winston was completely lucid only in the late morning after his a.m. nap. He would arise from his nap, come down to the Great Hall, sit in his favorite armchair, pour some brandy into a large snifter, swirl the brandy in the snifter, take a lingering sniff, and then a slow swallow. He would then take his mammoth cigar, uncover it carefully, roll it around by his ear, snip off the end, light it slowly, and gather in his first puff of the morning. He was now ready for a visit with a head of state. When the cigar was about two-thirds spent and the brandy goblet empty, in almost exactly 35 minutes, he would abruptly say that he was tiring and terminate the conversation. If I were in the house, he would tell me he was fading, with the full knowledge that he would not be alert until the next day's late a.m., and then sink into a profoundly confused state not to know where he was or who he was. Then the next a.m. he would again be lucid and see the next head of state."

THE END STAGE

The final stage of the disease is marked by a shrunken brain and the loss of vital functions. The victim, now in a vegetative stage, may remain fixed in a fetal position, incontinent of urine and feces. If, as is common, a respiratory infection develops, little will usually be done to maintain life, a form of passive euthanasia. Family members and nonfamily caretakers are usually heard to say that death at this time is a blessing.

PART FIVE

A Brief Forward Look

Two kinds of futures will be covered; first, the future of the current cohort of oldest old people as exemplified by the Sampsons; and second, the future of upcoming cohorts of oldest old people. Some future cohorts are known to us; for example the adult children of those now of advanced old age, the next generation, which was reared during the years of the Great Depression and now is in the late middle and younger old years; and the baby boomer generation, born after World War II and now in the middle adult years.

CHAPTER 11

The Futures of the
Oldest Old People

The Current Oldest Old People

Members of the current cohort of the oldest old people face variable futures. Some will be able to maintain their current levels of functioning and adaptation until death occurs at the limit of our genetic life span. Others will die suddenly before this limiting age of 110 to 115 years or so. Still others will experience lengthy periods of preterminal deterioration, many with Alzheimer's disease. The Sampsons however, were holding their own when they attended Suzie's wedding:

I Knew If I Lived So Long, It Would Be Wonderful

"We made it to Susie's wedding," said Marilyn Sampson with a big smile on her face. "Let me tell you from the very beginning. The plane trip was easy. They met us with wheelchairs at our gate. Its too long a walk to where the luggage is. We stayed at Davie's, our eldest son's, house. He brought in two beds for the first floor, but we had to go up some stairs to the bathroom. Davie took some time off from work to drive us to see friends and to a poker game at my sister's house. Jack can't drive in the city anymore. Davie also took us to a wonderful fish restaurant. We rested a lot. This was the first week. Then came the wedding. The prenuptial dinner was lovely. Larry's father, Larry was the groom, paid for the dinner at a nice Italian restaurant. Counting the members of the wedding party and out-of-town guests, there were about 63. Susie looked beautiful, and Larry is tall and handsome. He is so sweet. They make a lovely couple. There were a few toasts to them, and

we first had finger foods, little pizzas and shrimps. Dinner began with soup, we had salad, pasta, and then delicious veal. When the meal was over, and I couldn't eat anymore, they wheeled out a dessert cart. I stuck with the strawberries. After dinner, Howie's friend, the magician, performed for us. Howie is my youngest son, the father of the bride. The magician put on a performance like I've never seen before. He stood up and did his show and then sat at our table to do tricks with his hands. I was 2 feet away from him and couldn't tell how he did those things, like put an ashtray under a bowl and made it disappear or tore up playing cards that later he put together."

"It wasn't all so nice. Larry's father and mother are divorced. Larry's father is nice, but his mother is a no-goodnik. She's lousy. A bitter face. Doesn't talk nice to anyone, not to anyone. So many divorces nowadays. Howie and my Bobbie just got divorced. Why couldn't they wait until after the wedding? But they acted nice, like they were still together."

"The wedding was on Sunday afternoon. Susie's gown must have cost her a fortune. And the flowers? Larry's father paid for the flowers, too. They were something special. We did not march down the aisle. We sat on the aisle, and when it was our turn we stood up. Everyone said my dress was just right for the wedding. Everyone in the wedding party wore black and white. The men wore tuxes. The ceremony was just right, just like Suzie planned it. Then there was a bar. Then there was dinner with nice toasts. My Bobbie, Howie's wife, well no longer his wife but still my sweet daughter-in-law forever, was all choked up, and tears were coming down her face when she toasted Larry and Susie. Sometimes you go to a wedding when you know it won't work. This one will. They have lived together for 2 years and get along real well. So it was a real happy wedding."

"After dinner the band played. They were too loud. We were too tired to walk around and when people came to our table to see us, we couldn't carry on a decent conversation. Everybody came by. Three of our grandchildren came from out-of-town and also a niece with her husband. There were so many. My brother came too. Marvin, he's 90 now. Of course, Hannah couldn't come. She's my sister, really my stepsister. Didn't I tell you? My mother had to marry my father when her sister died and left four small kids. That's how it was in the old country. If your sister died you had to marry her husband. So when I was born, Hannah was already 13. She's now 99 and has all her mental faculties but is too sick to leave the convalescent center. I didn't dance. Jack danced once. He's still a good dancer. But the orchestra was too loud and too bad. They took pictures, video, and will have a 40-minute video of the wedding. We will get a copy."

"I knew if I lived so long it would be wonderful. It was! I put my dress away. Everyone said it was beautiful. I had my hair done, and the girls said it was perfect. Maybe I'll wear the dress again. I don't think so. I'm hoping that Susie's brother, my grandson Sam, will marry soon so I can go to another wedding and wear my expensive dress. He's going with a nice girl, but I don't know. He's 32 and acts like he's 15. My other grandchildren are too young. Sid got married late. Maybe something else will happen in the family, something very special to look forward to."

> *Jack Sampson had little to say, "It was great seeing the family. I hope it wasn't the last time. As long as my ticker keeps ticking, I'll be okay. I had to rest too much. There were some things I didn't like. The music was so loud. Then there were some people I didn't want to talk to, like my brother-in-law, but I had to be nice."*

Marilyn Sampson was hoping to live until a next glorious family event. Her long-lived family suggests several more years of life, which was unlikely for Jack because he was in failing health and suffering from congestive heart failure. Their futures reflect the normative pattern: Marilyn was caring for Jack and was likely to become a widow who eventually would be cared for by her children in their young-old years. This pattern began to emerge. Three days after the wedding, Marilyn celebrated her 86th birthday, the next day they returned to Florida, and 13 days later Jack died.

Jack's Death

> *Marilyn said, "He died suddenly. We had breakfast. After breakfast he didn't want to take one of his pills, but later he took the pill and went back to bed to rest. Later he did something he never does. He called me from the bedroom. He was sitting up. I knew something was wrong. He said my name and laid back on the pillow. Sort of flopped back. I called 911. They took a long time coming, more than 15 minutes. They worked on him for over an hour. Then I went with him in the ambulance. At the hospital they gave me a room to wait where I could lie down. After awhile a young doctor, a woman doctor, came in and told me he had died at home, and they couldn't revive him."*
>
> *"When I got home I called my sister to fly down. She said she would leave right away, and that we would both go north together, and I would stay at her house. But something terrible happened. The weather was bad, and she couldn't make it in that day. I had the worse night, being alone without Jack. Three days later we had the funeral, and then we sat Shiva at my sister's whose house I stayed at."*
>
> *"My kids were wonderful. Sid, the middle one, called to tell me he was going to call Dad that night to talk about a basketball game they each planned to watch on TV. He said that when the game was over, he forgot that Dad died and reached for the telephone. Like me. When I was looking for the airplane voucher and began to ask Jack where he put it. My friends said I would be doing that for a long while."*
>
> *"Also in the afternoon, my doctor, Dr. Fine, called and told me that I was better than any nurse in the way I took care of Jack. It really cheered me up."*

Marilyn decided while staying with her sister to sell her apartment in Florida and to move back home and into a congregate residence, euphemistically called a retirement hotel, to be near her family but to return to Florida for 3 months each winter to escape the cold she could no longer tolerate. This arrangement was chosen because she feared living in isolation away from her family and knowing that in a congregate residence, if she pulled the emergency cords in the bathroom, kitchen, or bedroom, someone would come immediately. Her family was also satisfied with these arrangements.

Ten days later Marilyn returned to Florida accompanied by her youngest son Howie. She was now quite depressed, unable to sleep or eat. Three weeks later she reported on how it was to return to Florida:

"I kept thinking Jack was dozing in the other room, and that any minute he will get up. I knew he was gone, but all his things were in place. Thank God Howie was with me. Then he left, after a week. I was alone. Friends and neighbors came to see me during the day. It was good to have company, but at night it was terrible. After so many years together to be alone. I would talk to him but he wasn't there. My neighbor, sweet Millie, said that she still talks to her husband, and he's gone 15 years. I got a little better. Still couldn't sleep, but I ate a little bit."

When another 2 months had past, Marilyn was beyond the phase of acute grief and had regained a semblance of her former self.

"I cleaned out much of the apartment when Davie, my eldest son, came down to help me out. Now I'm waiting to have my agent sell the apartment so I can move back home. I had a lot to do to get ready to move. I had to send out death certificates and even had to get my marriage license for the union. Otherwise they would not give me Jack's death benefits. I had to go to the broker to make sure I could afford to live in the new place. I can. I'm lucky Jack provided for me. I had to talk to the lawyer, the accountant and others, too. It was too much when I was so depressed. Without my kids and few friends, it would have been too much, too impossible."

"I eat better. So my strength is returning. But I still don't sleep well. Without Jack here I just don't sleep right. I don't know if I ever will sleep like I did when Jack was alive. It will probably be the same in my new place."

"I'm back to playing poker and going to the beauty shop every Saturday but shopping is a problem. I need a ride to get groceries. I pay Al to drive me when he is available. Jack drove everyone around, but people don't seem to remember. They're nice but don't put themselves out. I understand. They have their own lives. But I don't understand. They could help more. It will be different when I move. My family will make sure. And I know a few people there. Plenty play poker. The manager who went to school with my grandson and will make sure I meet compatible people."

Marilyn is a survivor who has become a widow and who is destined like most of the oldest old people to live among very old widowed women. Although she anticipated widowhood, she was unaware of how alone she would feel and how dependent she would be on others. Yet she is rebounding from her loss of Jack and from the curtailment of her independence as she contemplates the niche she will carve out for herself in her next apartment. In returning to her former self, she is again able to use the processes she previously used to preserve her sense of self.

Future Old-Old Cohorts

The Sampson's children will reach their advanced old age in 2 decades or so. How might they fare? Like the Sampsons, they were born and reared in difficult times, during the Great Depression. In these difficult times, they were inculcated with greater expectations. Their parents told them that their lives would be better than theirs, especially if they took up a profession, preferably medicine or law, and made a handsome living. The Sampson children, in common with most others of their generation, were thus raised to achieve more than their parents but only through hard work. If then achieving, they would surpass their parents in status and wealth and feel successful during their advanced old age. Fortunately, by the time the economy turned sour in the late 1970s, they had launched their children and most likely retired early to look forward to their later years.

The world in which they will live for the next two decades is, however, unpredictable. It may be sunny or it may be cloudy depending on the economy and certainly depending on whether chance adversities occur. They now have concerns about their children's futures. The economy does not look good, and two incomes are essential for a family to live comfortably.

If the economy worsens, not only will their life satisfaction be affected but also possibly their acceptance of death. They may feel that their life's tasks are incomplete if the family's next generations are experiencing difficulties. Concurrently, many may find death unacceptable because of unfinished business from self-assigned life goals. If they continue to seek to be productive or creative as artists do, they will be less willing to go gently into that good night. As each generation becomes more educated and use more of their leisure time for intellectual avocational pursuits, there may be less willingness than in previous generations to accept the finality of life at the end of the life cycle. Their religious beliefs may be different, not as facilitory for acceptance of death. Still, beliefs in a long life as a reward for service and hereafters with reunions can be expected to persist.

The baby boomers, however, evoke troubling concerns. They were raised with expectations of living in a rosy world. Reared in the late 1940s and early 1950s by parents who saw themselves as successful in an expanding economy, the expectations of the baby boomers could easily have become thwarted in their adult years from a worsening economy. How they will fare in their advanced years is certainly unpredictable.

With some certainty, however, we can foresee an extension of the active life span providing more healthy young-old years and delaying the age for the onset of the old-old years. Few predict Ben Franklin's alternative, "All would be long lived but none would grow old." Only by finding cures for Alzheimer's disease and musculoskeletal degeneration, by correcting each person's genetic faults, and by creating environments free of toxicity can we expect to have vitality until the end of our life span at 110 years or so. Until then, there is likely to be a variable period of advanced old age marked by increasing incapacities to carry out the activities of daily living. Spouses will continue to provide care and also children, who are likely to be closer to 70 than to 60. With, however, the delay of childbirth, some children will be younger and daughters may be less willing to withdraw from paid employment to become parent-carers. But in all likelihood, most will have retired by the time that care of parents becomes urgent.

During these years of advanced old age it can be expected that the facilitory adaptative processes used by the current cohort will also be used by future cohorts. Control in day-to-day life and assertiveness in coping with adversities will continue to be facilitory for adaptation. Reconstructions of the past will continue to be useful for affirmation of identity and for achieving a congruence between expected and achieved life goals. And religious beliefs will continue to enhance a sense of specialness when surviving to the oldest years and to assure reunions in the hereafter. An aura of survivorship will surely be displayed by future oldest old cohorts and surely will be greatly admired by all those in their surrounds.

References

Allport, G. W. (1961). *Pattern and growth in personality*. New Haven, CT: Yale University Press.

Angelou, M. (1978). *And still I rise*. New York: Random House.

Atchley, R. C. (1989). A continuity theory of normal aging. *Gerontologist, 29*, 183–190.

Baltes, P. B. (1993). The aging mind: Potential and limits. *Gerontologist, 33*, 580–594.

Baltes, P. B., & Baltes, M. M. (1990). Psychological perspectives on successful aging: The model of selective optimization with compensation. In P. B. Baltes, & M. M. Baltes (Eds.), *Successful aging: Perspectives from the behaviorial sciences*. New York: Cambridge University Press.

Bandura, A. (1977). *Social learning theory*. Englewood Cliffs, NJ: Prentice-Hall.

Becker, E. (1973). *The denial of death*. New York: The Free Press.

Berezin, M. (1987). Reflections on psychotherapy with the elderly. In J. Sadovoy, & M. Leszcz (Eds.), *Treating the elderly with psychotherapy: The scope for change in later life*. Madison, CT: International Universities Press, Inc.

Blazer, D., Hughes, D., & George, L. (1987). The epidemiology of depression in an elderly community population. *Gerontologist, 27*, 281–287.

Brechling, R. G., & Schneider, C. A. (1993) Preserving autonomy in early stage dementia. *Journal of Gerontological Social Work, 20*, 17–33.

Brody, E. M., Kleban, M. H., Lawton, M. P., & Silverman, H. A. (1971). Excess disabilities of mentally impaired aged: Impact of individualized treatment. *Gerontologist, 11*, 124–133.

Buhler, C. (1968). The general structure of the life cycle. In C. Buhler, & E. Massarik (Eds.), *The course of human life: A study of goals in a humanistic perspective.* New York: Springer.

Bumagin, V. E., & Hirn, K. E. (1979). *Aging is a family affair.* New York: Crowell.

Burnside, I. M. (1981). *Nursing and the aged.* New York: McGraw-Hall.

Butler, R. N. (1963). The life review: An interpretation of reminiscence in the aged. *Psychiatry, 26,* 63–76.

Callahan, D. C. (1987). *Setting limits.* New York: Simon & Shuster.

Chatters, L. M., & Taylor, R. J. (1994). Religious involvement among older African-Americans. In J. S. Levin (Ed.), *Religion in aging and health: Theoretical foundations and methodological frontiers.* Thousand Oaks, CA: Sage.

Cicero. (1982). Cato the elder on old age. In M. Grant (translator) *Cicero: Selected works* (pp. 214–215). Harmondsworth, England: Penguin Books.

Coe, R. M. (1987). Communication and medical care outcomes: Analysis of conversations between doctors and elderly patients. In R. A. Ward, & S. S. Tobin (Eds.). *Health in aging: Sociological issues and policy directions.* New York: Springer.

Cohen, D., & Eisendorfer, C. (1986). *The loss of self.* New York: Norton.

Cohen-Mansfield, J. (1996). Inappropriate behavior. In Z. S. Khachaturian & T. S. Radebaugh (Eds.), *Alzheimer's disease: Cause(s), diagnosis, treatment and care.* Boca Raton, FL: CRC Press.

Cohler, B. J. (1982). Adult developmental psychology and reconstruction in psychoanalysis. In S. I. Greenspan, & G. H. Pollock (Eds.). *The course of life Vol. III.* Washington, DC: NIMH.

Costa, P. T., & McCrae, R. (1984). *Emerging lives. Enduring dispositions.* Waltham, MA: Little, Brown.

Costa, P. T., & McCrae, R. R. (1997). Set like plaster? Evidence for the stability of adult personality. In T. Heatherton, & J. Weinberger (Eds.), *Can personality change?* Washington, DC: American Psychological Association.

Csikszentmihalyi, M., & Rochberg-Halton, E. (1981). *The meaning of things: Domestic symbols and the self.* Cambridge, MA: Cambridge University Press.

Dobrof, R. (1983). *Training workshops on caring for the mentally impaired elderly.* New York: Brookdale Center on Aging of Hunter College.

Eaton, M., Mitchell-Bonair, I. L., & Friedman, E. (1986). The effect of touch on nutritional intake of chronic organic brain syndrome patients. *Journal of Gerontology, 41,* 611–616.

Edelson, J. S., & Lyons, W. (1985). *Institutional care of the mentally impaired elderly.* New York: Van Nostrand Reinhold.

Elder, G. H., Jr. (1974). *Children of the great depression.* Chicago: University of Chicago Press.

Erikson, E. H. (1950). *Childhood and society*. New York: Norton.

Erikson, E. (1978). Reflections on Dr. Borg's life cycle. In E. Erikson (Ed.), *Adulthood*. New York: Norton.

Erikson, E. H. (1982). *The life cycle completed*. New York: Norton.

Feifel, H. (1977). Death in contemporary America. In H. Feifel (Ed.), *Meanings of death*. New York: McGraw-Hill.

Femia, E. E., Zarit, S. H., & Johansson, B. (1997). Predicting change in activities of daily living: A longitudinal study of the oldest old in Sweden. *Journal of Gerontology: Psychological Sciences, 52B,* 294–302.

Gallup, G., Jr., & Castelli, J. (1989). *The peoples' religion*. New York: Macmillan.

Gatz, M., & Zarit, S. H. (1999). A good old age: Paradox or possibility. In V. L. Bengtson, & K. W. Schaie (Eds.), *Handbook of theories of aging*. New York: Springer.

Geisel, W. (1986). *You're only old once*. New York: Random House.

Gergen, K. (1977). Stability, change and chance in understanding human development. In N. Datan, & H. Reese (Eds.), *Life span developmental psychology: Dialectic perspectives on experimental research*. New York: Academic Press.

Goldfarb, A. I. (1959). Minor maladjustments in the aged. In S. Arieti (Ed.), *American handbook of psychiatry Vol. I*. New York: Basic Books.

Gorney, J. (1968). *Experience and age: Patterns of reminiscence among the elderly*. Unpublished doctoral dissertation, University of Chicago, Chicago.

Grunes, J. M. (1982). Reminiscence, regression and empathy-a psychotherapeutic approach to the impaired elderly. In S. I. Greenspan, & G. H. Pollock (Eds.), *The course of life Vol. III*. Washington, DC: NIMH.

Grunes, J. (1987). The aged in psychotherapy: Psychodynamic contribution to the treatment process. In J. Sadovoy, & M. Leszcz (Eds.), *Treating the elderly with psychotherapy: The scope for change in later life*. Madison, CT: International Universities Press.

Gurland, J. J., Deen, L., Cross, P., & Golden, R. (1980). The epidemiology of depression and dementia in the elderly: The use of multiple indicators of these conditions. In J. O. Cole, & J. E. Barrett (Eds.), *Psychotherapy of the aged*. New York: Raven.

Gutmann, D. (1964). An exploration of ego configurations in middle and later life. In B. L. Neugarten (Ed.), *Personality in later life*. New York: Atherton.

Gutmann, D. (1987). *Reclaimed powers: Toward a new psychology of men and women in later life*. New York: Basic.

Hasselkuss, B. R. (1988). Meaning in family caregiving: Perspective on caregiving/professional relationships. *Gerontologist, 28,* 686–691.

Hayflick, L. (1996). *How and why we age*. New York: Ballantine.

Hughes, L. (1926). *Selected poems of Langston Hughes*. New York: Knopf.

Idler, E. L. (1987). Religious involvement and the health of the elderly: Some hypotheses and an initial test. *Social Forces, 66*, 226–238.

Idler, E. L., & Kasl, S. V. (1992). Religion, disability, depression and the timing of death. *American Journal of Sociology, 97*, 1052–1079.

James, W. (1892). *Psychology: The briefer course*. New York: Henry Holt.

Johnson, C. L., & Barer, B. M. (1997). *Life beyond 85 years: The aura of survivorship*. New York: Springer.

Kane, R. L., Ouslander, J. G., & Abrass, I. B. (1989). *Essentials of clinical medicine 2nd ed*. New York: McGraw Hill.

Kark, J. D., Shemi, G., Friedlander, Y., Martin, O., & Blondheim, S. H. (1996). Does religious observation promote health: Mortality in secular vs. religious kibbutzim in Israel. *American Journal of Public Health, 86*, 341–346.

Karp, D. A. (1985). A decade of reminders: Changing age consciousness between fifty and sixty years old. *Gerontologist, 28*, 727–738.

Kastenbaum, R. (1966). On the meaning of time in later life. *Journal of Genetic Psychology, 109*, 2–25.

Katzman, P. (1987). Alzheimer's disease: Advances and opportunities. *Journal of the American Geriatrics Society, 35*, 69–73.

Kaufman, S. R. (1987). *The ageless self: Sources of meaning in late life*. Madison, WI: University of Wisconsin Press.

Kierkegaard, S. (1957). *The concept of dread*. (Original work published 1844) (W. Lourie, Trans.) Princeton, NJ: Princeton University Press.

Kleemier, R. W. (1961, September). Intellectual changes in the senium, or death and the I.Q. Presidential address to Division 20 of the American Psychological Association, New York.

Koenig, H. (1994). *Aging and God: Spiritual pathways to mental health in midlife and later years*. New York: Haworth Pastoral Press.

Koenig, H. G., George, L. K., & Siegler, I. C. (1988). The use of religion and other emotion-regulating coping strategies among older adults. *Gerontologist, 28*, 303–310.

Kulys, R., & Tobin, S. S. (1980). Older people and their responsible others. *Social Work, 25*, 138–145.

Langer, E. J. (1989). *Mindfulness*. New York: Addison-Wesley.

Langer, E., & Rodin, J. (1976). The effects of choice and enhanced personal responsibility for the aged: A field experiment in an institutional setting. *Journal of Personality and Social Psychology, 34*, 191–198.

Leary, T. (1957). *Interpersonal diagnosis of personality*. New York: Ronald Press.

Lecky, P. (1945). *Self consistency: A theory of personality*. New York: Ronald Press.

LeFevre, P. (1984). Toward a theology of aging. *Chicago Theology Seminary Register, 74*, 1–12.

Lieberman, M. A., & Lakin, M. (1963). On becoming an institutionalized person. In R.H. Williams, C. Tibbitts, & W. Donahue, (Eds.),

Process of aging Vol. 1: Social and psychological perspectives (pp. 475–503). New York: Atherton Press.

Lieberman, M. A., & Tobin, S. S. (1983). *The experience of old age: Stress, coping and survival.* New York: Basic Books.

Lopata, H. (1979). *Women as widows: Support systems.* New York: Elsevier North Holland.

Lyons, W. (1982). Coping with cognitive impairment: Some family dynamics and helping roles. *Journal of Gerontological Social Work, 4,* 3–21.

Mace, N. C., & Rabins, P. V. (1981). *The 36-hour day.* Baltimore: Johns Hopkins Press.

Mittleman, M. S., Ferris, S. H., Shulman, J., Steinberg, G., Ambinder, A., Mackell, J. A., & Cohen, J. (1995). A comprehensive support group: Effect on depression on spouse caregivers of AD patients. *Gerontologist, 35,* 792–802.

Monahan, D. J. (1995). Informal caregivers of institutionalized demented residents. *Journal of Gerontological Social Work, 21,* 652–681.

Montgomery, R. J. V. (1982). Impact of institutional care policies on family integration. *Gerontologist, 22,* 54–58.

Montgomery, R. J. V. (1983). Staff-family relations and institutional care policies. *Journal of Gerontological Social Work, 6,* 25–38.

Munnichs, J. M. (1966). Old age and finitude: A contribution to psychogerontology. *Bibliotheca Vita Humana, No. 4.*

Myerhoff, B. (1978). *Number our days.* New York: E. P. Dutton.

Myers, W. A. (1984). *Dynamic therapy of the older patient.* New York: Jason Aronson.

Nemiroff, R. A., & Colarusso, C. (Eds.). (1985). *The race against time: Psychotherapy and psychoanalysis in the second half of life.* New York: Plenum.

Neugarten, B. L. (1974). Age groups in American society and the rise of the young-old. In F. Eis (Ed.), *Political consequences of aging.* Philadelphia: American Academy of Political and Social Sciences.

Neugarten, B. L., & Datan, N. (1974). The middle years. In S. Arieti (Ed.), *American handbook of psychiatry.* New York: Basic.

Neugarten, B. L., Havighurst, R. J., & Tobin, S. S. (1961). The measurement of life satisfaction. *Journal of Gerontology, 16,* 134–143.

Neugarten, B. L., Wood, V., Kraines, R. J., & Loomis, B. (1963). Women's attitudes toward the menopause. *Vita Humana, 6,* 140–151.

Palmore, E. (1980). The social factors in aging. In E. Busse & D. Blazer (Eds.), *Handbook of geriatric psychiatry.* New York: Van Nostrand Reinhold.

Perlin, S., & Butler, R. N. (1963). Psychiatric aspects of adaptation to the aging experience. In J. E. Birren, R. N. Butler, S. W. Greenhouse, L., Sokoloff, & M. R. Yarrow (Eds.), *Human aging: A biological and behavioral study.* Washington, DC: NIMH.

Pietrukowicz, M. E., & Johnson, M. M. S. (1991). Using life histories to individualize nursing home staff attitudes toward residents. *Gerontologist, 31,* 102–106.

Pillemer, K., & Moore, D. W. (1989). Abuse of patients in nursing homes. Findings from a survey of staff. *Gerontologist, 29*, 314–320.

Poggi, R. G., & Berland, D. I. (1985). The therapists' reactions to the elderly. *Gerontologist, 25*, 508–513.

Pollock, G. H. (1987). The mourning-liberation process: Ideas on the inner life of the older adult. In J. Sadovoy, & M. Leszcz (Eds.), *Treating the elderly with psychotherapy: The scope for change in later life.* Madison, CT: International Universities Press.

Revere, V., & Tobin, S. S. (1980/81). Myth and reality: The older person's relationship to his past. *International Journal of Aging and Human Development, 12*, 15–26.

Rodin, J., & Langer, E. (1977). Long-term effects of a control-relevant intervention with the institutionalized aged. *Journal of Personality and Social Psychology, 35*, 897–902.

Rowe, J. W., & Kahn, R. L. (1998). *Successful aging.* New York: Pantheon Books.

Ryff, C. D. (1993). The self in later life. *Gerontology News, 11.*

Sacher, G. A. (1978). Longevity, aging and death. *Gerontologist, 18*, 112–120.

Safford, F. (1980). A program for families of the mentally impaired elderly. *Gerontologist, 20*, 3–11.

Saunders, C. (1963). The treatment of intractable pain of terminal cancer. *Proceedings of the Royal Society of Medicine, 56*, 191–197.

Schlesinger, M. R., Tobin, S. S., & Kulys, R. (1981). The responsible child and parental well-being. *Journal of Gerontological Social Work, 3*, 3–16.

Schulz, R., O'Brien, A. T., Bookwala, J., & Fleissner, K. (1995). Psychiatric and psychological morbidity effects of dementia caregiving: Prevalence, correlates and causes. *Gerontologist, 35*, 771–791.

Schwartz, A. N. & Vogel, M. E. (1990). Nursing home staff and residents' families role expectations. *Gerontologist, 30*, 49–53.

Sherman, E. (1987). Reminiscence groups for community elderly. *Gerontologist, 27*, 569–572.

Sherman, E., & Newman, E. (1977/78). The meaning of cherished possessions for the elderly. *Journal of Aging and Human Development, 8*, 181–192.

Shneidman, E. S. (1973). *Deaths of man.* New York: Quadrangle/New York Times.

Simmons, L. W. (1945). *The role of the aged in primitive society.* New Haven, CT: Yale University Press.

Simonton, D. K. (1989). The swan-song phenomenon: Last works effects of 172 classical composers. *Psychology and Aging, 4*, 42–47.

Smith, G. C., Smith, M. F., & Toseland, R. W. (1991). Problems identified by family caregivers. *Gerontologist, 31*, 377–382.

Steele, K., Gertman, P. M., Crescenzi, C., & Anderson, J. (1981). Iatrogenic illness on a general medical service at a university hospital. *New England Journal of Medicine, 304*, 638–642.

Steinitz, L. Y. (1980). *The church within the network of social services to the elderly: Case study of Laketown.* [Unpublished doctoral dissertation], University of Chicago, Chicago.

Taylor, S. E. (1989). *Positive illusions: Creative self-deceptions and the healthy mind.* New York: Basic.

Tellis-Nayak, V., & Tellis-Nayak, M. (1989). When the world of the nurse's aide enters the world of the nursing home. *Gerontologist, 29,* 307–313.

Teri, L. (1996). Managing problems in dementia patients: Depression and agitation. In Z. S. Khachaturian, & T. S. Radebaugh (Eds.), *Alzheimer's disease: Cause(s), diagnosis, treatment and care.* Boca Raton, FL: CRC Press.

Tobin, S. S. (1991). *Personhood in advanced old age: Implications for practice.* New York: Springer.

Tobin, S. S. (1995). Fostering family involvement in nursing homes. In G. C. Smith, S. S. Tobin, E. A. Robertson-Tchabo, & P. W. Power (Eds.), *Strengthening aging families: Diversity in practice and policy.* Thousand Oaks, CA: Sage.

Tobin, S. S., Ellor, J. W., & Anderson-Ray, S. (1986). *Enabling the elderly: Religious institutions within the services system.* Albany, NY: State University of New York Press.

Tobin, S. S., & Gustafson, J. (1987). What do we do differently with elderly clients? *Journal of Gerontological Social Work, 6,* 29–46.

Tobin, S. S., & Lieberman, M. A. (1976). *Last home for the aged: Critical implications of institutionalization.* San Francisco: Jossey-Bass.

Troll, L. (1994). Family-embedded vs. family-deprived oldest old: A study of contrasts. *International Journal of Aging and Human Development, 38,* 51–64.

Vaillant, G. E. (Ed.). (1977). *Adaptation to life.* Boston: Little, Brown.

Wacker, R. (1985). The good die younger: Does combativeness help the old survive? *Science 85, 6,* 64–68.

Weissert, W.G. (1985). Estimating the long-term care population: Prevalence rates and selected characteristics. *Health Care Financing Review, 6,* 83–91.

Yalom, I. (1987). Foreword. In Sadavoy, I., & Leszcz, M. (Eds.), *Treating the elderly with psychotherapy: The scope for change in later life.* Madison, CT: International Universities Press.

Zarit, S. H., Orr, N. K., & Zarit, J. M. (1985). *The hidden victims of Alzheimer's disease.* New York: New York University Press.

Zinberg, N. E., & Kaufman, I. (1963). Cultural and personality factors associated with aging. In N. E. Zinberg & I. Kaufman (Eds.), *Normal psychology of the aging process.* New York: International Universities Press.

Index

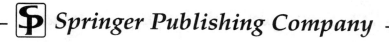 **Springer Publishing Company**

Working With Toxic Older Adults
A Guide to Coping With Difficult Elders
Gloria M. Davenport, PhD

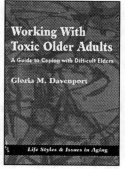

According to Dr. Davenport, toxicity in older adults manifests itself in negative behaviors and attitudes that can adversely impact interactions with health professionals, caregivers, and family members. Dr. Davenport presents theories and case examples to help us understand this phenomenon and provides useful techniques for caring for toxic elders.

This book is certain to be a valuable practice guide for social workers, therapists, caregivers, and students.

1998   312pp   0-8261-1223-4   hardcover

536 Broadway, New York, NY 10012-3955 • (212) 431-4370 • Fax (212) 941-7842

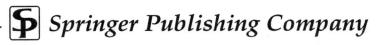 **Springer Publishing Company**

Life Beyond 85 Years
The Aura of Survivorship

Colleen L. Johnson, PhD
Barbara M. Barer, MSW

Those 85 years and older — the oldest old — are now the fastest growing group in the U.S. Using their original research, the authors examine how the oldest old adapt to daily challenges and what competencies are needed to survive and continue living in the community. The authors address the topics of health and physical status, family and social relationships, and quality of life, as well as the implications of increases in life expectancy for families and society. The book features illuminating vignettes that illustrate how the oldest old perceive and interpret their world, and thereby convey the aura of their survivorship.

Contents:

Springer Series on Life Styles & Issues in Aging
1997   267pp   0-8261-9540-7   hardcover

536 Broadway, New York, NY 10012-3955 • (212) 431-4370 • Fax (212) 941-7842